Taming the
Atlantic

Taming the Atlantic

*The History of Man's Battle with
the World's Toughest Ocean*

Dag Pike

Pen & Sword
MARITIME

First published in Great Britain in 2017 by
PEN & SWORD MARITIME
An imprint of
Pen & Sword Books Ltd
47 Church Street
Barnsley
South Yorkshire
S70 2AS

Copyright © Dag Pike, 2017

ISBN 978-1-52670-083-4

A CIP catalogue record for this book is available from the British Library.

Typeset by Concept, Huddersfield HD4 5JL.
Printed and bound in England by TJ International Ltd, Padstow, Cornwall.

Pen & Sword Books Limited incorporates the imprints of Atlas, Archaeology,
Aviation, Discovery, Family History, Fiction, History, Maritime, Military,
Military Classics, Politics, Select, Transport, True Crime, Air World,
Frontline Publishing, Leo Cooper, Remember When, Seaforth Publishing,
The Praetorian Press, Wharncliffe Local History, Wharncliffe Transport,
Wharncliffe True Crime and White Owl.

For a complete list of Pen & Sword titles please contact
PEN & SWORD BOOKS LIMITED
47 Church Street, Barnsley, South Yorkshire, S70 2AS, England
E-mail: enquiries@pen-and-sword.co.uk
Website: www.pen-and-sword.co.uk

Contents

Acknowledgements

A lot of people have helped with both information and photos for this book, particularly the historical pictures that have been collected over the years, and I would like to express my grateful thanks to all of them. I would also like to thank Sir Richard Branson for the *Virgin Atlantic Challenger* project, Paulo Vitelli of Azimut for the *Azimut Atlantic Challenger* project and HH Aga Kahn for the *Destriero* project, all of which I was involved with both as 'weatherman' and in some cases as navigator.

Equally important are the experiences of the millions of people who have crossed the Atlantic in a wide variety of ships and boats – many have shared their experiences both good and bad. I share with them the triumphs and traumas of Atlantic crossings in fair winds and foul and acknowledge the information of their experiences. With three shipwrecks on the Atlantic and several near misses, I know the Atlantic in all its moods and acknowledge my grateful thanks to those who have come to the rescue and all those who have shared in Atlantic dramas.

Chapter One

Winds, Currents and Wild Seas

The wind was screeching through the rigging, the note rising higher and higher as the storm grew in strength. Out to windward the white-crested waves were advancing in relentless fashion, rising to the height of the top of the funnel. The wind was going off the scale in the fierce gusts, causing the ship to heel under the hammer blows of the wind. It was a typical day on the Atlantic in winter and the cargo ship *Marjata* was hove to, riding out the storm while tossed and battered by the huge waves. Then from out of the blue came two larger waves, the towering crests hovering above the ship before crashing down onto the deck. As the ship rolled heavily to these waves there came a groaning, grinding sound from the bowels of the ship and she took on a list to leeward that made her even more vulnerable to the advancing waves.

In the lonely seas as she approached the Bay of Biscay the *Marjata* was in deep trouble. The horizon seemed to be playing tricks as it rushed up to meet the mast as the ship rolled over, further and further. That mast seemed intent on matching the horizontal line of the horizon and then only slowly, ever so slowly, did the roll stop and the ship hang for what seemed an eternity before mast and horizon parted company again and started to restore their normal relationship. That grinding sound was the shifting boards carrying away allowing the cargo of grain to slide over to leeward and causing the ship to list. These shifting boards are designed to stop the grain moving in the holds but first it was the boards in No. 2 hold that gave way, followed moments later on the next wave by the boards in No. 3 hold. A shift in one more hold would have been the end for us and there was no chance of survival in those wild seas if the ship had capsized.

It was a heart-stopping, knuckle-whitening moment as the ship fought for survival against the elements intent on her destruction. There was nothing we could do. Filling the ballast tanks would have created a free surface that would only have made matters worse; perhaps such an act would have been the straw that might have broken the camel's back. Trying to shovel the sea of grain that filled the holds back into its rightful position would have been futile, since the shifting boards erected to keep the grain in place were now lying in a tangled and useless mess.

A French deep sea trawler at the mercy of an Atlantic storm. (*Author*)

For thirty-six hours the ship fought for her life out there on the lonely Atlantic, a battle made even more critical by the fact that her sister ship had capsized and sunk, having lost a similar fight only months before. On every roll it could have been the end; a roll that would have carried on until the ship capsized. As a young apprentice, ignorance, perhaps, prevented me from recognizing all the potential consequences of what was happening, or perhaps it was a form of fatalism inherited from generations of seafarers who have taken on the Atlantic and either won or lost at the whim of a capricious mistress.

Gradually the storm eased and four days later we limped into Liverpool Docks and safety. On one level, we became just another statistic, and a not very important one at that; a vessel whose cargo had shifted in heavy seas, just one of the thousands of ships that have got into difficulties in the North Atlantic. On a personal level the experience of spending thirty-six hours not knowing whether the next minute would be your last was one that was going to live with me throughout my seafaring days. It taught me respect and humility for the North Atlantic and it gave me an understanding of how centuries of seafarers, most of them far less well equipped than we were to cope with the situation, have battled with storms out on the lonely wastes of the Atlantic.

Certainly the experience taught me to observe due reverence and respect for the Western Ocean, a wild stretch of sea that for centuries has been both a route for commerce and a barrier to trade. Even in more modern times the Atlantic still takes its toll; one of the latest mysteries is the loss of the modern container ship *Munchen*, apparently overwhelmed in mid-Atlantic despite having size on her side plus all the latest safety equipment. The Atlantic has been, and still is, a challenge to new maritime developments and technology, but above all the Atlantic Ocean is a testing ground for seamanship. It is an ocean with many changing moods, sometimes calm but more often rough and occasionally possessed of the blind and senseless violence of a major storm. While sailors may call her 'The Pond', with typical understatement, no seaman worth his salt is going to take the Atlantic for granted. The seabed of the Atlantic is littered with wrecks, some caused by war but most from ships that simply lost the battle with the storms of this mighty ocean.

There was a time, so the geologists would have us believe, when the Atlantic wasn't even there. Long before history began, there was a single large land mass on Earth from which the continents as we know them today slowly separated out. This movement continues today at an infinitesimally slow but measurable rate, the chain of volcanic activity running down the centre of the Atlantic being visible evidence of shifts and change in the Earth's crust.

The Atlantic is no respecter of size as these large warships struggle with storm conditions.

Perhaps the legends of the lost lands of Atlantis represent dim, distant folk memories of such times; however, the main visible changes in the Atlantic are not those affecting the land features on the ocean's rim but those arising from the daily, sometimes hourly, changes in the sea and the weather that can affect the largest and stoutest of modern ships. The mighty cruise ships, container ships and tankers that ply these waters treat the Atlantic with respect and plan their routes with caution.

It is the wind that is the main cause of waves at sea and it is the waves that create most of the problems for shipping, but these elements are just two of the many factors that can make the surface of all the oceans such wild and inhospitable places at times. The North Atlantic, like other oceans, is a constantly churning, constantly moving body of water with ocean currents shifting huge volumes of water in three dimensions. Added to this mixture of wild waters are the hazards created by fog, icebergs and off-lying rock shoals, all of which lie in wait for the unwary ship. It is easy to see why the Atlantic Ocean has established a fearful reputation over the years and why it has been so respected and feared by seamen throughout the ages. With largely overcast skies during the winter months, navigation was always a mixture of experience and guesswork until the introduction of first the Loran electronic navigation system and more recently the highly-accurate GPS. Now at least ships know where they are with a degree of certainty unknown in the past, making the Atlantic a safer place for the navigator trying to make a landfall in challenging conditions.

The Plimsoll line painted on the hull sides of all cargo ships is an indication of this respect for the Atlantic. Introduced in the 1800s, the Plimsoll line appears as a series of horizontal lines marked on the hull showing how deeply the ship can be loaded in different oceans and different conditions. It was introduced to prevent ships from being dangerously overloaded by unscrupulous owners seeking higher profits. A series of lines is necessary to allow for the different water densities and the different sea conditions in various oceans with the top line allowing for a deeper draft in less dense fresh water. Then come load lines for normal summer and winter use in sea water, and right at the bottom is a line marked with the letters WNA, standing for Winter North Atlantic. This is the only ocean region that has its own special load line, reducing the amount of cargo that can be carried on North Atlantic routes in the winter months and adding a bit extra to the safety margins. It is a reflection of the awesome sea conditions that can be found during the winter in the North Atlantic. Here the authorities have decreed that extra safety margins are required in order to try to ensure the safe conduct of shipping.

The Atlantic has earned itself this reputation over the centuries as trade routes have developed across the globe. This ocean has taken a higher toll on

Storm conditions south of Iceland. (*Author*)

shipping than any other, and not solely because of the density of shipping crossing this stretch of water between the Old and New Worlds. Initially the dream of European sailors was just to find what lay on the other side of this great oceanic divide. Then it was the prospect of riches in the form of gold and silver, spices and other valued products that lured adventurous seamen across the ocean. They were followed in time by colonists and traders and the need for regular communication. Two-way trade between the two main industrial regions in the world added to the shipping traffic as North America itself developed a commercial base. For passengers wanting to make the journey there was intense competition between shipping companies to offer the fastest crossings. High speed and rough seas are not a happy combination for the large ocean liners and if you throw fog and icebergs into the mix the risks are high. The captains of Atlantic passenger ships were required to maintain tight schedules even in adverse conditions so that in some, perhaps in many cases, the need for speed and keeping to schedules overcame common sense and seamanlike caution.

At the same time, the Atlantic has always been the prestige route for passenger traffic, and technological advances have taken place largely under the impetus of the speed, luxury and size requirements of making the crossing in the shortest possible time. The Atlantic Ocean has always been a testing arena and a proving ground for both man and his technology. Providing some of

The North Atlantic Ocean stretches from the Tropics to the Arctic.

the most challenging sea conditions for seamen, it is small wonder that the Atlantic has also been chosen as the arena for those who want to pit themselves against the forces of nature in smaller craft. There are men and women who are always looking for new challenges and new worlds to conquer and the Atlantic, because of its raw power and unpredictability, is still able to offer such an opportunity. In some of these personal challenges there can be a narrow line between a challenge that can be a worthwhile risk and foolhardiness that may ignore the dangers. Over the years people have attempted to cross the Atlantic in almost every conceivable type of craft and in some cases the authorities have made attempts to stop some of the more hare-brained attempts. However, it is very difficult to draw the line between potential success and disastrous failure and the truth of the situation appears to be that if you get away with it and make the crossing you are a hero; fail, and you may be called a fool for even thinking you could take on the might of the Atlantic Ocean.

The record of fine, well-found ships coming to grief in the stormy waters of the Atlantic is far too extensive for comfort. Perhaps surprisingly, although fewer in number, the small boat sailor has a safety record which matches or even betters that of commercial vessels, but such men and women are often unfairly criticized for trans-oceanic voyaging. To set a new record across the Atlantic is probably more of a personal matter than a risk but where criticism can be levelled is in the experience of some of the protagonists who take on the Atlantic. Experienced seamen may not want to attempt some of the more extreme Atlantic ventures, however, and thus these then tend to be left open to the inexperienced or foolhardy. This is where the risks can arise and where the element of foolhardiness enters into the equation, but such is the unpredictability of the Atlantic that a surprising number of these inexperienced sailors succeed in making safe crossings. It is worth noting though that most of the early small boat crossings were made by sailors who were experienced, knew what they were doing and relished the challenge.

The Atlantic Ocean is a setting of immense proportions for any attempt to cross it, whether it be for ship cargoes crossing on a safe and regular basis, to transport passengers at high speed, or simply an individual seeking to prove that something can be done. In this book we are looking mostly at the North Atlantic because the main trade routes have crossed this ocean for centuries and this has been the primary arena for both the personal and the technical challenge to the power and might of the oceans.

The North Atlantic stretches roughly from the Equator to the Arctic. There are no hard boundaries to this mighty ocean except the land, and the division between the North and South Atlantic oceans varies with the time of year. Because the Caribbean Sea, the South Atlantic and the Arctic Ocean

The power of the sea is very evident from this photo of a warship in a storm.

contribute to the water circulation of the North Atlantic, these have to be considered in the equation and in reality oceans know only the limits set by the land at their edges.

The wind and water circulation of the North Atlantic played a very important part in the way the exploration of the New World occurred. We are talking here about the water circulation on the surface of the oceans that affects shipping directly, but in fact the water circulation throughout the oceans is very much a three-dimensional affair and there are deep ocean currents that keep the whole of the ocean on the move. Surface currents are largely generated by the prevailing wind patterns that pick up the surface water and force it along in the same direction as the prevailing wind. The combination of wild winds and mighty ocean currents means that the Atlantic is an ocean in turmoil and never easy to predict.

If the world was an ideal place, then there would be a predictable wind pattern across the Atlantic. With the Earth being much hotter at the Equator than at the poles through the differential heating of the sun, the air at the Equator rises as it becomes heated and this warm upper air then flows northwards and southwards towards the poles, with colder air from the poles flowing at a lower level towards the Equator to take its place. This north/south air flow is the basic pattern in the Northern Hemisphere but nothing is simple when it comes to weather and in fact there is a sort of circular flow of air around the Atlantic, generally flowing to the east in the northern parts and to the west in the southern parts towards the Equator.

Much of the weather found in the North Atlantic starts life over the extensive mainland of North America. Here, heat differences combined with the major air flows start off a series of depressions that start to whistle their way out to sea and across the ocean. The main meeting-point between the winds flowing to the north and those flowing south is an area of turmoil and this is the location of the mighty jet stream that acts as a catalyst for those areas of low pressure which are a constant feature of Atlantic weather and generate most of the violent winds in the region. They tend to follow the line of the jet stream which pours eastwards high in the stratosphere and the meeting line between the two winds, the hot and the cold, will vary according to the season, moving north in the summer and drifting south in the winter. The drift south in the winter brings the area of violent winds right across the major trade routes and helps to give the North Atlantic the fearsome storm reputation discussed earlier. The deeper and more violent depressions produce winds that quickly reach gale force or more and they generate the mighty waves that roll across the ocean.

Therefore in the northern areas of the Atlantic, the general pattern of the weather shows a series of depressions running across from west to east, while further south the Azores high-pressure area brings more moderate winds and more predictable weather. If the Azores high strengthens, it pushes the depressions further north and this can bring fine weather to most of the maritime routes across the Atlantic. More frequently, this high-pressure area is beaten south and it is rarely able to fend off for long the assault from the depressions, determined in their eastward path across the North Atlantic in winter.

Between the Azores high and the Equator you get the north-east trade winds; predictable and consistent winds that were so favoured by sailing ships. South of these winds are the Doldrums, an area of fitful, unreliable winds where ships can experience violent thunderstorms creating an area that was and still is a major problem region for sailing vessels.

In many ways the surface currents in the North Atlantic follow the pattern of the winds with the Gulf Stream flowing from the coasts of Florida bringing warm water to the shores of the British Isles and further north. To the south there is the return flow across the ocean some way north of the Equator providing favourable currents for an east/west crossing spurred on by the reliable Trade Winds. These two currents set up a sort of circular flow around the North Atlantic centred roughly around the Azores High that can be used by low-powered ships to get a helping hand on ocean voyages. Added into this mix is the cold Labrador Current that flows down from the Arctic along the shores of Canada and across the Grand Banks, bringing with it the series of icebergs and fog that can be such a hazard to shipping in the North Atlantic.

The cold Labrador Current has a lot to answer for when it comes to creating difficult sea conditions for shipping. Flowing down through the Davis Straits from the icy wastes of the Arctic, it brings with it large quantities of floating ice. Much of the region through which this current flows is so cold in the winter that the sea freezes over and is a mass of solid ice, but in the early summer the ice starts to break up and melt. This 'first-year' sea ice is not too much of a hazard to navigation and most of it melts before it is carried very far south in the Labrador Current, but each summer huge sections break from the glaciers that run down from the Greenland ice cap into the Davis Strait and it is these icebergs heading south in the current that present a major hazard to shipping.

It may take a couple of years for an iceberg to reach the Grand Banks of Newfoundland and then head even further south into the major shipping lanes. Many of these icebergs are so large that they ground on the shallow waters of the Grand Banks of Newfoundland, which stretch some 300 miles to the seaward of Newfoundland. Such huge bergs may stay grounded until they melt sufficiently to continue their southward journey over the shallow water. Eventually they are caught up by the relatively warm waters of the Gulf

The build-up of ice on ships is a constant threat in the seas around Iceland. (*Author*)

Icebergs are a threat in many of the shipping routes across the Atlantic. (*US Coast Guard*)

Stream when melting is rapid. Few icebergs reach more than 35° west before they are picked up and destroyed by the warm Gulf Stream, but the bergs that stay closer inshore, in the colder current, may occasionally get down as far as 40° north. Most of the icebergs that keep inshore tend to congregate just south of Cape Race on the south-east corner of Newfoundland where they eventually break up or melt.

The movement of icebergs is affected by both currents and winds and is difficult to predict. The RMS *Titanic* disaster brought home to the public at large the risks posed to shipping by icebergs. In the days of sailing ships and in the early days of steam ships most vessels took a course directly across the Grand Banks when coming from Europe in order to pick up the favourable Labrador Current which could help them down the coast towards the ports of Boston and New York. This took ships through the ice zone during a large part of the year but as the speed of shipping rose and the consequences of a collision with an iceberg increased there were attempts to route ocean traffic away from the ice danger. An international conference on the safety of life at sea, held in London in 1913 following the *Titanic* disaster, led to the introduction of the International Ice Patrol and although this is a service managed by the US Coast Guard, it is funded by most of the major maritime nations. The ships and aircraft of the Ice Patrol keep track of all the icebergs each season and use computer programs to predict their future positions, so warning vessels in their path. Yet ice still remains an ever-present danger, particularly when the fog often found in these latitudes reduces visibility. Fog and icebergs are not a happy combination for shipping.

Fog can be a hazard to shipping throughout much of the North Atlantic but it is particularly prevalent on the coasts of North America. Here, once again, it is the Labrador Current that is the main culprit. The meeting of the cold water of this current with the warm moist air sweeping up from the south-west creates prime conditions for fog to form. During the summer months fog on the east coast and out over the Grand Banks can occur as often as one day in two and the fog can stretch for hundreds of miles. In addition to the hazards of fog and ice, the fact that the fog is generated by a wind-against-current situation can give nasty sea conditions and it is small wonder that here is an area dreaded by seamen. Ships coming from Europe meet this fog region just at the time when they need good visibility for a landfall and fog-reduced visibility has been responsible for many disasters in Atlantic waters. Hazards such as Sable Island off Nova Scotia and the extensive Nantucket Shoals off Cape Cod compound the navigator's problems in this region.

It was an American naval officer, Lieutenant Maury, who in the 1800s collated information from a mass of ships' logs to produce a picture of the ocean winds and currents. For the first time this gave ships' captains the information required to optimize their routes using the winds and currents to best advantage. This was the first type of weather routing used on the Atlantic and while not as sophisticated as the computer-generated systems used by ships today, it

Big following seas were a challenge on our sailing record attempt across the Atlantic. (*Author*)

allowed ships to gain maximum advantage from the winds and currents and hopefully reduce the chance of encountering storms en route.

With the major circular flow of water around the North Atlantic, there is an area of relatively static water left in the centre. Lying at the centre of the North Atlantic circulation, the Sargasso Sea, as it is known, tends to be an area where debris, seaweed and, in more recent times oil slicks, tend to congregate. Here large patches of Sargasso or gulf weed float on the surface. This weed often looks like low-lying land from a distance and it supports its own ecosystems. It is easy to imagine the effect of such a region on early sailors who were often sailing into unknown waters where anything different or unusual was looked on with suspicion or even dread. Since the region is also bedevilled by calms, it is easy to see why the early, highly superstitious sailors tried to give the Sargasso Sea a wide berth.

There are many more localized areas that can be found along many of the coasts bordering the northern parts of the Atlantic Ocean that have a reputation for wild seas and dangerous waters. The culprit in many of these areas is usually the currents in the sea that are generated by strong tides. These strong tides can be found flowing in and out of the Gulf of St Lawrence in Canada, in the English Channel between England and France, and the water that pours in and out of the North Sea twice a day, all of which generate very strong water flows. When the wind flows against the tide you can get areas of violent sea conditions, short steep waves that can often be dangerous for ships and boats. Through the Pentland Firth in the north of Scotland the tides can run at up to 9 knots, quickly creating maelstrom conditions particularly when the west-going ebb tide flowing out of the North Sea meets the full force of a westerly gale sweeping in from the Atlantic. Conditions such as this can make the coastal waters on both sides of the Atlantic some of the most violent found anywhere in the world. In such seas, ships can find themselves in trouble even when they have almost reached the security of harbour. In the days when I was employed testing new designs of lifeboat I took a 70-footer through the Pentland Firth in a westerly gale and these were probably the most extreme sea conditions I have ever experienced.

Bad weather and wild sea conditions are not confined to the northern parts of the Atlantic. The mainly balmy waters of the Horse Latitudes located several degrees north of the Equator are the breeding ground for hurricanes at certain times of the year. These can be the most violent storms to be found anywhere in the world and pose a considerable threat to shipping. Officially known as tropical revolving storms, hurricanes are similar to a depression or low-pressure area, with the wind circulating (in the Northern Hemisphere) in an anti-clockwise direction, but in a hurricane the pressure is a lot lower than that found in a depression with the isobars much more concentrated.

It is the breaking crests of the waves that can be the biggest threat to shipping and boats on the Atlantic. (*Author*)

Hurricanes are usually highly-concentrated areas of wild winds extending out about 200 miles from their centres, although some spread out over a much larger area. Within 50 miles of the centre of the hurricane, the wind speed can exceed 150 knots, creating conditions where it is difficult to tell where the sea stops and the air begins. You can almost feel like drowning because the air is so full of water and a hurricane is nothing short of a seething mass of water and wind, seemingly intent on destroying everything in its path. Forecasters have become better at predicting the path of hurricanes so they can give warning to shipping but with a hurricane nothing is certain, their tracks can be highly unpredictable and their effects devastating.

For the most part, tropical revolving storms occur on the western side of the northern oceans and in the Atlantic they are found generally in the West Indies and Caribbean and then heading up along the Eastern Coast of the United States. Here they are most frequent during the late summer and early autumn with an average of five hurricanes occurring each year. Most of the hurricanes occurring in the Atlantic start off somewhere off the coast of Africa at around latitude 20° north. At first they are just local disturbances rather like a very active thunderstorm, but as they pick up energy from the warm waters of the Tropics they can intensify and track west before turning north, striking land in a devastating maelstrom of wind, rain and tidal surges. Thus they may head in towards the islands of the Caribbean, sometimes sweeping right in across the Gulf of Mexico or, at other times, head north up the east coast of the United States and then out into the Atlantic. Nothing seems certain about the path of a hurricane and historically their recorded tracks cover most of the western half of the Atlantic Ocean. Hurricanes tend to weaken slightly when they touch land but many end up heading out into the Atlantic in a north-easterly direction, perhaps calling in at Bermuda on their track to the north where they then tend to weaken and become just another intense low-pressure area heading towards Europe.

Today, with aircraft and satellite coverage, hurricanes can be detected at an early stage and closely monitored with warnings broadcast to shipping in time for them to take avoiding action. In the past the first warning a ship might have of a hurricane approaching would be a rapidly falling barometer and a darkening threatening cloud mass. Even sixty years ago, by the time a hurricane had been detected by a ship it was probably too late to escape it and the fight for survival would begin. In my sixty-five years at sea I have experienced two hurricanes, one in harbour and one at sea, and the extreme conditions are beyond description. Even in harbour a ship is not safe from the ravages of these violent winds and the tidal surges and for early sailors who lacked warning systems, to be caught in one must have been worse than any nightmare.

The area known as the Bermuda Triangle falls within the hurricane region, covering much of the eastern seaboard of the United States right down to the tip of Florida. It is small wonder that it has gained a reputation for unpredictability when you consider the hurricanes that sweep the area and the very strong currents generated by the Gulf Stream. These two features in themselves are enough to generate unpredictable and violent sea conditions, often at short notice. Much of the Sargasso Sea also falls within the so-called 'Triangle'. Small wonder then that superstitious seamen have felt that supernatural causes lay behind some of the major disasters that have occurred in the region. Such reputations tend to be self-perpetuating, with any unexplained happening helping to further the myth with the line between reality and imagination becoming blurred.

An additional Atlantic hazard for small vessels comes from whales. In recent times, with the increase in small craft on the ocean, there have been a number of incidents in which whales have damaged or even sunk boats. The vessels used by early sailors were often little larger than many of the yachts that sail the Atlantic today and no doubt whales aroused their wildest fears, perhaps accounting for many of the early tales about sea monsters.

The Atlantic can indeed be an inhospitable place for a number of reasons, but it is not all bad. There are large areas with reliable and predictable winds that can be of tremendous benefit to sailing ships and the wily seaman takes advantage of winds and currents that can be in his favour. Steam-powered ships have less need to follow the dictates of the winds and currents but these features can still be friends or foes and it still pays to maintain a healthy respect for the sea. Despite its reputation for violence and unpredictable weather, for calms and fog and for icebergs, the North Atlantic has become the major trade route of the world with ships and boats of all descriptions crossing it every day. Modern technology has not been able to tame the Atlantic but improved weather forecasting and improved ship designs and technology have made it possible to cope with the extremes of this unpredictable ocean; however, the Atlantic is always waiting to catch the unwary sailor who lets his guard down.

Chapter Two

The Early Explorers

It is hard for us to picture a world in which the huge land mass of America stretching almost from pole to pole was unknown. When Columbus set off from Spain on a westward course he was looking for China and Japan rather than any new land in between and his much-heralded 'discovery' of America was almost a mistake. Navigation was pretty basic in those days with estimating the distance travelled each day largely a matter of intelligent guesswork. Nobody knew just how far you might have to travel west across the Atlantic before you found land and even when you did you would not know which land it was. There was even some doubt remaining about whether the world was indeed round and if it was, what was its size. The West Indies were so named because the early explorers thought that they had found land somewhere in the vicinity of India and the native population of North America were called Indians for the same reason. It might be termed exploration by accident but it certainly took some brave sailors to sail off into the blue without a destination, without any charts and without knowing where and how they might end up. This was real exploration in its most basic sense and it does suggest that some of the early discoveries of America were accidental rather than by design. Although Columbus is usually credited with the discovery of the American continent, there had been legends and rumours of its existence for a long time and it is even possible that the 'lost continent of Atlantis' could have been the American continent.

I doubt that we will ever know for sure who was the true first 'discoverer' of America, but almost certainly the initial discovery of this continent across the Atlantic was not a planned event. When you look at the current and wind circulation in the Atlantic as we know it today, it is not hard to imagine a primitive fishing boat being picked up by the North Equatorial Current and the prevailing westerly winds as it sailed off the coast of Africa and the crew being carried helplessly across the Atlantic without any means of turning back. Bear in mind that the early sailing vessels could make very little progress against the wind when under sail and if you combine the winds and currents that were running strongly to the west in this region, then there would be little hope that a boat caught up in the system would be able to make any headway back to where it started. It is likely that most of these early

'explorers' would have died on the long crossing but there is a distinct possibility that some would have made it.

Such an accidental voyage across the Atlantic is credible and Columbus,
on one of his later voyages, reported finding white-skinned natives in the
northern regions of South America, which is the area where any boat drifting
across the Atlantic would most probably have ended up. Thor Heyerdahl set
out to demonstrate through his *Ra* expeditions that the ancient Egyptians
could have had links with the advanced cultures found in Mexico and Peru
and Heyerdahl re-enacted a possible crossing of the Atlantic in a craft constructed in the manner and style of the time and deduced from this that direct
links between the two civilizations on the widely-separated continents could
have existed.

Heyerdahl's voyage was a courageous attempt to confirm historical theories
by practical demonstration but it seems to fall down in two areas. Heyerdahl
set out knowing that America existed and one must assume that the ancient
Egyptians didn't, and it is therefore hard to picture them setting out deliberately on such a voyage in such a craft. It is known, however, that they explored
down the coast of Africa after passing through the Straits of Gibraltar and it
is perhaps more likely that they could have been caught up in the winds and
currents and made the voyage across the Atlantic by accident rather than
by design. This assumes that they could perhaps have survived the voyage by
catching fish and drinking rainwater. Heyerdahl, of course, knowing the
distance involved, was able to store his boat with the appropriate requirements to make the voyage without the threat of thirst or starvation. Also any
replica boat re-enacting an Atlantic crossing is secure in the knowledge that
they know where the destination is, they have radio communication and safety
equipment and the knowledge that there is a good chance someone will come
to their aid if they get into trouble. This takes away the not inconsiderable
mental challenge involved in just heading off into the blue with slim chances
of survival on what might have seemed to be a futile voyage.

Even assuming that the ancient Egyptians made the trip across, there's
an old saying that 'you haven't discovered something until you have told somebody about it.' An astronomer, discovering a new star, only has to let someone
else have a look through his telescope to confirm the discovery. An explorer,
on the other hand, has to make the return journey back to his or her civilization to tell people about his find before it becomes a discovery. This is the
worrying aspect of Heyerdahl's theory and while it is comparatively easy to
accept that a boat made from fragile papyrus could have crossed the Atlantic
from east to west and Heyerdahl demonstrated that this was possible, it is
much harder to visualize the same craft making the return journey. The only
feasible route would have been to pick up the Gulf Stream and make the long

journey north-about back to Europe, and that really doesn't seem to be a possibility in such a craft and with a crew totally ignorant of currents and ocean navigation. If the arrival in the New World was accidental then it is hard to picture such an advanced civilization as existed in Mexico or Peru being developed from a few shipwrecked sailors who were probably all men. We may never know for sure the origins of these civilizations, but I think we can reasonably assume that the first early voyages across the Atlantic were made from east to west and by accident.

One of the first records of purposeful voyages of discovery out on the Atlantic is found in the voyages of Saint Brendan. There were claims that around 570 AD, Saint Brendan crossed the Atlantic to America from Ireland and in the manner of Thor Heyerdahl a reconstruction of such a voyage was carried out by Tim Severin in 1976–77 in a replica craft made from the same basic materials and construction techniques available at the time. The general consensus, however, is that Saint Brendan managed to reach the southern shores of Iceland and also sailed southwards to the Azores, but that he didn't

The fragile replica of the *Brendan* boat that crossed the Atlantic (note the wireless antenna at the stern).

make it the whole way across the Atlantic. This is not to detract from what were certainly brave voyages of discovery in such a fragile craft and Severin demonstrated that it was possible to sail the Atlantic in his replica craft but again he knew where he was heading and had modern resources on board to cope with potential disaster. It was nearly 400 years after Saint Brendan did his Atlantic roaming that the Vikings made what is now generally taken to be the first European landing on the American continent and this does appear to have been the result of a navigational error rather than a planned voyage of discovery.

Many of the early craft sailing on the European side of the Atlantic were fishing vessels and it is easy to imagine these vessels sailing further and further offshore in the pursuit of their catch. It is likely that the Azores, Madeira and the Canary Islands were discovered in this way and it is possible that some of these vessels made it all the way across the ocean when caught up in the prevailing winds and currents. There have been reports that the wreck of an ancient Basque fishing boat was found in the waters off Labrador and the fish-rich waters of the Grand Banks have always been a Mecca for fishermen.

By the year 900 AD the Vikings had moved out across the oceans to Iceland and Greenland from their Norwegian home waters and gained much experience of sailing in these inhospitable northern waters. This far north, the currents, if not directly in their favour, were at least not against them. A big plus in their favour was that their craft were capable of being propelled by oars as well as sails, so these Viking ships were not entirely reliant on favourable winds. It is speculated that the first sighting of the North American continent by Bjarni Herjulfsson came about because he steered the wrong course or was diverted from his course by unusual winds and not because he had any exploratory motives. Herjulfsson had set out from Iceland to make the trip to the newly-established colonies on Greenland and the Viking sagas record that he landed in a strange land. Later researchers have suggested that this first landing-point was in the Cape Cod area. In terms of the prevailing winds and currents, this seems an unlikely landfall for somebody making for Greenland, even taking into account the rudimentary navigation techniques of the time. Although strong currents run down both sides of Greenland that could have taken the boat to the south and made it miss Greenland altogether, the most likely landfall then would be in the region of Newfoundland or Labrador, assuming the boat was steering a reasonably consistent heading.

Herjulfsson apparently didn't take the trouble to explore the new lands, but was irked by his navigation mistake and was more intent on getting back to Greenland rather than exploring the new lands. It was an Icelander, Leif Erikson, who has the claim to being the first European to set foot on American soil. This was some seventeen years after Herjulfsson had made his

A replica Viking ship. With both sails and oars, this craft was less at the mercy of the wind than pure sailing vessels.

landfall and Erikson's voyage to America may have been for a purpose as mundane as collecting wood for the Viking colony on Greenland. Erikson actually established a colony on the new continent, although its exact location has never been clearly identified. This was a seasonal colony and for several years thereafter the Greenland Vikings visited the area to collect timber. Thus this so-called 'first discovery' of America was a fairly casual affair and the significance of the discovery was not really appreciated. However, the word 'discovery' is correct because both boats and crews returned to tell the story.

These first two crossings of the Atlantic followed the most practical routes for low-powered vessels that would have difficulty sailing against the wind. While the southern route was longer but favoured by consistent winds and currents and warmer temperatures, the northerly route across the Atlantic allowed a degree of island-hopping which was a help with the basic navigation techniques available and it had reasonably favourable currents. However, this northern route is also prone to storms and cold which must have made the Viking voyages pretty daunting affairs. Even today, smaller craft hesitate to venture into these seas and certainly not in the open craft used by the Vikings. We tend to hear about the ones that made successful voyages rather than those that didn't simply because they lived to tell the tale. These early sailors had no knowledge of ocean currents or wind patterns and their navigation

A Viking replica at sea. These were surprisingly seaworthy craft for the early explorers.

skills were pretty basic since they lacked compasses, but it has been suggested that they could work out latitudes from the sun and stars. In the circumstances it is quite easy to see why Herjulfsson raised the American coast rather than Greenland and it is a tribute to his navigation skills that he was able to find his way back to Greenland. The reduced distances involved in the northern island-hopping route would have helped, of course.

The voyages of Columbus across the Atlantic were even more daring and courageous because he set out into the unknown with a well-defined purpose; namely to find China and/or Japan by going 'the wrong way round the world'. Columbus has gone down in history as a famous explorer with good cause but it should be remembered that at the time he set out westwards across the Atlantic, the Azores had already been discovered and, since they lie some 700 miles to the west of Spain, it is clear that ships were already ranging well out into the Atlantic. The Canary Islands to the south were also well known and these islands were the first stopping-off point for Columbus on his voyage of discovery.

Columbus took a fleet of three ships. This was a sensible precaution on a voyage into the unknown where there was an obvious risk of losing ships through storm or through grounding; three ships increased the likelihood

A replica of the *Santa Maria*, the flagship of the Columbus fleet.

that one or two would survive the voyage and this was a feature of several early voyages. In the light of present-day shipping experience, the vessels taken by Columbus were remarkably small, being little bigger than many of the yachts that sail the Atlantic today. The flagship of the fleet, the *Santa Maria*, ranks as one of the most famous ships in history, but in fact few details have survived. Her overall length is believed to have been around 85ft and when you consider that this includes the bowsprit, the hull itself was probably no more than 70ft in length, but as Columbus says in his account of the voyage, 'smaller ships are desirable on voyages of discovery because of their handiness when sailing in strange and uncharted waters.'

Once Columbus left the Canary Islands, he headed on a course that was almost due west. Navigation techniques were still elementary but the elevation of the Pole Star above the horizon enabled navigators to maintain a fairly consistent latitude. Indeed, the starting-point of the Canary Islands and the landing-point at San Salvador are on almost the same latitudes. Columbus set out with the intention of finding China/Japan and since the southern islands of Japan are only slightly further north in latitude than the Canary Islands, he was on the right track, although he was several thousand miles out in his calculation of longitude!

What must have been most worrying for Columbus on his outward voyage was the constant presence of favourable winds. Favourable winds are fine if you want to get somewhere quickly, but there must have been the nagging doubt that it would be necessary to find the way back against these same consistent breezes. Columbus would not have known about the currents that were also helping him and against which he would also have to battle on his return journey.

On his arrival in what became known as the West Indies, Columbus spent some time exploring among the islands but his crews were getting restless and the *Pinta* deserted the expedition to sail back for Europe. Later the *Santa Maria* was lost after being wrecked on a sandbank at an anchorage and this left Columbus with only the diminutive *Niña* to make the voyage back to Spain. After establishing a settlement, the remaining members of the expedition set off in the *Niña* heading on a north-easterly track which represented the best course that could be maintained in the prevailing wind conditions. On this northerly route both the *Niña* and the *Pinta* ahead of her experienced tremendous seas, perhaps encountering a hurricane, the first Europeans to do so.

The *Niña* overtook the *Pinta* on the return journey, enabling Columbus to arrive back in Spain first with the news of his discovery. It was an epic voyage into the unknown but perhaps most significant for future exploration was the fact that Columbus returned with gold artifacts. Even though he hadn't discovered the riches of the east, there was sufficient promise of riches from the new lands to whet the appetite for further voyages. Columbus himself made three more voyages to the New World, the first of these with seventeen ships and 1,500 men. On this major expedition he discovered many of the islands comprising the West Indies and on his third voyage he found the mainland of South America where he came across the white-faced natives.

Columbus has gone down in history as the discoverer of America, but the reality is that both he and many subsequent explorers, when they realized that these new lands were not the Chinese or Japanese coastline that they were seeking, spent much of their time trying to find a way round or through the huge American continent to get to the Far East. News of the voyages of Columbus spread and from Britain John Cabot set out in the *Matthew*, a small three-masted trading vessel about 65ft in length, to find some of the fabled riches for Britain. Cabot set out from Bristol in 1497 and after little more than a month on the Atlantic sighted either Newfoundland or Cape Breton Island. For an east-west passage across the North Atlantic, this voyage by Cabot was remarkably quick and he probably took a fairly northerly route with more favourable winds and currents. While this may have been more by accident than design, there is some evidence that the fisheries of the Grand Banks area were already being exploited by British vessels. Indeed, one is led to the conclusion that the expeditions that led to recorded landfalls on the coasts of America were probably preceded by many earlier wide-ranging voyages. It is

Columbus sights land on the far side of the Atlantic.

more than likely that land had been sighted on such earlier journeys and while these sightings have not been recorded for posterity, they may have encouraged early explorers to embark on deliberate voyages of discovery.

Like Columbus, Cabot, after his first expedition to North America with just a single ship, managed to get a lot more support for a second expedition and he set off the following year with a fleet of six vessels. However, Atlantic storms seem to have caught up with the fleet and little is known about their fate except that one put into an Irish port. The significant aspect of Cabot's voyage was not so much the rediscovery of mainland North America after the Viking voyages many years before, but the establishment of the Grand Banks fisheries. By the year 1500, fleets from many of the south-western British ports ventured out across the Atlantic to fish in these prolific waters. Only eight years after Columbus made his historic voyage, small fishing boats were making the arduous trip across the Atlantic with the prosaic motive of catching fish rather than glamorous ideas about discovering new lands. History has endowed many of the early discoverers with high and pure motives for their voyages into the unknown but in all probability the motives were essentially those of greed and personal gain; the prospect of finding untold wealth was always a powerful motivating force.

For the Spaniards, who continued to explore and exploit the lands around the Caribbean Sea, wealth was found among the riches of the Inca and the

Fishing boats were reported to be sailing the Atlantic to the prolific Georges Bank fishing grounds in the early days of discovery.

Aztec civilizations during the sixteenth century. Spanish ships made regular voyages taking settlers across to establish colonies in the new lands and returning to Spain laden with looted treasure. It is small wonder that the British and the French cast envious eyes at these Spanish treasure ships and it was not long before what amounted to piracy on the high seas was under way as these nations attacked returning Spanish ships in order to get a share of the riches of the new territories. By the early sixteenth century the Atlantic was being crossed regularly, but the ships involved were still very small and history tends to record the successful voyages rather than the ones that didn't make it. These small and, by present-day standards, very primitive vessels must have been extremely tough on their crews and, in the North Atlantic, storms must have taken a heavy toll. Even in the better conditions on the sailing route that followed the North Equatorial Current, the Spanish ships and later their attackers from northern Europe must have experienced hurricanes and other navigational hazards. Sailing the Atlantic remained a venture into the unknown and for the superstitious sailor the long days at sea without sighting land, the bad weather, basic food and very limited water must have created conditions where death was a constant companion.

The vessels used by the early discoverers were ungainly sailing ships by modern standards.

The lure of new lands and new riches, however, maintained a high level of exploration. In 1534 the French explorer Jacques Cartier was the first to sail up the St. Lawrence River. Like many early explorers, Cartier was looking for a way around the American continent and was rather less interested in exploring it. Although he is credited with the 'exploration' of this part of North America, European fishing vessels were already using the lower reaches of the river for shelter and indeed on Cartier's first voyage a French fishing schooner dropped anchor close by in the mouth of the St. Lawrence.

Even before Cartier's journey, the French ship *La Dauphine* commanded by an Italian, Giovanni da Verrazzano, had explored much of the continental coastline further north and discovered what is now New York harbour where his name is perpetuated in the bridge across the narrows at the entrance. Verrazzano was one of the first to realize that the American continent was not in fact the Far East, although many years would elapse before it was appreciated that America was cut off from Asia entirely.

One of the most notable Atlantic voyages of this time was the crossing by the *Mayflower* in 1620. This crossing was organized by the Pilgrim Fathers to escape religious persecution and set up a new base in Plymouth in the United States. This crossing in a 100ft-long three-masted ship highlights the appalling conditions on board ship in those days. Of the 102 passengers and 30 crew who started the journey, just half this number survived, although this was not entirely due to the conditions on the crossing as they had to endure a tough winter on arrival. The journey across the Atlantic took sixty-six days, giving an average speed of a shade over 2 knots. The first indication of land on the American side was probably the tide rips over the Georges Banks and then landfall was probably at the tip of Cape Cod before making for what is now Plymouth. This was probably the best recorded of the early Atlantic crossings and gives us an insight into conditions at sea in those days. A replica *Mayflower* seems to have had a much easier time of it when it crossed in 1955 but that reflects the 'luxuries' that were carried on board such as fridges, and

A replica of the *Mayflower* under full sail.

more hygienic and comfortable conditions as well as a considerably reduced number of people on board.

Increasing trade across the Atlantic and further voyages of exploration led to the development of larger ships. When ships had been following coastal routes, the need was for smaller, handy ships to cope with the difficult coastal conditions, but for ocean travel the need for larger ships was recognized. Expanded maritime trade routes and the associated national wealth and prestige that went with them increased the importance of naval power and led to the development of such warships as the *Henry Grace à Dieu* in England and in France, *Grand François*. In Sweden, a large warship 174ft long and with a beam of 40ft was named, appropriately, the *Elefant*. The technology developed in the construction of these flagships of the fleet spilled over into the design of merchant vessels which also continued to increase in size. Increasingly too, trading vessels were required to be heavily armed for defence against the ships of other nations sailing on Atlantic waters which had become something of a battleground. By the mid-sixteenth century sailing ships with a length between 100ft and 120ft were regularly used for trans-ocean voyages. They were also being built to more seaworthy forms with much more attention being paid to rigs which were strong and divided up into smaller sails for easy handling in bad weather conditions. Three- and four-masted vessels became common but making headway with the wind anywhere forward of the beam still remained a major problem.

For their size, all of these ships carried enormous crews and life on board must have been miserable in the extreme, particularly in cold northern waters. There would be no heating on board except for the galley fire and that would normally be on deck and have to be put out in bad weather. Hot food would not be available when it was needed most and with all the other risks of sailing in uncharted waters it is small wonder that mutiny was never far away. The popular and romantic picture of seamen ready to fight for king and country was a long way from the reality of the very primitive conditions that existed on board. For the captains there was the prospect of making a fortune out of a successful voyage and this was the incentive that made the risks and hardship worthwhile.

With the increasing number of ships making the Atlantic crossing during the sixteenth century, an understanding of wind and current patterns steadily developed. Navigation was still more of an art than a science and no means of measuring longitude had been developed other than by checking the distance travelled. With the introduction of the astrolabe, latitude could be determined with reasonable accuracy and ships gained basic compasses to give them an idea of direction. A pattern of voyages developed in which ships would leave Europe and head south with favourable winds and currents to the coast of Africa where they would pick up the North Equatorial Current and the north-east trades to make the Atlantic crossing to the west. Returning, the ships would pick up the Gulf Stream and the prevailing south-westerlies to make the trip back to Europe across a more northerly track and thus a circular pattern of trade developed; a pattern that was to persist throughout the history of the sailing ship on the Atlantic. Even today, modern yachts with their adequate windward capability still tend to follow this basic Atlantic routing.

Since navigators could measure only latitude with a reasonable degree of accuracy, ships tended to follow due east or west courses across the Atlantic, maintaining a steady latitude until they found land that would give them an indication of their longitude. Once the landfall had been made they would then either follow the coast 'up' or 'down' to the latitude of their destination, or alternatively head due north (or south) until they hit this new latitude and then head east or west as appropriate. These courses assumed that the winds would allow them to sail in the desired direction and in many cases prolonged storms could blow the ship a long way off course. It is small wonder that shipping casualties were frequent in the sixteenth century, particularly as vessels were making landfall in largely uncharted waters.

One of the biggest problems facing shipping was the inability of the sailing ship to make progress to windward. Almost inevitably when the vessel was approaching land it would be approaching with the wind from somewhere abaft the beam and there was always the risk of the vessel becoming embayed and unable to beat out to windward to escape from the clutches of the land. The American coastline was probably not as dangerous in this respect as the European coastline where the Bay of Biscay became much feared by seamen heading home. Ships were often trapped in the Bay of Biscay by the prevailing westerly winds and found themselves driven remorselessly towards and eventually against the shore, unable to beat to windward and clear the ensnaring arms of the coastline.

By the mid-sixteenth century, when Magellan had shown that the world was round by sailing round Cape Horn and out into the Pacific, the broad exploration of the American coastline was largely complete and numerous settlements existed in the New World. In the south the Spaniards established their superiority over the local population with strong demonstrations of force, but the northern colonists on mainland America had a much more difficult time with the aggressive native Indians. Gradually, however, the colonies were established and voyages of discovery across the Atlantic became increasingly voyages of trade or piracy.

In the second half of the sixteenth century the British became particularly bold on Atlantic and Caribbean waters. These were the days of Hawkins,

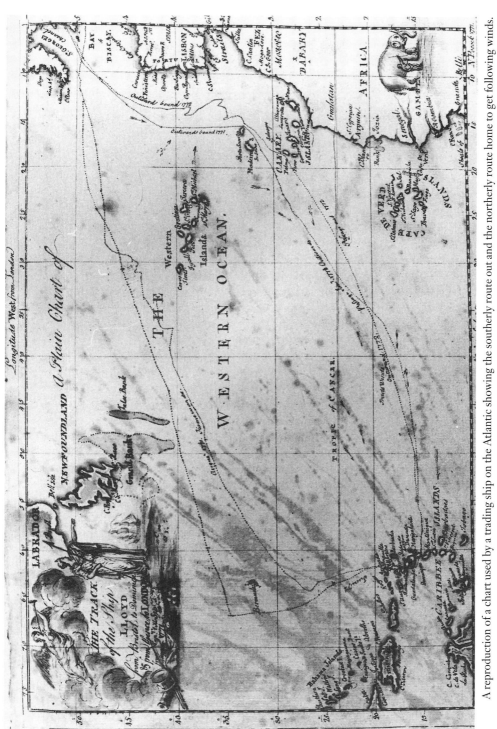

A reproduction of a chart used by a trading ship on the Atlantic showing the southerly route out and the northerly route home to get following winds.

Drake, Frobisher and Howard who set out with official sanction to attack Spanish shipping. It was John Hawkins who effectively began the slave trade across the Atlantic. Sailing out from England he would head south down the coast of Africa to pick up slaves and then take the favourable winds and currents across the Atlantic to the West Indies and to the Americas where surviving slaves could be sold off. After attacking Spanish galleons and loading up with treasure, he would take the favourable Gulf Stream to make a quick passage back to Europe. This triangular trade pattern was to be followed for the next century and a half, although more latterly ships would load up with legitimate cargoes of tobacco or cotton from the New World for sale in the markets of Europe instead of plundered Spanish goods.

The first passenger services across the Atlantic, if they can be called such, involved the shipping of parties of colonists to found settlements in North America. On these early 'passenger' trips the conditions must have been appalling. Bad as the conditions were for sailors on the Atlantic, for the passengers the conditions were worse and they were often battened down below for days on end when weather conditions were bad. Food and water would be restricted and poor in condition to the extent that scurvy was a major problem among seafarers and passengers alike on long ocean crossings. Privation and disease were the rule rather than the exception on both slavers and ships carrying colonists.

By 1600 British ships were firmly established on the Atlantic and the Spanish influence was starting to wane. However, there was now another seafaring nation on the scene and the Dutch, after a late start, were beginning to make their mark. By 1630 they had seized a number of West Indian islands from the Spaniards and were established in New Amsterdam, later to become New York. British colonies too were beginning to flourish and the Pilgrim Fathers made their famous voyage across the Atlantic in the *Mayflower* to establish their colony at Plymouth in 1620. As with the passengers on the *Mayflower*, many colonies in North America were established on a religious basis in order to escape persecution or the lack of freedom in Europe and it must have been the prospect of a new life that kept them going. Around 200 years later as the huge emigrant trade developed, conditions on board some vessels would not have been much better and it was a long time before luxury and better schedules started to prevail.

The British were the dominant nationality among the colonists and by the same token British ships were dominant in the Atlantic trade, but the American Revolution and the Declaration of Independence in 1776 marked a turning-point. From this point the traffic became two-way in as much as the colonists' own 'American' ships started to participate in the trade across the Atlantic. The emphasis for trade gradually switched from the Caribbean up to

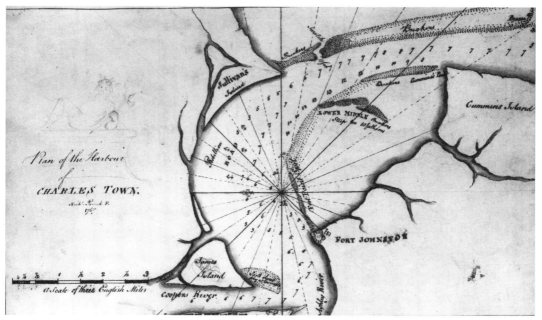

An early chart of Charlestown Harbour on the US east coast showing the basic navigation information.

the increasingly productive American and Canadian east coasts. It was also around this time that another significant event took place: the partnership of Watt and Boulton that would lead to the development of the steam engine which was to change the design of ships and the crossing of the Atlantic forever.

Meanwhile colonists continued to head west, frequently paying the lowest fares to take over what was normally cargo space, but for the favoured passenger who was prepared to pay the right premium there was cabin accommodation in the officers' quarters. This was still very basic by any stretch of the imagination but it offered a measure of civilized living as far as this could be obtained in a rough ship tossing and pitching its way to the Americas. Navigation was becoming more scientific (the chronometer and nautical almanac were developed around 1760) but the Atlantic Ocean retained its awesome reputation for bad weather. Each voyage across the Atlantic in the trading ships was a constant battle for survival and the biggest achievement was to arrive safely. Ships were completely isolated from the land unless they happened to meet another ship with which they could exchange messages. If a ship ran into difficulties there was no one to turn to for help. At best the life-saving appliances on board would be a couple of rowing boats, as often as not, totally inadequate for the number of people on board, especially when colonists were being carried. In any case the chances of survival from a ship that was in distress were small. The best that could be hoped for was that a passing ship would see their plight and rescue them, but the odds were against them. With the increasing traffic on the Atlantic this chance was also increasing, but shipping casualties remained high with up to one in five vessels being lost each year. Only the lure of the large profits that could accrue from successful voyages encouraged ship-owners to continue to send their vessels across the Atlantic. Throughout the history of Atlantic travel, the profit motive has been used to justify the risks involved but the cost, in terms of human life, must have been considerable.

Chapter Three

Emigration and the Sailing Packets

At the end of the eighteenth century and the beginning of the nineteenth century there were periods of considerable political turmoil on both sides of the Atlantic. In America the colonists were coming to terms with their new-found independence after kicking the British out, while further north Britain had taken over Canada from the French and so retained territorial rights over at least part of the continent. In the south the Spaniards were retreating from territories in Central and South America and in the Caribbean the British and the French were still in hot competition for the various islands and the southern shores of what is now the USA. In Europe the French Revolution was under way and Napoleon made his bid for power. The Battle of Trafalgar took place in 1805 on the edge of the Atlantic but it was 1815 before the Battle of Waterloo restored peace to the European scene and commerce across the Atlantic could resume a more normal pattern.

Over the three centuries since Columbus sailed across the Atlantic, commerce across the ocean had developed into a regular although highly risky business. Trading ships were small, rarely exceeding 150ft in length, and the achievement lay in completing a passage rather than in making fast passages or establishing records. Ships were often in poor condition, they sailed with comparatively small crews and the life expectancy of both ship and crew was short. The shipping newspaper *Lloyd's List* records that in a six-year period from 1793, some 4,344 British ships were captured by 'the enemy' and 2,383 were lost through shipwreck, grounding or fire. Probably Atlantic waters accounted for half these numbers and the figures demonstrate that it was not just shipwreck that was the danger. The Atlantic was a dangerous place for many reasons.

Despite the political upheaval, trade across the Atlantic continued. By 1800 it was very much a two-way operation with manufactured goods and luxuries being taken out from Europe and the ships returning loaded with tobacco, cotton and sugar from the south and timber, fish products and furs from the northern regions of the new continent. The timber trade is particularly significant because it demonstrates the shortage of timber that existed in Europe, particularly timber suitable for shipbuilding when most ships were still being built from this material. This shortage was a major factor behind the move by

European yards to build the first composite ships with iron framing and wooden planking, followed by ships built completely of iron.

On the American side of the Atlantic there was timber to be had for the taking from the vast forests and a large export trade developed. Shipyards were established in North America to take advantage of the timber reserves and these yards were eventually to produce some of the most magnificent sailing ships ever seen on Atlantic waters. Even as early as 1700 North American yards were building roughly half the sailing ships that were trading across the Atlantic and towards the end of the eighteenth century nearly a third of British-owned ships were built in North America to take advantage of the lower costs of raw materials. Most of the new timber was of the softwood variety and the ships were built using new techniques to match this wood.

At this time European warships were being built in the magnificent three- and four-deck style typified by HMS *Victory*, best known as Nelson's flagship. These warships were a throwback to the vessels of the Spanish Armada in which firing power from the cannons was considered more important than speed and manoeuvrability. On the other side of the Atlantic a much handier, faster type of warship was being developed and epitomized by the frigates *United States* and *Constitution*, both of which were launched in 1797. When fighting in the War of Independence ceased, the shipbuilders again turned their attention to the requirements of trade. Square sails were giving way to the much handier fore and aft sails to make ships capable of sailing into the wind and North American shipyards developed the famous schooners that both served the fisheries on the Grand Banks of Newfoundland and carried dried fish to the markets of Europe. Although equipped with fore and aft sails to give them a much better ability to make progress to windward, it was their fine underwater lines that gave them their speed and served as prototypes for the great tradition of the American clipper ships and the speed they brought to the crossing of the Atlantic under sail.

Attention invariably tends to be focused on the fast vessels, even though these were actually quite a small minority of the vessels plying Atlantic waters. The vast majority of vessels trading the Atlantic at the beginning of the nineteenth century were full-bodied, comparatively slow and unwieldy craft with the accent on cargo-carrying capacity rather than elegance and speed. Trading vessels remained at risk from attack by the ships of unfriendly nations and convoy systems were used to give mutual protection. Even then, other factors could still bring about disaster. One such convoy set out from Cork in 1804 with sixty-nine merchant ships and two warships bound for the West Indies and headed south to pick up the favourable winds and currents. However, twenty-nine of the ships in this convoy subsequently ran aground, with heavy loss of life, on the coast of Portugal. This disaster demonstrates that accurate navigation was still a problem, even when a whole convoy of ships was involved. The chronometer required for calculating longitude did not come into universal use until late in the eighteenth century.

The more settled situation in North America after the War of Independence and the vast tracts of land available for colonization were in stark contrast to the crowded cities of Europe and the starvation levels of subsistence in parts of the European countryside. The earlier colonists gave way to a rising tide of emigrants across the Atlantic that was to be a feature of Atlantic shipping for the next 100 years. The emigrant trade took in people from most European countries and built up slowly at first, although by 1850 more than 1 million emigrants a year were making the passage across the Atlantic. This new emigrant trade brought increased business for the ship-owners and formed what were probably the first real passenger-carrying services across the Atlantic, although passenger accommodation still left much to be desired. Emigrant ships were usually converted cargo ships with temporary accommodation built below decks for the passengers. On the return journey the ships would revert to their cargo-carrying role and be loaded with timber or other produce destined for Europe. While functioning as emigrant ships the accommodation would be basic with two or three tiers of bunks constructed in the holds. Space was at a premium because the greater number of emigrants carried, the more the ship-owner got paid, so the travellers would be packed as tightly as the ship-owners dared and cooking and toilet facilities would be as primitive as the owners thought they could get away with.

Seasickness must have been a major problem with the emigrants battened down below decks in anything but the finest of weather. Death on the crossings was a common occurrence and as the fare had to be paid before boarding, there was little incentive for the ship-owners to improve conditions to ensure that their 'passengers' survived. Thus the emigrant trade was in direct contrast to the slave trade in which the ship-owner had every incentive to keep his human cargo in good condition so that they could be sold on arrival. With the emigrants there was no such motive and epidemics of cholera and other infectious diseases were quite common on board. Up to a quarter of the emigrants might die on a passage across the Atlantic but there was also a lively birth rate on board these vessels so that on occasion the number of emigrants on arrival might just exceed that of departure!

The emigrant trade was so lucrative for ship-owners that all sorts of vessels were pressed into service to take advantage of it. One record reports that the sailing ship *Vestal* which sailed from Scotland to Prince Edward Island in Canada arrived with 301 'passengers' despite being only 90ft in length. Even smaller was the *Peter and Sarah* which took emigrants to Prince Edward Island in 1818. She was only 50ft in length, about the size of a harbour ferry. It is

Immigrants arriving in New York. The reality was they would most likely be in very poor condition after the long voyage.

The ships on the immigrant trade were extremely crowded so arrival must have been a considerable relief. (Illustrated London News)

small wonder then that around 16 per cent of all those who emigrated to Canada in 1847 died either on the passage or shortly after arrival and these figures are by no means unusual for other years.

One of the big problems with the emigrant trade was the time taken for the westward passage. For many ships, particularly the smaller ones, a passage of fifty or sixty days was considered quite normal, battling for week after week against the hostile winds and currents. These adverse conditions were inevitable unless the ships took the option of the cold route to the north or the much longer but warmer route to the south, and neither of these was likely to improve the health of the emigrants. That the trade continued in the way it did says much for the life the new arrivals expected to find and a lot about the conditions they were leaving behind. Perhaps they kept to a minimum their reports about the journey in letters and news sent back to other potential emigrants and since few could write anyway, perhaps new travellers set off in blissful ignorance, buoyed up by the hopes and expectations of the 'promised land' on the other side of the ocean. Emigrant ships sailed summer and winter for the New World and shipwreck, fire and storms took their toll on the human cargoes. The barque *John* ran aground on rocks shortly after leaving Plymouth in 1855 and the master and crew abandoned the ship, leaving the emigrants on board to their fate with many of them drowning as the ship broke up. This is just one example of the hundreds of vessels that suffered severe damage or were totally wrecked on their passage across the stormy Atlantic. Emigrants took their chance between the conflicting perils of shipwreck and disease and with the absence of safety regulations and equipment, it is perhaps remarkable that enough of them survived the passage to populate the vast new continent across the ocean.

While much of North European coastline consists of high cliffs with few off-lying dangers making a landfall relatively safe, the North American coastline is much more challenging. It is mainly low-lying and there are extensive shoals offshore such as the dreaded Nantucket Shoals and Sable Island waiting for the unwary ship. If you add into this the extensive fog banks that lurk along this coast at various times of the year then many ships must have got into trouble on the last leg of their journey. The icebergs that floated down from the Arctic added another challenge to the ships with just very basic navigation aids.

In 1820 more than 1,000 journeys were made across the Atlantic with timber cargoes for the British Isles. Twenty years later that number had more than doubled. With a ship making perhaps only two return passages a year, this figure for 1840 equates to 1,000 ships and to this must be added a similar number of ships bringing cotton and other goods from America. This was only the trade to the British Isles and in total there were probably 5,000 or

The early ships on the Atlantic routes were full-bodied vessels with poor sailing qualities.

more ships regularly sailing on the Atlantic routes by the mid-1820s. One-way trade is rarely profitable but here they could carry traditional produce cargoes on the eastbound voyage and return westwards with a human cargo. These voyages became so profitable that as the emigrant trade increased the fares charged actually dropped, so that by 1840 an emigrant would be charged perhaps only £3 for the Atlantic passage (a figure equivalent to a seaman's wages for a month and a half). The American Civil War in 1861 brought a temporary halt to the emigrant trade and also introduced other restrictions to commercial activity, but by this time the governments on both sides of the Atlantic had in any case started to regulate the emigrant trade, calling for minimum standards and conditions on board ships. The steamship had also started to make its appearance on the Atlantic and these ships offered improved conditions and speed. The promise of regular and predictable passages across the Atlantic under steam provided competition that the sailing ships could not match. As far as the latter were concerned, the emigrant trade was coming to an end by 1860. From this point on, the significance of the trade carried by sailing ships across the Atlantic started to diminish, although their finest hour was still to come.

An excerpt from the logbook of a ship crossing the Atlantic in 1771.

Not all the passenger movement across the Atlantic was migrant traffic. With the Industrial Revolution taking place first in Europe and then in North America, there was an increasing demand from people with adequate means for a comfortable passage across the ocean. Emigrants who had made money wanted to return to see relatives in Europe and the demand for a regular passenger trade in both directions across the Atlantic began to expand. Passengers on sailing ships who could afford it would pay for a cabin located aft among the officers' quarters on the ship and this led to demands for regular and predictable passenger services and the same for the more rapid transport of valuable cargoes. From this the sailing packet ship was born. Now the emphasis for these sailing ships was on speed and reliability with sailing schedules being advertised and proper provision being made for passenger-carrying. Larger sailing ships were built for speed and in the passages of these packet ships we start finding references to fast crossings and record journeys for the first time.

The first record of an advertised sailing for a sailing ship carrying passengers dates from 1817 and announces that the 424-ton *James Monroe* would sail from New York to Liverpool on 5 January 1818. The same advertisement said that the *Couvier* would sail from Liverpool on 1 January for New York and that regular monthly sailings would continue. So began the era of regular advertised shipping services and the establishment of the famous Black Ball Line, setting the stage for the quest for speed across the Atlantic. These scheduled passenger services were made possible by the use of ships designed with a hull form to give maximum speed and a rig that would enable them to make progress in light breezes but still strong enough to cope with Atlantic storms. Driving these large and powerful sailing ships was a new breed of men: tough, ruthless, but above all excellent seamen who would push their ships to the limit in order to make fast passages.

The dividing line between driving a ship to its reasonable limits and reck-lessness is a narrow one, and the reputations for fast Atlantic crossings were made by those captains who could keep just on the right side of this line. The successful captains who established the records were treated like gods, both feared and respected by seamen, but their reputations were only as good as their last passage. The North Atlantic is no respecter of reputations and their dogged determination would prove the undoing of many captains should they take one chance too many and push their ships to the point of disaster, particularly with the tenuous navigation resources then available.

The packet ships, or 'clipper ships' as they became known in some trades, were largely an American development. They had their origins in the ship-yards on the east coast of North America and were generally larger than their predecessors. Average ship lengths rose from around 160ft to 200ft or more. The largest of the clipper ships was 250ft in length, still a small ship by com-parison with the ships we know today, but for ships built of wood and carrying vast areas of sail these vessels marked the peak of the wooden shipbuilders' art. For European owners the prospect of building a ship in North America offered numerous advantages, not least an initially attractive price and the ability to immediately pick up a timber cargo for the maiden voyage eastwards across the Atlantic.

At the beginning of the nineteenth century two Scottish naval architects and shipbuilders, John and Charles Wood (appropriately enough), took this practice to a logical extreme to avoid a tax on imported timber brought into Britain, conceiving the idea of importing timber into Britain by constructing a ship of solid timber, sailing her across the Atlantic with a full cargo and breaking her up for the timber on arrival. This ship was designed specifically for the purpose and was built as cheaply as possible in order to allow as much of the squared timber to be re-used once it had been brought to Britain. The fact that this timber was actually part of a ship meant that it would not be regarded as being imported as cargo and could thus evade the tax.

John and Charles Wood were not inexperienced: they had designed and built the steamboat *Comet* way back in 1812 and they travelled to Canada to build the *Columbus* and the *Baron of Renfrew*. The former, which was built in 1824, had a length of 301ft and a beam of 50ft, making her, in all likelihood, the largest ship of her day. Packed with solid timber and rigged as a four-masted barque, the *Columbus* was towed down the St. Lawrence but went aground and much of the timber had to be jettisoned to refloat her. The *Columbus* made the voyage across the Atlantic safely, although it was reported that there was 18ft of water in her hold on arrival in London, perhaps due to her poor construction standards. The timber cargo was discharged from the ship, but rather than break her up her greedy owners decided to send her back for another cargo and on this return voyage she foundered. You can't take chances with the Atlantic.

The *Baron of Renfrew* was slightly larger at 304ft long and with a beam of 61ft. Launched in 1825, she too successfully crossed the Atlantic on her maiden voyage but went aground in the Thames Estuary and eventually drifted onto the French coast where she broke up. In terms of size the *Columbus* and the *Baron of Renfrew* were well ahead of their time and it was thirty years before their size was eclipsed by the clipper ship *Great Republic* designed and built by the famous Donald McKay at Boston. The *Great Republic* as originally constructed had a length of 335ft and a 53ft beam and went on to make one of the fastest-ever sailing ship crossings of the Atlantic in 1855.

The Black Ball Line began packet ship operations with the *James Monroe*, *Couvier*, *Amity* and *Pacific* in 1818 and here we have the first mention of shipping 'lines'. These vessels made regular sailings, had comfortable cabin lay-outs and were specifically designed for passenger operation with cargo-carrying being very much a secondary consideration in their design. Although only a maximum of 500 tons, each ship was equipped with a large dining room, panelled in mahogany and satinwood, with seven passenger state rooms off each side. The success of their operation may be judged by the fact that after six months in service, four more ships were added to the fleet with sailings now advertised on the 1st and 16th of each month and a year later the fleet was expanded with four more vessels. During the first years of the Black Ball Line's existence the average eastbound crossing took twenty-three days and the westbound crossing forty days. The *Canada*, one of the later ships to be added to the fleet, set a record for the best crossing from New York to Liverpool in fifteen days and eighteen hours in 1823.

The captains of these and other packet ships were expected to drive them extremely hard and such was the pressure on the hull and rigging that few vessels lasted more than a few years in this demanding service. However, the Black Ball Line prospered in its endeavours and as the packet trade developed the ships being employed also grew in size from the initial 500 tons or so up to 1,500 tons. One of the fastest ships on the Atlantic in 1852 was the *Fidelia* of just under 1,000 tons, which made a record run from New York to Liver-pool in thirteen days, seven hours and a remarkably fast run on a westbound

Handling the sails on the larger sailing ships was a high-risk occupation.
(*American Merchant Marine Academy*)

passage of seventeen days, six hours. The *Fidelia* was built by William H. Webb of New York who, along with Donald McKay, was responsible for many of the fast and famous large sailing ships built in America.

Competition for the Black Ball clippers was not far behind as the speed of the passage became the critical factor in the minds of the passengers. The success of the Black Ball Line led to the establishment of other packet ship companies with the Red Star Line being founded in 1821 and the Swallow Tail Line the following year. The Red Star had sailings on the 24th of every month from New York, while the Swallow Tail Line sailed on the 8th, thus dovetailing their services comfortably into those of the Black Ball Line to give weekly crossings on the Atlantic route. All these early services went into Liverpool on the European side but later the Swallow Tail Line established services direct to London, taking the risk of sailing through the extensive shallows of the English Channel and Thames Estuary. The Black X Line was also established in the 1820s to operate the service between New York and London and used smaller ships but later went on to build more luxurious vessels such as the 1,000-ton *Victoria*, which caused a sensation with her luxurious accommodation.

The Dramatic Line was established in the late 1830s by Captain E.K. Collins who later gave his name to the Collins Line steamships. Despite the luxurious appointments of these sailing packets, a crossing must still have been quite a daunting experience, even for the first-class passengers. Driving a sailing ship hard to maintain the schedules would give it a very uncomfortable

The magnificent *Oriental* was typical of the US-built sailing ships on the Atlantic routes.

motion no matter how much effort was put into creating a luxurious environment and the risks to a sailing ship crossing of the North Atlantic, particularly in winter, could not be entirely disguised.

Despite the luxury for first-class passengers these packet ships continued to carry emigrants in the holds. As the passenger trade developed, a second-class passenger division was also introduced, thus setting the pattern for three classes of Atlantic passengers that would later be followed by the steamships.

Competition between the shipping lines soon became intense and by the mid-1830s there were forty or more ships sailing between North America and Europe on scheduled sailings. As rivalry increased it was inevitable that sailings would be made on the same day by different lines and thus develop into races across the Atlantic. One of the first of these races took place between the *Columbus* (not to be confused with the Canadian-built timber ship *Columbus*), the *George Washington* and the *Sheffield*. These three ships left New York on the same day, but the *George Washington* was the first to be sighted off Holyhead on the Welsh coast three hours in front of the *Sheffield* having made the crossing in seventeen days. Although the *Columbus* was the loser in this 1836 race, she challenged the Dramatic liner *Sheridan* to a race across the Atlantic for a stake of $20,000. On this occasion the *Columbus* made the crossing in sixteen days, with the *Sheridan* arriving more than two days later.

Despite the advertised reliability of the service, at least as far as departures were concerned, events often dictated otherwise, particularly on the passage westbound from England to America. The packet *Hendrick Hudson* took seventy days for one crossing and then foundered on a later westbound crossing when she was carrying a cargo of iron rails. Even if the total loss of a packet ship was fortunately rare, damage to spars and rigging was frequent, particularly when these vessels were driven hard. Owners, however, accepted rigging failures as part of the price they had to pay for fast crossings, even on the most well-constructed ships.

Public interest in fast crossings was sustained and fostered by the shipping companies since their popularity, and hence profits, largely depended on their reputation for speed and reliability. Sailing packet services were soon being offered from ports other than New York on the American coast with Boston and Philadelphia being important terminals for transatlantic sailings. On the European side, Liverpool remained the main port for the packet ships but London, the French port of Le Havre and some of the German ports soon entered the fray. On the main routes the size of ship continued to increase, as did the speed of the crossings. Sixteen days was quite a commonplace time for the Atlantic crossing on the eastbound trip by the 1850s. Anything under three weeks could be considered a fast passage against the prevailing winds and currents.

Towards the end of the sailing ship era, the ships were built for speed under sail.

Brown and Bell built all the early Dramatic Line ships and later the *Patrick Henry*, a 1,000-ton ship that made an Atlantic crossing in fourteen days. By 1846, however, their reputation was being challenged by the famous Donald McKay shipyard. One of the first vessels built at this yard was the *New World* which, at 1,400 tons, was one of the largest of the packet ships of the mid-1800s, a huge ship to be built of wood. Shipbuilder Donald McKay had firm ideas about design and was responsible for many improvements in the size, speed and performance of the packet ships. Born in Nova Scotia, he moved south to New York and by the age of 30 he was at the top of the ship-designing and building profession. By the age of 34 he had set up his own shipbuilding yard at Boston that was to produce many famous packet and clipper ships. The *Staffordshire*, of 1,817 tons, was built in 1851 and in 1853 the yard went on to build the *Star of Empire* and the *Chariot of Fame* which were the largest packet ships ever built at 2,050 tons. None of these vessels broke any records on the Atlantic but they set the pattern for the clipper ships for which McKay was to become famous.

American and Canadian shipyards were the birthplace of the clipper ship. These vessels were primarily designed for operating over the long-distance routes from Europe and USA to Australia, and from the east coast of the USA round the Horn to the gold-prospecting areas of the West Coast. However, by 1850 the writing was on the wall with competition from steam ships and

The *Great Republic*, the largest sailing ship on the Atlantic trade route. (Sea Breezes *magazine*)

the reliability of the steam ships was starting to take over the passenger trade on the relatively short Atlantic passenger routes. Steam still could not yet compete on the long-distance routes because of the need for frequent coaling. Nevertheless, many clipper ships, although designed primarily for other routes, made Atlantic crossings on their maiden voyage or early in their career. The huge *Great Republic*, for example, built by McKay in 1853, crossed from New York to the Scilly Islands off Land's End in just thirteen days, a time that the steam ships would be hard-pressed to equal.

One of the most famous of the big sailing ships regularly plying the Western Ocean was *Dreadnought*. Built for the Red Cross Line of New York, this ship had an equally famous captain, Samuel Samuels, one of the toughest skippers on the Atlantic, who became a legend. He was so successful with earlier ships of the Red Cross Line that the *Dreadnought* was built specially for him and became known as the 'wild boat of the Atlantic'. Her first passage to Liverpool took twenty-four days but she made her reputation on the return voyage with a fast passage of nineteen days. In December 1854 the *Dreadnought* crossed the Atlantic from New York to Liverpool in thirteen days, eleven hours, and five years later knocked another two hours off this time. Although these were not record crossings, the *Dreadnought*'s reputation came from her consistently fast crossings in both directions. The all-time record for a packet or clipper ship crossing of the Atlantic was set in 1864 by the *Adelaide* with a time of twelve days, eight hours between New York and Liverpool.

The *Dreadnought* was the pride of the Red Cross Line but the company had far less success with their other ships and their toll of losses between 1850 and

1855 is indicative of the risks that were sometimes run. The *St. Patrick* was wrecked in 1854 and the *Andrew Foster* was in collision in the Irish Sea and sank. The *Driver* was reported missing on the Atlantic with 600 people on board, while the *Racer* went ashore in the Irish Sea. At this distance in time it is difficult to determine whether these losses were the result of the captains taking extraordinary risks with their ships or whether other factors such as the unpredictable weather of the Atlantic or poor maintenance came into play.

Despite these fast passages and apparent regularity of the Atlantic services by the sailing packet ships, their time was coming to an end. The threat posed by the steamships is shown significantly on the rare occasions when the sailing packet ships managed to make faster crossings than their rivals. In 1846 the packet boat *Toronto* arrived ahead of a Cunard steamer that had left on the same day from England and the captain of the *Toronto* became a national hero. The *Adelaide* of the Black Star Line, in making her record passage across the Atlantic in 1864, beat the Cunard steamer *Sidonia* but this was a rare and notable achievement. Today's public may give its sympathy and affection to the sailing ship but the march of progress was inevitable. The speed and particularly the reliability of the steamships were steadily eclipsing the more erratic performance of the sailing packets and clipper ships. These sailing

The *Glory of the Seas* built by Donald McKay. (*American Merchant Marine Museum*)

ships were fighting a losing battle for passengers and gradually they were switched to cargo-carrying where they could still compete economically.

In the early days of the changeover from sail the ocean-going steamships competed only on the transatlantic route and the fast sailing ships could still find passenger-carrying employment on the longer routes to the Far East and Australia. As sailing ships sizes increased, wood construction gave way to iron and then steel, thus handicapping the American shipyards that were building in wood. The competitive edge that the wood building yards had hitherto enjoyed against competing European yards was being lost and by 1880 the freight rates available for the sailing ships had dropped significantly and sailing ships were increasingly relegated to low-class freights. Insurance rates for the softwood ships built in North America also rose, especially as they got older.

Nevertheless, the sailing ship took some time to die out on the Atlantic. The introduction of iron masts and rigging and later iron hulls allowed sailing ships to match the steamers in size. Even steam power was introduced on sailing ships, not to assist with propulsion but to help with the handling of the heavy sails and spars. Sail didn't die easily and iron and then steel construction of sailing ships enabled much larger vessels to be built. The French five-masted barque *France*, for example, was built in 1918 with a length of 430ft to become one of the last of a dying breed. In America, huge schooners were built with the *Thomas W. Lawson* being built in steel in 1902 with no fewer

The seven-masted *Thomas W. Lawson* built in steel towards the end of the era of sailing ships on the Atlantic. (Sea Breezes *magazine*)

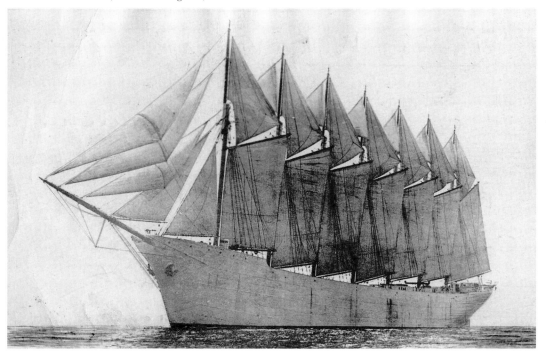

than seven masts. The six-masted *Wyoming* built in 1910 was the longest wooden sailing ship ever built with a length of 350ft and represented a game attempt by the wooden shipyards to stay in the running but steam and steel had really eclipsed their star by 1900.

Sailing ships continued to be seen on Atlantic waters up until the First World War and even in the 1920s and 1930s German and Scandinavian owners were still operating sailing vessels on the Atlantic but they were a rarity, no more than a relic of the era when the Atlantic had been dominated by sail for both the cargo and passenger trades. The best sailing ship in the world was no match for the speed and reliability of the steamer, however, and the record passages made by the sailing ships of this era should be seen as a memorial to the thousands of passengers and crews who lost their lives in creating and maintaining the vital trade routes linking the Old and New Worlds. The only sailing ships remaining today are training ships operated by a number of maritime nations and a few cruise ships that try to replicate the emotion of sail. These ships try to maintain the illusion of the romance of sail, operating without commercial pressures, unrealistic relics of a bygone age and they give little indication of the risks and perils of the sailing ship life on the Atlantic.

Chapter Four

Early Steam

Steam has a long history as far as its use as a means of propulsion for boats and ships is concerned. The first developments took place in the seventeenth century and towards the end of that century steam-powered boats were being built on both sides of the Atlantic but these were for operating on rivers and canals. It was 1808 before the first steamship ventured out to sea where the operating conditions are very different, both because of the motions of the vessel and the fact that the ships were operating in salt water. The *Phoenix* was designed for operating in the River Delaware but as she was built on the Hudson River she had to make a sea journey to get to her working territory. In Europe the *Comet* was launched in 1812 and operated first on the River Clyde and then out to the Scottish islands.

Builders and operators of steamships became more adventurous and it was not long before they were looking at the possibility of crossing the Atlantic. However, operating out on the ocean was a considerable challenge because of the need to carry huge amounts of coal to fuel the boilers and the fact that it was salt water that was not good for the boilers. The first steamship crossing of the Atlantic was made in 1819 but here the word 'steamship' needs qualifying because the *Savannah* was designed as a sailing ship and the steam engine was very much an auxiliary engine for use when winds were adverse and it was only used for a limited amount of time during the Atlantic crossing. Nevertheless, the 320-ton *Savannah* has gone down in history as the first steamship to make the Atlantic crossing. Built in New York in 1818, she was intended to operate the packet service from New York to Le Havre as a sailing ship but before she was completed she was purchased by the Savannah Steamship Company and fitted with a single-cylinder steam engine of 90 hp. This engine drove the 15ft-diameter paddle wheels which were collapsible and could be stowed on deck when not in use. Speed under steam alone under fair conditions was a modest 4 knots which was probably not much use against Atlantic waves.

With her steam engine and paddle wheels fitted the *Savannah* ran trials in March 1819 but at that time her owners decided that trade didn't justify her operation on the Atlantic and it was decided to send her to Europe for sale. Loaded with 75 tons of coal, she set off on 24 May and after loading more coal at Kinsale in Ireland, she arrived in Liverpool on 20 June having made the crossing at an average speed of 6 knots. It is reported that the engines were in use for a total of only eighty-five hours during the passage. Although the *Savannah* made the crossing of the Atlantic from west to east, her claim to the title of the first steamship crossing must not be taken too literally, and although designed to carry passengers she didn't actually have any on board during her Atlantic crossing so this was very much a tentative steamship venture onto the Atlantic.

The next ship fitted with steam power to cross the Atlantic was the *Rising Star* with a length of 123ft. She was built in London as a warship for use in the Chilean Revolution and was fitted with a twin-cylinder engine. The paddle wheels were incorporated inside the hull structure working through apertures in the bottom of the hull. She made the trip to Valparaiso that involved crossing the Atlantic, finally arriving in April 1822 after a voyage lasting nearly six months.

In 1824 the two-masted schooner *Caroline* owned by the French navy made a crossing of the Atlantic to French Guiana and later in 1827 made the return journey. This 121ft vessel was fitted with a steam engine to drive paddle wheels and has the distinction of being the first steam vessel to make a two-way crossing of the Atlantic but once again the engine was used very much in the auxiliary mode, usually only brought into operation when the winds were adverse, under which conditions progress under power was painfully slow.

The first attempt to use a steamship as a trading vessel across the Atlantic came with the building of the *Calpe*. Built for the American and Colonial Steam Navigation of London which is the first record of a company using the word 'steam' in its title, this vessel was sold to the Dutch navy in 1826 before she ever entered commercial service. However, she did make the passage across the Atlantic for her new owners in 1827 and went on to make two double crossings. Under Dutch ownership her name was changed to *Curaçao*. Her paddle wheels were equipped with extensions that could be fitted at sea so that as the coal on board was burned up during a passage and the vessel rose in the water, the wheels would continue to dig into the water and push the vessel along.

The next steam crossing of the Atlantic is also attributed to a naval vessel, this one being the paddle steamer *Rhadamanthus*, built for the Royal Navy in 1832. Four sister ships were also built to a similar design at the same time but it was the *Rhadamanthus* that had the distinction of covering a distance of 2,500 miles across the Atlantic at a mean speed of 6.1 knots, but once again steam power was used only intermittently to help the vessel along during adverse winds or in calm conditions. Steam was starting to make its mark on the Atlantic but not yet in any commercial applications.

The *Royal William* became the first Canadian-built steamship to make the Atlantic crossing. The largest steamship to be built at the time of her launch in 1831, she was designed to operate a regular passenger service between Quebec and Halifax in Canada and it is notable that Samuel Cunard was one of the directors of the company. Like the *Savannah*, the *Royal William* was then sent to Europe for sale and on this crossing the ship carried seven passengers, the first to be carried across the Atlantic on a steamship. However, the *Royal William*'s main claim to fame is the fact that she made virtually the whole crossing of the Atlantic under steam power with the sails being the auxiliary system. Leaving Nova Scotia on 18 August 1833, *Royal William* encountered severe gales off Newfoundland that disabled the starboard engine and for ten days the port engine alone was used. She eventually arrived at her destination on the River Thames twenty-five days later after putting into the Isle of Wight for repairs. Her average speed on this crossing was 6 knots, despite having to stop for one day out of every four to clear the salt from the boilers. Like the majority of early steamships operating in salt water, the *Royal William* was not fitted with condensers to recycle the steam and therefore had to use salt water in the boilers.

This problem and the ability to carry sufficient coal for an Atlantic crossing limited the application of steam power. You might need 500 tons of coal on a larger ship to fire the boilers on an Atlantic crossing which would reduce the amount of cargo that could be carried and also the time and effort taken to load the coal. Steam power might offer time reliability but there were also serious handicaps. Apart from the large amounts of coal that had to be carried, there was the valuable space in the centre of the ship that was taken up by the engines and boilers. The paddle wheels were also less than efficient and it should be remembered that these were primarily developed for ships operating in calmish waters. Out at sea in waves it could be a struggle to keep the paddles in the water to drive the ship along and they were fairly fragile and vulnerable to wave impact. Then on those early ships that had both sails and steam, one paddle wheel would come out of the water when the ship heeled under pressure from the sails affecting the steering with the ship wanting to turn away from the side where the paddle was driving. Those early paddle steamers must have been quite a challenge in the open ocean. On shorter routes the paddle steamers worked well and were starting to offer regular and reliable passenger services and it was this experience and the confidence it generated that led to the almost simultaneous formation of three companies to operate transatlantic passenger services by steamship despite the potential handicaps and ignoring the problems.

These companies, the British and American Steam Navigation Company of London, the Great Western Steamship Company of Bristol and the

Transatlantic Steamship Company of Liverpool, were the European answer to the American domination of transatlantic sailing packet traffic. British sailing ship companies had previously been concerned mainly with the emigrant trade, returning with non-human cargoes, leaving the prestigious packet ship routes to the Americans. The policies of these new steamship companies reflected the rapid development of and confidence in operating steamships in Europe. All three companies were formed in 1838, a fact that generated intense competition to operate the first regular transatlantic steamship service. Each company had a steamship designed and built for the transatlantic service, the *British Queen*, the *Great Western* and the *Liverpool* respectively; however, two of the companies decided not to wait for their new ships to be built and chartered ships to start the operation. This was an attempt to try to get a head start on the Great Western Steamship Company whose Brunel-designed *Great Western* had been launched in Bristol in 1837. The Transatlantic Steamship Company chartered the *Royal William* (not to be confused with the Canadian *Royal William*) and the British and American Steam Navigation Company chartered the *Sirius*, both these vessels having been built originally for the Irish Sea passenger service.

The *Sirius* takes a place in history as being the first steamer to cross the Atlantic under continuous steam power, this 208ft-long vessel making the crossing from Cork to New York in eighteen days, ten hours at a mean speed of 6.7 knots. Although she sailed from London, she called at Cork for more coal and to pick up passengers. The *Sirius* sailed from Cork on 3 April 1838 bound for New York and she was followed by the *Great Western* which sailed from Bristol just under a week later, having been delayed there for a day by unfavourable weather. The *Great Western* arrived in New York on 23 April, only a few hours after the *Sirius*. She made better speed but this margin of hours was enough to give the *Sirius* her place in the history books as the first.

It was not all smooth sailing for the *Sirius* though. While the captain is quoted as saying 'I am quite sold on the ship's security and speed far outstripping any mode of conveyance hitherto known', it seems that navigation was still the weak link. Approaching the home waters of the English Channel, she was in thick fog when in a sudden clearing of the fog she found herself almost upon one of the rocks of the Scilly Islands and only veered off at the last minute. This was possible in a steam ship but a sailing ship might not have been manoeuvrable enough to take such avoiding action. There must have been many such near misses.

However, the *Great Western* was a purpose-built ship designed to take on the North Atlantic. She was a magnificent ship for her day with a length of 235ft and she made the crossing in fifteen days, five hours with an average speed of 8 knots. She may not have been the first but she was the fastest with a time that beat most others set by the sailing ships and her time was one that could be relied on without dependency on the wind and weather. It was the *Great Western* that opened the door to steam on the Atlantic and demonstrated its potential and she ushered in a new era of Atlantic passenger travel comfort. She set high standards of accommodation for eighty passengers in luxuriously-appointed cabins and in comparison with the auxiliary power of the early Atlantic steamers, she had very powerful engines of 750 hp. Coal consumption was 30 tons a day but the bunkers could hold up to 800 tons. The *Great Western* went on to complete sixty-four crossings of the North Atlantic and served until 1846 when she was sold to the Royal Mail Steam Packet Company Ltd, with whom she continued to operate Atlantic services between Southampton and the West Indies.

The *Royal William*, the other chartered ship to enter service on the Atlantic steamship routes, was operated by the Transatlantic Steamship Company. She departed from Liverpool with thirty-two passengers on board and averaged 7.3 knots on her maiden Atlantic voyage. The *Royal William* completed three round trips on the Atlantic before returning once more to the Irish Sea service. With a length of just 175 ft, she was probably the smallest steamship ever to regularly trade on the Atlantic routes.

The second purpose-built Atlantic steamship to enter service was the *Liverpool*, built to take over from the *Royal William*. She left Liverpool on her maiden voyage in the autumn of 1838 with sixty passengers on board intent on a non-stop crossing, but was forced into Cork by a violent gale. It was sixteen days from her Liverpool departure before she finally left Ireland, covering the journey to New York at an average speed of 7.9 knots. The *Liverpool* was the first two-funnelled steamer to take on the Atlantic but her operations did not prove to be the hoped-for success and the Transatlantic Steamship Company was wound up two years after formation.

The *British Queen* was purpose-built for the British and American Steam Navigation Company and at the time of her launch in 1838 was the largest steamship afloat. Accommodation was provided for 207 passengers with 104 berths in the aft cabins and 103 in forward cabins. A large 60 ft-long dining saloon was situated between the two cabin areas, bringing a new measure of luxury to the Atlantic, but completion of this ship was delayed by financial problems with the engine-builders and the *British Queen* finally sailed from London in 1839. She averaged 8.4 knots on her maiden voyage across the Atlantic and made nine crossings in the service of the British and American Steam Navigation Company before being sold to the Belgian government, under whose auspices she continued in Atlantic service until 1842. For two years the *British Queen*, with her length of 245 ft, was the largest passenger ship in the world.

The *Royal William*, the first two-funnelled ship on the Atlantic.

Although steam power was used continuously on these crossings, all the early steamships were fitted with a full inventory of masts and sails and obviously used these to the fullest extent when the winds were favourable. These early ships were all paddle steamers built in wood and must have experienced considerable difficulty keeping the paddle wheels in the water when the ship was rolling in any sort of seaway. Contemporary reports suggest that there was continual trouble with paddle wheels being damaged and repairs having to be effected at sea. On the other hand, the problem of salt contamination in the boilers had largely been removed by the introduction of condensers that allowed fresh water to be recirculated throughout the system, condensing the steam from the boilers after use and pumping it back into the system. Nevertheless, machinery on these early ships was not particularly efficient with steam pressures, for example, rarely exceeding 5lb per square inch. The engines themselves were massive, with the bore and stroke being measured in feet rather than inches, and it is a remarkable testimony to the early engineering skills that the machinery could cope with the stresses and strains of an Atlantic crossing. In addition to the risk from the ravages of Atlantic weather, there was also a considerable fire risk on these wooden-hulled vessels.

However, these pioneering steamships on the Atlantic service captured the imagination of the public in a way that was to continue for more than a century through all the magnificent Atlantic liners to follow. The departure of ships on their maiden voyages attracted huge crowds and their arrival in

New York set the precedent for the receptions afforded later to all major new passenger ships making their first appearance in the harbour. The rivalry of the *Sirius* and the *Great Western* and their arrival within hours of each other in New York continued a trend set by the sailing packet ships and firmly established the pattern of Atlantic 'races' that intensified the competition between operating companies.

On one occasion in 1839 the *British Queen* and the *Great Western* sailed from New York on the same day and this time it was Brunel's ship that arrived home first in Bristol, but only hours ahead of the *British Queen*'s arrival in Portsmouth. In time such rivalry between ships and companies developed into a matter of national pride involving governments and politicians in the struggle for supremacy on the Atlantic Ocean. 'Fast' passages and luxurious accommodation were the criteria by which Atlantic passenger ships were judged, even though speeds were still a modest 10 knots, while safety, caution and respect for the ocean appear to have taken a back seat.

One of the greatest names in passenger shipping was that of Samuel Cunard, whose direct association with the Atlantic really began when he won the contract for the carriage of mail by steamship across the North Atlantic in 1838 (although he had also been linked with the *Royal William*). At that time he didn't have a ship with which to fulfill his mail carriage obligations, but with this contract in his pocket Cunard formed the British and North American Royal Mail Steam Packet Company, later to become the Cunard Steamship Company, and the paddle steamer *Unicorn* (which had been built in 1836) was purchased to operate the embryonic mail service. The *Unicorn*'s first Atlantic crossing took place in 1840 with twenty-seven passengers on board and the ship reached Halifax in fourteen days, averaging 8 knots in what are described as appalling weather conditions.

The 185ft-long *Unicorn* was kept on by Cunard to operate a service between Quebec, Pictou and Halifax, while the Cunard line had four new ships – the *Britannia*, *Acadia*, *Caledonia* and *Columbia* – built to maintain the Atlantic service. With four ships in his Atlantic fleet, Cunard brought a new pattern to the Atlantic passenger trade and the four vessels established a monthly transatlantic mail steamship service between Liverpool, Halifax and Boston. The first of these vessels to enter service was the *Britannia* but the other ships were of almost identical design. With a length of 207ft these ships didn't break any size records but when built in 1840 they offered a new degree of sophistication, particularly in their machinery. The boiler pressure was now raised to 9lb per square inch to supply steam to the 440hp engine. Although the speed of the vessel is given as 8.5 knots, the *Britannia* made her maiden voyage from Liverpool to Halifax in eleven days, four hours to give a mean speed of 10 knots, perhaps indicating that she must have had considerable help from the wind on this crossing. The *Britannia* was received with great enthusiasm in both Halifax and Boston, these ports being delighted to be on the receiving end of a passenger service that was eclipsing the service provided by the sailing packet ships departing from New York. On the return voyage to Liverpool the *Britannia* took just over ten days for the crossing, a record for any vessel at that time, although of course the distance from Boston to Liverpool is shorter than from New York.

Much was made of the regularity and reliability of these passenger services, but aboard such comparatively small ships the North Atlantic must still have been very uncomfortable at times, particularly during the winter storms. Steamships could make progress against the wind and they helped to reduce the danger of being stranded on a lee shore but the hazards of nature that had plagued the sailing ships remained. Violent storms, icebergs and fog, the latter particularly over the Grand Banks and the waters down to Nova Scotia, did not suddenly disappear, so perhaps it was almost inevitable that eventually disaster would strike the all-conquering steamships.

In 1843 the *Columbia* ran aground on rocks off Cape Sable at the south-east tip of Nova Scotia but, amazingly, all the passengers and crew were saved as well as the mail and cargo! This incident demonstrated that navigation techniques had not kept pace with the advent of the steamship. However, even before this incident Cunard had ordered another ship that was even larger. This was the *Hibernia*, and a sixth ship, the *Cambria*, was added after the loss of the *Columbia*. These two new ships were faster and more luxurious than the first four, and for seven years the Cunard Line had established a virtual monopoly of the transatlantic steamship services carrying the mail and high-profile passengers on what was still a risky Atlantic crossing. Even with the monopoly, the Atlantic services were not profitable and it was only the mail subsidies that enabled operations to continue. Despite this lack of profit, it was inevitable that Cunard supremacy would eventually be challenged and that the challenge was to come from the United States.

This time it was the proposed award of mail contracts from the United States government that prompted the construction of the paddle steamer *Washington* by the US Ocean Steam Navigation Company in 1847. When she was commissioned the *Washington* became the largest ship afloat and was reputed to be the fastest and on her first sailing from New York, with 120 passengers on board, she found herself racing the Cunard liner *Britannia* which had left Boston on the same day bound for Liverpool. Perhaps it was experience that counted but the *Britannia* completed the crossing a massive two days ahead of her rival; however, since New York to Southampton is a considerably longer distance than Boston to Liverpool, there can have been little difference in speed between the two vessels. In fact the performance of the

Washington was quite creditable considering that this was her maiden voyage and she needed time to bed down. A second ship, the *Hermann*, was added to the Ocean Steam Navigation Company fleet in 1848 and made a record crossing from New York to Southampton in eleven days, twenty-one hours and now the speed challenge on the Atlantic passenger services had started, setting a pattern that was to survive for the next 100 years.

Not to be outdone by this American competition, Cunard obtained a contract to operate a Liverpool to New York route and alternated this on a weekly basis with Halifax and Boston. Four new ships were built to maintain this service, named *America*, *Niagara*, *Europa* and *Canada*. The last two of these ships both set new Atlantic records with the *Canada* taking just nine days, twenty-two hours to cross from Liverpool to Boston. Cunard supremacy was re-established but the Americans were not taking things lying down and with support from government sources the Collins Line was established to build five large and fast mail steamers for the Atlantic routes, thought to be the first time that government support or subsidy was given to ships on the Atlantic passenger routes.

It was not only speeds that were increasing but also size. Tiny by modern standards, the *Atlantic* was the first of this new fleet to be built in 1849 with a length of 300ft, but construction was still in wood in the American tradition. She was followed by the *Pacific*, *Arctic* and *Baltic*, while a fifth ship was planned but never built. Luxurious accommodation for 200 passengers was provided but these vessels could also carry 450 tons of cargo and the paddle wheels

The *Europa*, the liner that helped Cunard re-establish their Atlantic supremacy.

The *Atlantic*, one of four sister ships built for the Collins Line in 1849.

were powered by an 800 hp engine. The *Atlantic* left on her maiden crossing in 1850 but suffered considerable mechanical problems, only managing to redeem herself on the return voyage with a record run of ten days, sixteen hours to New York to beat the Cunard record. Cunard retaliated with even faster speeds from their ships, putting more pressure on the machinery. As the pace of the ships increased, so did the casualty rate and the Collins Line *Atlantic* was an early victim. She was reported overdue on a mid-winter voyage but was sighted by another Cunard ship, stopped with her main paddle shaft broken. With only sail power now available, the *Atlantic* had to return to Cork.

Despite these setbacks, attempts to set new records did not diminish and the four Collins Line ships now dominated the Atlantic as far as speed was concerned with crossings in less than ten days to gain what soon became known as the Blue Riband; a title given in later years to all speed record-holders and believed to have its origin in the blue of the garter sash worn by Knights of the Garter. Average speeds for a crossing soon rose to around 13 knots and the effects of speed on passenger traffic can be seen by the fact that patronage of the slower Cunard ships fell off by 50 per cent while the Collins' ships held the record.

Cunard tried to tackle this problem by commissioning the *Arabia* but this wooden paddle steamer could not compete with the all-conquering Collins

The *Arabia*, the last wooden vessel built for Cunard in 1851. (*American Merchant Marine Museum*)

Line ships. The stage seemed set for Collins' dominance when the Cunard ships were taken out of Atlantic service after requisition by the British Admiralty for military use during the Crimean War. This left the Collins Line ships with the Atlantic routes to themselves until 1854 when disaster struck and the *Arctic* collided with the 200-ton steamer *Vesta* in dense fog 60 miles south of Newfoundland in the Grand Banks area. The *Vesta* made port safely and it was only after she had steamed away that the *Arctic* realized her own damage was so extensive that the ship was sinking fast. There was no way to call the *Vesta* back and the captain of the *Arctic* headed for Cape Race in attempt to beach the ship, but she sank 20 miles from land with only a handful of the 391 passengers and crew surviving in the two lifeboats. This led to public condemnation of the 'high speeds' of these record-breaking ships in fog, but little comment was made about the lack of lifeboats. Two years later in 1856 the *Pacific* was also lost at sea and despite the fitting of additional watertight bulkheads on the *Baltic*, the Collins Line could not cope with the adverse publicity of these disasters and collapsed in 1858.

The way was open for British Cunard to make a comeback and this they did with a vengeance by introducing the *Persia* in 1855. She was the first iron vessel for the company and the first iron paddle steamer on the Atlantic routes, and she also represented a considerable leap forward in size, being 376ft in length. More attention was paid to safety features such as watertight

The Collins Line's *Arctic* held the Blue Riband for four years but sank after a collision off Newfoundland. (Sea Breezes *magazine*)

bulkheads in an attempt to restore public confidence in Atlantic liners and the *Persia* crossed the Atlantic from Liverpool to New York at an average speed of 13.82 knots, giving her the Blue Riband which she held until 1862.

Disasters tend to be quickly forgotten and the increasing demand for passenger places from both sides of the Atlantic led to new companies entering the fray and for the first time ships from outside Britain and the US entered the fray. Notable among these was the Hamburg Amerika Line from Germany but from Britain there was the Inman Line and the US was represented by the Vanderbilt European Line established by Cornelius Vanderbilt. Initially Vanderbilt used his own 2,000-ton private yacht for passenger-carrying, but the reputation of the company was established by the purpose-built *Vanderbilt* launched in 1855 which came close to setting a new Atlantic record but could not quite break the supremacy of the Cunarders.

Since the introduction of steam on the Atlantic the design of ships had not changed a great deal except increase in size. Paddle wheels were still the favoured propulsion system and wood construction was still used, although iron ships were starting to be introduced. Now design was starting to change reflecting the increase in size with Cunard using iron construction and more importantly for the first time introducing propeller propulsion in 1843. Paddle wheels were never a very successful solution in the rough seas that were associated with Atlantic weather and the introduction of the screw propeller on the SS *Great Britain* was to set a pattern for the future. Built in Bristol for the Great Western Steamship Company, she was notable for her technological innovation and her length of 322ft, but her speed did not match that of the paddle steamers and her potential for competing on the Atlantic routes ended abruptly when she was stranded on the coast of Ireland. Nevertheless, the design of the *Great Britain* set the pattern for future successful Atlantic liners with the combination of wrought-iron construction and screw propellers.

Her sister the *Great Eastern* was launched in 1858 and has been described as the most ambitious failure in the whole history of naval architecture. Once again, Brunel was the designer and this ship was five times the tonnage of any ship then in use: she was close to 700ft in length, a monster for the time. A hybrid screw and paddle wheel system of propulsion was proposed for this giant ship to give her a speed of 15 knots. One of the advantages of this size of ship was that sufficient bunkers could be carried for very long passages without compromising cargo and passenger-carrying ability. Accommodation was provided for 4,000 passengers, a huge number for the time compared with the 500 or so carried by rivals and comparable to many modern cruise ships. However, her speed did not come up to expectations and she was never a commercial success, perhaps making a leap too far into the future in one step. Still, her time on the Atlantic was not over and she was used to lay a number of transatlantic telegraph cables.

These pioneering designs predicted the changes on the Atlantic, however, and the last wooden steamship built for Atlantic passenger service was the

The huge *Great Eastern* in a gale south of Ireland.

Adriatic built for the Collins Line in 1856. Five years later saw the last of the paddle steamers, the *Scotia*, enter Atlantic service. From then on it was iron followed by steel combined with propellers for propulsion powered by steam from high-pressure boilers.

The American Civil War greatly curtailed Atlantic passenger traffic and it was not until 1863 that the *Scotia*, ironically a paddle steamer, set a new Atlantic record with a crossing from New York to Cork at an average speed of 14 knots. On the westward crossing she set a speed of 14.54 knots and both records lasted until 1867. The Cunard Line stuck to paddle steamers because their contract with the Admiralty for carrying mail had stipulated the use of such vessels. Eventually the Admiralty relented and Cunard were able to introduce their first screw steamer, the *Russia*, which set a new record on the eastbound crossing with a speed of 14.22 knots. Note it was now speed and not time that defined the Atlantic record-holders and this took into account the different distances from alternative ports.

Competition on the Atlantic was still fierce and the *City of Paris*, owned by the Inman Line, took the Blue Riband in 1867. When the *Russia* and the *City of Paris* left New York together they made their crossings of the Atlantic within minutes of each other. The Inman Line was riding high by 1870 but then came the White Star Line which commissioned four ships to be built for

Life on board was often far from pleasant when a liner was rolling in a storm.

the Atlantic trade: the *Oceanic, Atlantic, Baltic* and *Republic.* The *Baltic* set a new Atlantic record in 1873 and made history by being the first ship to exceed an average speed of 15 knots on the Atlantic crossing, still very slow by modern standards but a milestone at the time.

Once again though, it was disaster that slowed progress and this time it was the loss of the *Atlantic*. Five days out from Liverpool the *Atlantic* ran into wild winter gales that caused her to reduce speed. With bunkers dwindling and still 460 miles to go to New York, the captain decided to put into Halifax in Nova Scotia for more coal. Reputedly without adequate charts and little past experience of the port approaches, the *Atlantic* went aground about 20 miles from Halifax and over half the nearly 1,000 passengers and crew on board lost their lives. A letter written in 1875 and quoted in the maritime publication *Ships Monthly* states that 'none of the officers had ever taken a vessel into Halifax, and few knew anything about it. Placed in an unknown position, they were ignorant of the rocks and shore and so this appalling catastrophe happened.'

Accidents such as this appeared to affect only the shipping company involved rather than having any lasting effect upon the transatlantic trade in general. In this respect the Cunard ships seemed to bear a charmed life, although they must have been equally exposed to the risks of fog and ice and the shoals of Nantucket and Sable Island. The Inman Line cashed in on the discomfiture of the White Star Line by building the *City of Berlin*, the largest and longest liner to enter Atlantic service when she made her maiden voyage in 1875. An overall length of 520ft made her an impressive vessel and accommodation for 1,700 passengers, most of them in steerage, made her a significant force in the Atlantic trade and a sign of how the technology of ship design was developing.

The *City of Berlin* set a new Atlantic record within her first year of service but the White Star Line was not to be outdone and ordered two new ships, the *Britannic* and the *Germanic.* The *Germanic* claimed the Blue Riband with a record crossing and then had to hand the title over to her sister ship a few years later. Once again, the White Star Line was at the top of the tree and at the forefront of Atlantic travel.

The British Guion Line (also known as the Liverpool and Great Western Steamship Company) had been operating on the Atlantic for thirteen years, focusing mainly on the immigrant trade before they decided in 1876 to build a ship to attempt the Blue Riband. The result was the *Arizona* which upped the record speed for a crossing to 15.96 knots, a record that she held for three years. However, she hit the headlines for all the wrong reasons by colliding with an iceberg in 1879 while travelling at 14 knots. Her bow was crushed for a length of 26ft but a collision bulkhead built into the forward part of

The White Star liner *Celtic* in a winter storm on the Atlantic.

the hull saved her from sinking. After putting into St. John's, Newfoundland, a temporary wooden bow was fitted and the liner continued her voyage to Liverpool!

In 1881 the Cunard Line made a brief reappearance in the record charts with another pioneering development, the first steel ship for the Atlantic routes, the *Servia*. The Guion Line responded with the largest ship then in service, the *Oregon*, which upped the Atlantic record to 17.48 knots. Despite this success, the Guion Line was running into financial difficulty and the *Oregon* was sold to arch rivals Cunard, for whom she went on to set further records. However, she was in a collision and sank off Fire Island near New York but all the passengers and crew were rescued by the German liner *Fulda*. This was Cunard's first major ship casualty but their reputation remained largely intact because everyone was rescued. No one seemed to question the cause of the collision, which was likely to have been the speed of the *Oregon*.

From 1880 or so until the end of the century a ding-dong battle started for the Atlantic speed record with the prestigious title of 'fastest on the Atlantic' changing almost every year. The *America* built for the National Line of Liverpool took the title from the *Oregon* but then lost it back to the (now) Cunard ship. Cunard maintained their service with the *Etruria* and the *Umbria*, the former ship coming very close to breaking the 20-knot barrier with a speed of

The *Oregon* was built for the Guion Line but sold to Cunard. She was a holder of the Atlantic record but sank in a collision off New York.

19.9 knots for an eastbound crossing in 1887. It was the second *City of Paris*, however, owned by the Inman Line that finally crossed this threshold in 1889 on a westbound crossing, going on to break the 20-knot barrier on the eastbound crossing as well later the same year. Two years later the new White Star Line twins *Teutonic* and *Majestic* each held the westbound Atlantic record for brief periods. These two famous sister ships claim a special place among the distinguished ranks of the Atlantic liners. They were the first White Star liners to have twin screws but they were also the last ships to be ordered by this company to attempt the Blue Riband.

By the turn of the century the whole concept of Atlantic liners was changing. The size of ships was steadily increasing and much more reliance was now placed on the engines' auxiliary sails being abandoned entirely. Many vessels now had at least twin screws and it was increasingly felt that engines were sufficiently reliable, even at speeds of 20 knots or more. The steam engines used were compound reciprocating engines operating with high steam pressures but coal was still the primary fuel.

The technical advances were important but in the eye of the public the attention was on the ever more luxurious accommodation. The *Teutonic* and her sister ship *Majestic* owned by Cunard were especially impressive in this respect. These ships were seen as epitomizing national pride, for although the Guion Line's *City of New York* and *City of Paris* operated under the British flag, the company and their ships were, to all intents and purposes, American-owned. The rivalry between these four ships aroused tremendous public interest. Cunard tried to stand publicly aloof, but they were equally guilty of

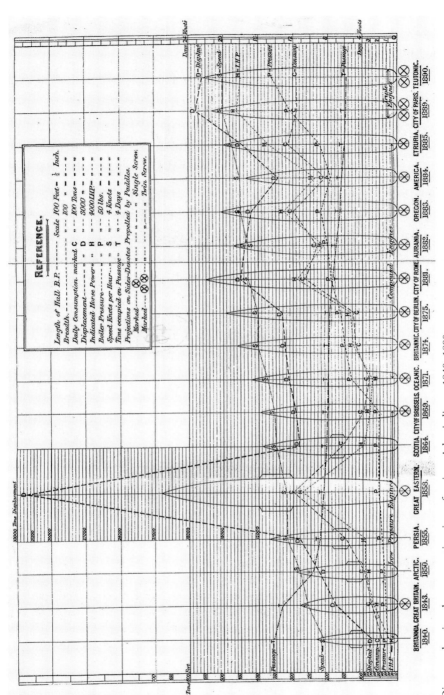

Diagram showing the comparative sizes of various Atlantic liners, 1840–1890.

forcing their ships to maintain schedules, no matter the conditions thrown up by the Atlantic. On one occasion the *City of New York* and the *Teutonic* left Cork almost simultaneously and arrived at New York within four hours of each other, with the *Teutonic* setting the pace and claiming a new Atlantic record in the process.

The Inman Line eventually transferred to the United States flag in 1893 in order to qualify for a subsidy to carry American mails. Cunard, meanwhile, commissioned two new ships for the Atlantic route, the *Lucania* and the *Campania* which were completed in 1893. Both went straight out to set new records for the crossing of the Atlantic, taking the record close to 22 knots. It was British and American ships that were fighting it out for the Atlantic record at this time but then a German challenger appeared.

The early ships of the German ship-owners Norddeutscher Lloyd and the Hamburg Amerika Line were built in Britain, but when it came to building Blue Riband contenders, national pride dictated that ships had to be built in home yards. By 1897 these two German companies were carrying consider-ably more passengers across the Atlantic than the British with the numbers being swelled by the immigrant trade. For the Blue Riband two new ships were ordered: the *Kaiser Wilhelm der Grosse* and the slightly smaller *Kaiser Friedrich*. The *Kaiser Wilhelm der Grosse* with a length of 627ft was the largest passenger liner in the world at the time of her launch and, as events were to prove, also the fastest. Her machinery comprised two sets of four-cylinder triple-expansion steam engines producing a total of 28,000 hp. To supply these engines, coal consumption was a massive 250 tons a day and the design speed of the ship was 22.5 knots. On her maiden voyage the liner didn't take the record but towards the end of 1897 she managed an eastbound crossing at an average speed of 22.35 knots and a year later set a westbound record of just over 23 knots.

The focus on the Atlantic trade was on the passenger ships but there was a huge traffic in moving cargoes across the Atlantic. The sailing ships main-tained their position by still carrying a considerable proportion of the cargo because it was not time-critical and sail was a cheaper alternative. However, steamships were moving into the cargo trade as well and, as said in the last chapter, the days of the sailing ship, even for cargo-carrying, were numbered.

So the nineteenth century ended with ever larger and faster passenger ships on the Atlantic but shipping companies were treading a narrow line between operating advertised fast services on schedule and avoiding the bad publicity that would result from any accident. Communications were still by line-of-sight flags and signals and navigation was still very basic, relying on sextant positions that in turn relied on clear skies, making landfalls on both sides of the Atlantic a risky business. Fog and icebergs were still a threat that did not diminish and the crowded mixture of slow sailing ships and fast steamships on the Atlantic was an unhealthy one. Many of the sailing ships that disappeared without trace at this time are likely to have been victims of collision with steamships, which would perhaps hardly have noticed the impact as they thundered across the Atlantic. The Atlantic was a crowded and dangerous ocean by the turn of the century and while the luxurious passenger ships dominated public attention, the number of shipping casualties was still unacceptably high and navigation technology had not kept pace with advances in ship design.

Chapter Five

The Grand Liners Dominate the Atlantic

The twenty years between 1890 and 1910 saw the Atlantic liner come of age. With ships now approaching 700ft in length, passengers were at last largely isolated from the rigours of going to sea, or so at least the liner companies would have their customers believe. By surrounding their passengers with all the comforts of the shore, the risks of an Atlantic crossing such as ice and collision were made to appear minimal and ship-owners could pretend that the often violent weather of the North Atlantic Ocean and its associated risks could be shrugged off with impunity. We still see the same approach today with modern cruise ships.

The reality was otherwise, of course, because no matter what size the ship, the storms outside could not be ignored and as average speeds rose above 20 knots the captains of the liners were challenged to maintain speeds and schedules in rough seas. The captains were faced with an appalling dilemma, trying to find a balance between safety and maintaining schedules, and in most cases it was the schedules that were more important. This challenge was particularly significant on westbound crossings when ships were ploughing into the prevailing westerlies. The fine bows shape needed for speed had reduced buoyancy at the front of the ship and so would tend to plough through a wave rather than rise over it and on even the largest liners the foredeck would be totally submerged in the oncoming seas and the crests of the waves would roar down the deck to crash dangerously against the superstructure. Damage to the fittings and fixtures on the decks was a common occurrence and ought to have served as a warning to captains that the time had come to slow down. This was a message that continued to be ignored by some captains in the interests of making a fast passage and damage to the bridge structure far above the waves was a disturbing feature of some of the more dramatic crossings. This type of damage could put the ships' very survival at risk, so balancing the demands of the ship-owners for regular schedules to be maintained and the dictates of safety, which demanded that ships eased down when the sea was rough, remained a real challenge for the liner captains. As any seaman will know, rogue waves can arrive unannounced and when the bow descends into the first

The smashed-in bridge of the *Lusitania* after she was struck by a rogue wave in 1910. (*Frank Braynard Collection*)

large wave even the mightiest ship could be dwarfed. The Atlantic takes no prisoners in its violent storms.

In severe weather, the more responsible crews might try to reduce the motion of the vessel by reducing speed to ensure passenger comfort. The elite first-class accommodation was placed amidships where the motion would be less but there was no hiding from the plunging motion when heading into waves at speed. If the sea was on the beam then the ship could roll heavily because this was in the days long before computer-controlled stabilizers had been developed. Passenger loyalty to individual liner companies was only as good as the last trip across, and a passenger who had suffered discomfort on one trip would think nothing of switching his or her allegiance to another line in the hope of better treatment. Passengers were unlikely to appreciate that all ships become equal when faced with the might of an Atlantic storm.

The techniques of navigation of these ocean greyhounds had not kept up with their increase in speed. By the beginning of the twentieth century the sextant and the chronometer had been fully refined, so that observations of

The fine-looking *Aquitania*, a classic Atlantic liner.

sun and stars could give positions with a good degree of accuracy, certainly to within 1 mile in fine conditions. However, the North Atlantic rarely offers these fine conditions with clear skies and sharp horizons that enable a sextant fix to be achieved. Skies could remain overcast for the whole crossing, meaning that after a trip lasting five days or so a liner might get no more than one or two fixes on the way across the Atlantic and yet she would be expected to make an accurate landfall on schedule. On the European side landfalls were made slightly easier even in modest visibility because the majority of dangerous rocks such as the Scilly Isles were marked by lighthouses by this time but on the American side, the Nantucket Shoals stretching 50 miles out to sea from Nantucket Island were one of many traps waiting to ensnare unwary vessels as they neared the land on the way into New York. Even in fine weather an accurate landfall here is difficult but in fog it must have been a nightmare. Approaching land on either side of the Atlantic in poor visibility in a large liner at speeds around 20 knots with thousands of passengers on board and working on dead reckoning from positions two or three days old must have taxed the navigation skills of any ship's officers to the maximum.

Radar that could help to fix positions in fog was non-existent until after the Second World War. A large ship travelling at 20 knots takes several miles to be brought to a stop and even if ships slowed down as they were supposed to in fog, then their very size and momentum could still make it difficult to take

avoiding action should other vessels suddenly loom out of the fog. It is therefore hardly surprising that there were numerous collisions between the liners
and other ships. The White Star liner *Olympic* collided with HMS *Hawke*
when approaching Southampton on 20 September 1907 but escaped with
comparatively minor damage. Perhaps because the liners invariably came off
best in these encounters with relatively superficial damage, they received little
publicity and little adverse comment was made.

Several liners struck icebergs on their Atlantic voyages. The highly-
publicized sinking of the RMS *Titanic* in 1912 could almost have been
foreseen long before the event occurred, for several earlier ships suffered collision and damage. In 1907 the *Kronprinz Wilhelm* was travelling at 16 knots
when she struck an iceberg a glancing blow and was lucky to do so, for at that
speed a more direct impact could have resulted in very severe damage or
sinking. In 1911, less than a year before the *Titanic* went down, the Anchor
Line ship *Colombia* hit an iceberg on her way from Glasgow to New York.
The captain's terse message over the radio was 'August 4th 1911 – 1,800 miles
east Cape Race. During intermittent fog collided with iceberg, damage bow,
proceeding on voyage, weather fine, position today noon – 43° 40 north –
28° 22 west. Signed Mitchell.'

The *Colombia* was fortunate because she had slowed to 8 knots in the known
iceberg region. Even so, when she hit the berg the bow plunged 12ft into the
ice and tons of ice fell on to the deck. The liner was carrying 520 passengers
and although none suffered injury, this must have been a dramatic and worrying moment for Captain Mitchell who was on his first command of an
Atlantic liner.

The White Star liner *Baltic* also collided in fog when she rammed an oil
tanker 1,000 miles out into the Atlantic from New York. The bow was badly
damaged but fortunately the bulkheads held and the liner was able to make
New York safely, although not without considerable panic among the passengers on board. The crew of the *Baltic* was able to patch up the hole in the
liner, but nothing is recorded about the fate of the tanker which was last seen
from the *Baltic* drifting away in the fog, apparently sinking.

The speed and potential of the liners was outgrowing the means to operate
them safely, particularly in poor weather conditions. A letter published in the
American magazine *Atlantic Monthly* in 1910 from an officer on a transatlantic
liner illustrates the problems:

I have been left in charge of a liner carrying a crew of 500, 2,200 steerage
passengers, 300 second class and about 300 firsts, in all about 3,300 souls.
These, in addition to the valuable ship and freight have been under my
charge at a time when I have been from 30 to 40 hours on my feet and

without sleep or rest. The safety of all depended upon my vigilance at a time when soul, mind and body have long been worn out. To keep awake at such times is torture; one must walk, walk, walk and get through somehow and all this in waters crowded with shipping and where vessels are subjected to the whims of the tide. At no other time in their lives perhaps, are passengers in such jeopardy. Some years ago elaborate plans were drawn up for the safety of liners. I refer here to the tracks which were agreed by the leading steamship companies. These tracks no doubt are a good thing and do minimise the risks of an ocean passage, but the gravest and most unwarrantable risks are taken in the very worst places in the world, the English Channels, and under the worst possible conditions.

The tracks referred to in this letter were internationally agreed routes across the Atlantic that would separate eastbound and westbound vessels and thus help to reduce the risk of collision. These tracks were designed to keep the liners well to the south of the ice and fog dangers but the distance across the Atlantic following these recommended routes was longer than the optimum 'Great Circle' routes and liners intent on a new Atlantic record would follow the Great Circle rather than the recommended route, thus putting their passengers at additional risk for the sake of prestige. Indeed, it is thought that most liners followed the Great Circle lines rather than deviate to the south in order to make the fastest passage.

A letter in the *New York Times* in 1910 states boldly: 'Knowing what goes on behind the scenes I have no hesitation in declaring that *Mauretania*'s latest record, 26.08 knots was faked. I do not believe for a moment, nor do the officers aboard her, that she made that average covering the official distance.'

In hindsight it seems as if the Blue Riband of the Atlantic took on a sort of magical quality in the eyes of the travelling public and shipping companies alike, for to hold the Blue Riband was the key to passenger revenue and commercial success of a ship and a company. A generation of magnificent transatlantic liners was designed and built to compete for the Blue Riband. For many observers, again with the benefit of hindsight, this competition and race was to culminate in what now appears to be the almost inevitable calamity in which the White Star's *Titanic* took the principal tragic part.

The size and speed of the *Kaiser Wilhelm der Grosse*, discussed in the previous chapter, made the German shipping companies incredibly popular in the first decade or so of the twentieth century, and it was perhaps fortunate for their competitors that the *Kaiser Friedrich*, the second of the pair, didn't quite match up to the performance of her companion. The Hamburg Amerika Line's *Deutschland* was even larger than this pair with a length of 661 ft and on her maiden voyage the *Deutschland* set a new record in both directions and

September 1900 saw what the world's press billed as a race between these two German ships. *Kaiser Wilhelm der Grosse* left New York ninety minutes before her rival and arrived off the Lizard at the entrance to the English Channel about four hours ahead. Although stories of such races were denied by the respective owners, there must have been a tremendous incentive for the captains to keep speed up to a maximum on such voyages and one report of this 'race' suggests that the two liners ran neck and neck with only a few miles between them in the middle of the Atlantic.

The *Deutschland*'s high speeds were only obtained at the expense of severe vibration that was probably a propeller balance problem. Vibration was a common problem on these liners and it is likely that the technical capabilities of her designers had been stretched to the limit. Later in her life the *Deutschland* was to suffer constant machinery breakdowns. Meanwhile, not to be outdone by the apparent success of the *Deutschland*, the Norddeutscher Line launched a companion for the *Kaiser Wilhelm der Grosse*, the *Kronprinz Wilhelm*, in 1901. This ship had several innovations, one of the most notable being the extensive use of electricity throughout the vessel. It was also one of the first ships to be equipped with the new wireless telegraphy. On her maiden voyage the *Kronprinz Wilhelm* could only manage an average of 19.74 knots because of appalling weather, but on her return she averaged 23.1 knots to take the Blue Riband and she went on to take the westbound record the following year.

The introduction of radio transmitters to these liners was a considerable safety bonus. It did not save ships from collision or from weather damage or grounding, but at least if things went wrong they could call for help and this was evident to a certain extent in the *Titanic* disaster. Things would have been a lot worse if ships had not picked up the distress message from the ship and

The German liner *Deutschland* suffered from severe vibration caused by her propellers.

come to the aid of the *Titanic* survivors. Radio could also allow warnings of the position of icebergs but initially its use was spasmodic and it took many years for radio to become a commonplace fitting on ships.

At this time German dominance on the Atlantic routes seemed likely to persist, for the White Star Line had been sold to the American company International Mercantile Marine and the prospect of Cunard going down the same route seemed likely. To the British this would have been a national disaster, and in an effort to counter the twin American and German threats to Atlantic dominance the British government advanced a hefty loan to Cunard, enabling them to place an order for two new liners designed from the keel up to regain vital Atlantic prestige. The result was the commissioning of two of the most famous ships ever to sail the Atlantic: the *Lusitania* and the *Mauretania*. These ships were the largest and fastest on the Atlantic route with a length of 790ft and a design speed of 24.5 knots. By any stretch of the imagination these were superships and when the *Mauretania* reached 27.4 knots on trials and then set a new Atlantic record soon after her launch, there was national rejoicing. What is amazing about this magnificent ship is that she was to hold this record for an unprecedented twenty-two years.

These two liners marked a turning-point in ship design as they pioneered the use of steam turbine engines rather than reciprocating steam engines that had been in use up till that time. The reciprocating engines were huge and heavy compared with the compactness of the turbines and the turbines were also much smoother with little vibration. When they were launched both these liners were still burning coal in their boilers, with the stokers have to

The *Mauretania*, one of the finest of the Cunard Atlantic liners.

shovel up to 900 tons of coal per day. In 1922 the two ships had their turbine power upgraded to around 90,000 hp and the boilers were converted to using oil as a fuel. Up to this time virtually all liners had been built with compound reciprocating steam engines but with a massive 70,000 hp being required to propel these new vessels, the lighter and more efficient steam turbine was the logical solution. The most powerful turbines that had previously been fitted to ships were only 12,000 hp units, so to make the quantum step up to the huge power output required for the new ships was a very brave step indeed but one that was amply rewarded and following their success turbines were used on virtually all subsequent ocean liners.

The *Lusitania* was the first of the 'twins' to take to the water to test the new powerful turbines and almost immediately set a new Atlantic record, but she was outclassed by her sister's maiden voyage. The *Mauretania* set several records on the Atlantic and was the first vessel to complete a crossing in less than five days.

Once more the Cunard Line was back in control on the Atlantic and when the White Star Line ordered two new ships for the Atlantic service, the *Olympic* and the *Titanic*, they were designed to focus on luxury rather than speed. These two ships had a length of 882ft, nearly 100ft longer than the *Mauretania*, but the trial speed was only 21.75 knots and no attempt at Atlantic speed records was ever made with these liners. Tragically the *Titanic* only achieved fame and even notoriety through her highly-publicized collision with an iceberg on her maiden voyage in 1912 when more than 1,500 lives were lost. This appalling disaster was to have a lasting effect on all forms of shipping with new legislation regarding lifeboats and safety equipment on ships and the establishment of the International Ice Patrol being positive actions to accrue from a maritime disaster of unprecedented proportions. These new safety requirements were rather like 'closing the stable door after the horse has bolted' and even today safety at sea regulations are largely dictated by previous accidents rather than trying to anticipate them.

Many liners making record attempts would deviate from the officially-recommended routes in order to make faster passages. However, there was little reason for the *Titanic* to make such a change of course, because with her limited speed potential there was no possibility of her making a record crossing. What is surprising about the *Titanic* disaster is the fact that she did not significantly slow her speed, despite warnings about ice in her vicinity. The Cunard liner *Carmania* ran into an area of icebergs interspersed with growlers (small bergs) and lesser ice and was brought to a halt in the same area. The French liner *Niagara* had also run into this ice field, apparently some 70 miles by 35 miles in area, and had been damaged both below and above the waterline. Her crew managed to stem these leaks with temporary patching and the ship and her 100 passengers completed the voyage. Certainly this ice field was a major hazard to shipping in the North Atlantic and, in addition to the three liners that ran into trouble, there are reports of numerous other ships either being entrapped in this ice or in collision with icebergs.

Meanwhile, the *Lusitania* and her sister in the Cunard fleet, *Mauretania*, were not without problems. Both ships had fine bows and demonstrated a tendency to plough into head seas, often pitching quite violently. On one occasion the *Lusitania* shipped an enormous sea over the bow that broke in the wheelhouse windows and bent the steel of the superstructure. The wheelhouse on the *Lusitania* was 80ft above the waterline and several of her lifeboats were smashed in this incident, suggesting perhaps that it was a rogue wave she encountered. Both ships also rolled much more heavily than anticipated, despite company blandishments that all was sweetness and light on these wonderful new liners. Among their problems, which also included the loss of one of the *Mauretania*'s propeller blades in 1908, these two magnificent liners became known as 'The Incomparables'. They dominated the Atlantic service until the First World War during which (in 1915) the *Lusitania* was torpedoed and sunk by a German U-boat with the loss of 1,198 lives. In 1913 the pair had been joined by the *Aquitania* which was the first liner to exceed 900ft in length. Despite her impressive length, the *Aquitania* never matched the speed and performance of 'The Incomparables' and her fastest crossing at 25 knots was well below the record set by the *Mauretania*.

Wartime camouflage on one of Cunard's Atlantic liners.

The counter-stern of the *Aquitania* with one of her four-bladed propellers.

In 1914, at the outbreak of war, an even larger liner was being built in Germany to bring that nation back into the reckoning for the Blue Riband. Built and launched as the *Bismarck* in 1914, this ship was not finally completed until 1922 when she was handed over to the White Star Line as part of a war reparations deal and renamed *Majestic*. She was the largest ship on the Atlantic for many years (at 954ft in length), but she never managed to break any records, despite a design speed above 25 knots. The White Star Line tended to be more concerned with size than speed and back in 1911 they had proposed the construction of a new ship, the *Gigantic*, which was to have been the first ship to exceed 1,000ft in length and designed to carry more than 4,000 passengers! With twelve decks, the proposed design included facilities for golf, tennis and cricket matches, but this boat was to be no ocean greyhound and was planned to make leisurely seven-day crossings of the Atlantic. In reporting the possibility of building this ship, the *New York Times* newspaper noted: 'There are no technical difficulties about building a ship with these unprecedented dimensions, but there are commercial difficulties and new docks would have to be built to take ships of this size.' Presumably these economic factors and the gathering clouds of war prevented the ship from ever being built.

The war set back German attempts to increase their share of the lucrative Atlantic passenger trade, but the nation defeated on the battlefield was not to be outdone in her quest for the Blue Riband of the Atlantic. In 1928 the *Bremen* and the *Europa* were launched with the specific objective of taking the title from the *Mauretania*. This was achieved in a convincing manner in 1929 when the 938ft *Bremen* made her maiden voyage across the Atlantic at an average speed of 27.83 knots. With 130,000 hp available from her turbines, the *Bremen* and her slightly larger sister *Europa* dominated the Atlantic passenger routes and in 1934 raised the record to 28 knots. Facilities on board included swimming pools, a sports arena, ballroom, cinema and shopping centres that were all available to passengers much as on a modern cruise liner. When the *Europa* joined the *Bremen* in 1930 she captured the Blue Riband with a speed of 27.91 knots on the westward crossing, but in 1933 the record went back to the *Bremen* when she raised the speed to 28.51 knots.

This German domination could not go unchallenged and new contenders from France and Italy were being planned as well as new ships in Britain. Indeed, the early 1930s saw intense activity in the offices of naval architects around Europe and the stage was being set for the most competitive period ever in the history of the Atlantic liner. The Cunard Line had been resting on the laurels of the ageing *Mauretania* and the *Aquitania* but in December 1930 work began on vessel No. 534, later to be named *Queen Mary* at John Brown's shipyard on Clydeside. A few weeks later the keel of the French liner *Normandie* was laid, and earlier that year work had started in Italy on two

The German liner *Europa* briefly held the Blue Riband in 1930.

superliners, the *Rex* and *Conte di Savoia*. Although ordered together, the two Italian ships were quite different in character. The *Conte di Savoia* was a fine vessel in the traditions of Atlantic liners but it was the larger and faster *Rex* that was clearly designed to take the Blue Riband. Sailing from the Mediterranean, the Atlantic crossing for an Italian ship would begin at Gibraltar and end in New York and in 1933 the *Rex*, which operated out of Genoa, completed this passage in four and a half days at an average speed of 28.92 knots. On her builders' trials the *Rex* had come close to the magic 30-knot mark, but she never managed to sustain this sort of speed on Atlantic crossings.

Both the Italian and the French liner building programmes continued during the economic recession of the early 1930s, despite the severe effect that this had on Atlantic passenger traffic. In Britain the Great Depression led to the postponement of the building of the *Queen Mary* with construction halted for twenty-seven months. It had been the Cunard tradition to build Atlantic liners in pairs, but government funding for two vessels was only forthcoming after the enforced merger of the Cunard and the White Star companies. Work resumed on the *Queen Mary* in 1936 and the same year, the keel of the *Queen Elizabeth* was laid.

Meanwhile the *Rex* held both the Blue Riband and the newly-awarded Hales Trophy (awarded by British MP Harold K. Hales in 1935 for the fastest Atlantic crossing). The French launched their Atlantic giant, the *Normandie*, which was the largest and fastest Atlantic liner in 1933 with a total length of 1,029ft. Largely financed by the French government, the *Normandie* was finally completed in 1935 and achieved a remarkable speed of 31.9 knots on sea trials. This ship was a stark departure from the upright dignity of earlier Atlantic liners: her smooth-flowing lines and steam turbo-electric propulsion represented a revolution in ship design for the Atlantic service. The accommodation also surpassed anything seen before, with a grand hall extending to three decks in height. On her maiden crossing from Cherbourg to New York, she averaged 29.94 knots, marginally under the magic 30-knot barrier, but on the return voyage to Cherbourg she was the first to exceed that figure with an average of 30.35 knots. Like many other liners before her, the *Normandie* experienced vibration problems from her powerful propellers but when these were replaced with a new design, the problem was largely eliminated.

Having soundly beaten the Germans and Italians in terms of size, speed, appearance and appointments, this magnificent French liner now had to face the challenge from the first of the British contenders, the *Queen Mary*. This event was eagerly awaited by an expectant public who looked on it not just as a question of speed, but as a contest between the traditional values represented by the design of the *Queen Mary* and those of the brave new era represented by the *Normandie*. The *Queen Mary* finally left her building yard in 1936 after nearly six years in the making and began her trials. The speeds achieved on these trials were kept a closely-guarded secret and when she began her maiden voyage on 27 May, great things were expected. However, she didn't beat the *Normandie*'s time and it was another two months before she finally achieved a record crossing and gained the Blue Riband, the outward passage being completed at an average of 30.14 knots and the return at 30.63 knots, the first time both crossings had been made in excess of 30 knots. The *Queen Mary* was awarded the Hales Trophy, but the canny Cunard/White Star directors refused to accept it on the grounds that it implied that they were taking part in ocean racing and this was not consistent with the company's policy of safety first! In view of the fact that the company had built a ship with the implicit purpose of breaking the Atlantic record this is a somewhat pompous attitude, but as it turned out they would not have held the trophy for long anyway because in 1937 the *Normandie* increased her speed with a best crossing at 31.2 knots. The following year the 'non-racing' *Queen Mary* regained the record with her fastest-ever crossing at 31.69 knots.

To the *Normandie* remains the distinction of being the first ship to complete a crossing in less than four days, but there was little to choose between these two magnificent ships. Once again, however, Cunard managed to come out on top, perhaps through a combination of good luck and good judgement,

Three Atlantic liners together in New York. From top, *Normandie*; middle, *Queen Mary*; and bottom, *Queen Elizabeth*.

The *Queen Elizabeth* on her speed trials in the Firth of Clyde after launch.

for the *Queen Mary*, pressed into war service, held the record for the duration of the Second World War. The second of the Cunard pair, the *Queen Elizabeth*, was not completed in time to make passenger crossings before the onset of the Second World War and she was to make her first Atlantic crossing to New York in conditions of utmost secrecy in March 1940 and was to serve as a high-speed troopship throughout the conflict.

The Battle of the Atlantic took on a new meaning during the Second World War. Submarines and surface warships were an additional hazard for merchant ships bringing vital supplies to Europe and the carnage among ships and crews was far greater than anything inflicted by Atlantic weather and icebergs in the past. Once more ships sailed the Atlantic in convoy for mutual protection. Often sailing far to the north to escape the enemy, they found themselves running into trouble with the weather and ice. This war, like the previous world conflict, took its toll on the Atlantic liners and many other fine ships. The *Normandie* caught fire and sank in New York Harbour and was finally scrapped. The *Bremen* was damaged in an air-raid in 1941, as a result of which she too was scrapped, and a similar fate overtook the *Rex*. The two Cunard 'Queens' ran the gauntlet of many Atlantic crossings, their high speed generally keeping them out of trouble, although the *Queen Mary* did collide with an escorting cruiser, HMS *Curaçao* on 2 October 1942, coming out virtually unscathed herself but slicing the cruiser in two.

The *Europa*, *Queen Mary* and *Queen Elizabeth* survived the war and again war reparations were made. *Europa* was transferred to the French Line and operated under the name of *Liberté*, while peacetime saw the *Queen Elizabeth*

The fine bows of the *Mauretania* were needed for speed but not the best solution in rough seas. (*Swan Hunter Shipbuilding*)

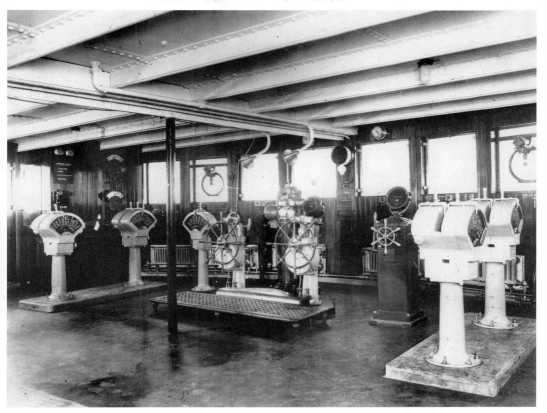

The bridge of the *Queen Mary* showing little advance in technology from that of the *Lusitania* shown in an earlier photo.

make her maiden passenger voyage on the Atlantic run in 1946 but at the by then moderately sedate pace of 28 knots.

The Cunard/White Star Company made no further attempts on Atlantic records, perhaps because there was little competition but also because such affluent behaviour was not in keeping with post-war times of austerity. The two '*Queens*' dominated the Atlantic service, but a new rival had arrived to challenge them. Transatlantic air transport had arrived to offer a new way of crossing the Atlantic for those in a hurry.

Before air travel got fully into its stride, however, the Americans once more cast their eyes on the Atlantic passenger routes and under the guise of building a vessel that could double up as a troopship in wartime, heavy subsidies were contributed towards the building of the SS *United States*. Because of her military capability, information on this ship was kept secret but it was known that she had been designed with a very high speed potential and that she was propelled by engines approaching nearly 250,000 hp. Slightly smaller than the '*Queens*', she was built with a superstructure in aluminium to keep the overall weight down. Her full potential was soon realized when she made her maiden voyage in 1952 in three days, ten hours and forty minutes at an average speed of 35.59 knots, a significant increase in the record speed. However, such speeds meant little in commercial terms against those achieved by jet aircraft over the same route.

For the transoceanic liners the writing was on the wall and the times set by the *United States* were never to be equalled again by any Atlantic liners. Although the *United States* continued in service for the next seventeen years, no attempts were made to improve on her maiden voyage speeds and the ageing '*Queens*' had no answer to the newer vessel. To all intents and purposes, interest in Atlantic records faded along with the magnificent ships that had participated in them. So came to an end the long era of passenger traffic on, as opposed to above, the Atlantic. The size of the ships, their sumptuous accommodation and their speed rivalries were to become part of Atlantic history and legend. When national prestige is at stake, normal financial considerations do not always come into the reckoning and there is little doubt that the most magnificent liners were built to a standard and with a speed potential that far exceeded commercial sense. They became almost dinosaur-like, too large to support their own weight and importance. The lighter, more commercially flexible aeroplane took the passengers that were the lifeblood of the liners. Perhaps from the safety point of view this is just as well, because the Atlantic itself hadn't changed and speeds in excess of 30 knots plus schedules to keep would eventually have resulted in disaster as navigation equipment aboard ships had improved relatively little. Radio direction-finders and echo-

The SS *United States*, the last of the Atlantic liners to be built and the holder of the Hales Trophy for many years.

sounders were introduced in the 1930s and wartime saw the development of more sophisticated electronic aids so that the '*Queens*' (during and after the war) and the *United States* were equipped with radar to aid navigation. These vessels also had electronic position-finding systems, but this equipment never reached current levels of reliability during the heyday of the ocean liner. This became evident in 1956 when two Atlantic liners collided in fog off the Nantucket Shoals. The Italian liner *Andrea Doria* and the Swedish liner *Stockholm* collided and the former sank in what a board of enquiry termed a 'radar-assisted collision'. Of the 1,700 passengers and crew on the two ships, 46 lost their lives.

By the mid-1960s, the days of the Atlantic liners were coming to an end. Cunard was building new ships but these were cruise liners capable of speeds around 25 knots. Cruise liners were taking over passenger traffic, enabling passengers to go to sea at a more leisurely pace while the aircraft served those who were in a hurry. The *Queen Mary* is ending her life as a hotel ship on the US West Coast while the *Queen Elizabeth* was to become a floating university before catching fire and sinking. The SS *United States* remains laid up in America, gently rusting away, and is currently being considered for conversion to a cruise ship fitted with diesel engines so high speeds on the Atlantic are now only possible in smaller high-speed vessels and the era of luxury high-speed Atlantic crossings is at an end.

Chapter Six

Small Boats and Yachts

The history of yachting as a sport and recreational pastime goes back to the seventeenth century but it was 1720 before the first recorded regatta was held. Yachts were designed for pleasure, for social events and mainly for safe sailing in inshore waters. Why would a yacht want to take on the uncertain waters of the Atlantic? Perhaps the answer lies in the challenge and we find that the history of yachting is full of daring sailors who have embarked on long and challenging voyages mainly for their own satisfaction. This is what may have persuaded the owner of *Cleopatra's Barge*, the 83 ft yacht that is credited with a passage across the Atlantic Ocean in 1817, to take on the challenge. There was little difference between this yacht and the commercial vessel on which it was based apart from the comfort and luxury of the accommodation and its intended purpose, so in crossing the Atlantic it was doing much the same as matching commercial versions. Owner George Crowningshield made the Atlantic crossing, stopping off at the Azores on the way and carrying on to cruise in the Mediterranean. The following year she returned to the US and was sold to become a coastal packet ship.

This first Atlantic yacht crossing started a tradition that was to make the Atlantic crossing the ultimate test for yachts and yachtsmen and inevitably it was not long before yachts were being specially built to make fast passages and to race across the Atlantic.

One of the most famous yachts in history, the *America*, was built in 1850 and the following year this 102 ft-long schooner crossed the Atlantic in a fast twenty-one-day passage. She was built for the express purpose of competing in a series of races in England that were to become the famous America's Cup races, named after this US yacht. The design of *America* was to have a significant effect on future yacht design in Europe and she marked the start of transatlantic competition. The yacht later returned to the US to be fitted out as a Confederate dispatch boat and blockade-runner in the American Civil War.

America's first Atlantic crossing was the catalyst for a series of similar voyages by other yachts. The *Sylvie* was even faster than the *America*, taking just sixteen and a half days for her crossing the same year. Most of these early yachts venturing out onto the oceans were well-equipped craft, built to the

The yacht *Sylvie* which was one of the first larger sailing yachts to cross the Atlantic.

highest standards of the day and often larger than many of the commercial sailing vessels that regularly traded across the Atlantic at that time.

The first Atlantic yacht race took place in 1866 when James Gordon Bennett's *Henrietta* raced against the *Fleetwing*, owned by the Osgood brothers, and the *Vesta* owned by Pierre Lorillard. All three yachts were schooners of a similar size and the start of the race at Sandy Hook off New York attracted a huge spectator fleet. The race was held in December, a wild time to cross the North Atlantic, but chosen out of bravado to raise the stakes of the competition.

Stormy Atlantic winter conditions soon took their toll of the contestants and six of *Fleetwing*'s crew were lost overboard when a wave swamped the cockpit. *Henrietta* and *Vesta* battled it out in a very close contest with the two yachts being sighted off the Scilly Isles on Christmas Eve only fifteen minutes apart. After 3,000 miles of racing this was a remarkably close race and the finish line was at Cowes still 300 miles further on! *Henrietta* reached Cowes on the evening of Christmas Day having picked up a pilot off the Lizard but *Vesta*, following a similar track, became lost in fog on Christmas Eve and only made Cowes on Boxing Day, having by then been overtaken by *Fleetwing* which, despite her problems, had continued to sail the course. *Henrietta* had averaged 9.25 knots over the 3,106-mile course, which compared very favourably with the times put up by the fast packet ships.

After his success in this Atlantic race, Gordon Bennett had a new and larger schooner, the *Dauntless*, built and in 1870 this yacht raced in the second transatlantic race against the *Cambria* on a course from Ireland to Sandy Hook. The *Cambria* was also the first challenger for the America's Cup which was now scheduled to be held in US waters. In the westbound Atlantic race she came out on top, winning by the very narrow margin of just one hour, seventeen minutes, but she was beaten in the America's Cup races. Once again the Atlantic took its toll, with two of the crew of *Dauntless* lost overboard. One of the conditions of the America's Cup races for many years was that the challenging yacht should sail the Atlantic for the competition; a condition that put a heavy burden on the challenger yacht as she would have to be built strongly enough to take on the Atlantic before participating in the actual races for the cup.

Now smaller yachts were finding their way out onto the Atlantic. One of the first was the 43ft-long *Charter Oak* which crossed in 1856 with just a three-man crew. The *Charter Oak* goes down in history as the first small yacht recorded to have made the Atlantic crossing. A year later the slightly larger *Christopher Columbus* made the crossing from New York to Cowes in forty-five days, and eight years later the sloop *Alice* with a length of 49ft made a fast crossing from Boston to Cowes in nineteen days, returning the following year from Cowes to Boston and taking thirty-four days for that crossing.

Now people, perhaps looking for the ultimate in adventure, were looking at crossing the Atlantic in tiny boats under sail. Some of the first were two Americans, Donovan and Spencer (together with a dog called Toby), who set out to cross the Atlantic in a 14ft 6in-long dinghy called *Vision* in 1864. Despite its diminutive size, this craft was rigged as a brigantine with three square sails on the foremast and a main mast with fore and aft sails, an extraordinarily complex rig for such a small boat. *Vision* was sighted about 90 miles off New York after two days at sea, but after that nothing further was heard and the boat and crew were presumed lost at sea. Some contemporary reports put the length of *Vision* at 24ft, which would seem more reasonable in terms of the complex rig she was carrying, and this would make her similar in size to the next small craft to make an attempt to sail across the Atlantic, the patriotically-named *Red, White and Blue*. This vessel had even more complex sails, being square-rigged on all three of her masts.

The *Red, White and Blue* set out to sail the Atlantic to gain publicity for a new type of lifeboat design, Ingersoll's Improved Metallic Lifeboat on which she was based. With a length of 26ft she was built from galvanized iron and fitted with watertight compartments. She was quite well-equipped for the crossing despite her impossibly complex rig and she sailed from New York in 1866 and, like the *Vision* before her, carried a dog as well, probably the most useless passenger you could find for such a voyage. Thirty-five days and more than 3,000 miles later the *Red, White and Blue* arrived at Deal in Kent but many sceptics have doubted whether she actually made the crossing on her own, or whether she was perhaps lifted aboard another ship for part of the crossing, or was perhaps towed. History has given the crew the benefit of the doubt and the pair is credited with having made the first true 'small boat' crossing of the Atlantic.

The next in line for an adventurous Atlantic crossing was Captain Gould. His *John T. Ford* was 22ft 6in long and she sailed from Baltimore on 27 June 1867 with a four-man crew, which must have made this diminutive boat very crowded. After calling at Halifax the quartet set out across the Atlantic on 16 July – a little late in the year to get good weather in the North Atlantic –

There was some doubt about whether the *Red, White and Blue* had sailed all the way but she was credited with being the first small boat to cross the Atlantic.

The *John T. Ford* which completed its Atlantic crossing with no crew on board after they were rescued.

and the *John T. Ford* capsized in a storm on 5 August. Amazingly the boat was righted and continued on her voyage, only to be capsized again off the south coast of Ireland. This time her crew was overcome by exhaustion and three of them were lost overboard; one man, however, clung to the boat for three and a half days and was eventually rescued by a passing ship. The boat actually completed the crossing when it was later washed ashore on the Irish coast!

Yet this type of disaster did not dissuade other adventurers and another small boat voyage was a further attempt to demonstrate the capabilities of a new form of life-saving craft. The *Nonpareil* was a remarkable craft for her time, being constructed from three inflatable tubes 25ft long and 2ft 6in in diameter, linked together by a wooden platform. On this platform a canvas shelter was erected for the three-man crew. The *Nonpareil* was in fact a raft fitted with two masts and she was schooner-rigged. Crewed by three men named Mikes, Miller and Mallene, the *Nonpareil* set out from New York in June 1868. Although the vessel and her crew experienced their fair share of bad weather, they made the crossing all the way to Southampton in fifty-one

The *Nonpareil* based on three inflatable tubes made a successful crossing of the Atlantic in 1868.

days, so this unlikely craft has the distinction of being the first inflatable vessel to cross the Atlantic and also the first multi-hull. After her successful Atlantic crossing, there is no record of the *Nonpareil* having any success in the life-saving market for which she was designed.

All these early small boat crossings were made by Americans and made from west to east with the prevailing winds and currents, but in 1870 the first recorded small boat crossing from east to west was achieved by an American, John Buckley. Buckley made the crossing in the 20ft-long converted ship's boat *City of Ragusa* and took eighty-four days to cross from Cork to Boston. One picture of the *City of Ragusa* shows it with a large air propeller mounted on the aft mast. This was probably an experimental system in which the air propeller was connected to a water propeller to drive the boat along and it could have worked in conditions where the wind was ahead and the sails would not be of much use. As far as is known, this system was not used on the crossing and it must have been an incredibly arduous voyage; two men on a 20ft boat can have had very little space left after all the stores and water had been put on board, and they were battling against the prevailing westerly winds. Eventually the *City of Ragusa* was sailed back to England in a crossing that took only thirty-eight days, so this tiny vessel also goes down in history as the first double crossing of the Atlantic by small boat.

Six years later we come across the first single-handed crossing of the Atlantic in a sailing boat, a feat that is still regarded as a severe test of man and

The *City of Ragusa* fitted with an air propeller for propulsion. This was discarded for its Atlantic crossing.

boat even today. This first solo crossing was achieved by Alfred Johnson in a 20ft gaff cutter called the *Centennial*. It was the 100th anniversary of independence for the United States and the lone voyage was planned to celebrate this event, hence the name of the boat. Alfred Johnson was an experienced seaman, a Grand Banks fisherman, used to cold and icy conditions, and his boat reflected this experience, being a 20ft dory similar to those used on the Grand Banks, although for this voyage it was decked over. Despite some difficult weather, the *Centennial* made good time across the Atlantic until she was just 300 miles from the Irish Coast when a violent storm overtook the frail craft. Apparently the *Centennial* rode the big seas quite comfortably when hove-to, but was suddenly overwhelmed by a tremendous breaking wave that capsized her. Johnson struggled to right his craft and it was only with a superhuman effort that he finally achieved this and bailed her out. Cold, wet, close to exhaustion and without food, Johnson was tempted to give up the crossing when a ship hove in sight, but finding that he was only 100 miles from the Irish coast he decided to continue after being given food and water and arrived on the Welsh coast after forty-six days at sea.

A recurring name in the history of small boat crossings of the North Atlantic is William Andrews. He made no fewer than three Atlantic crossings in small boats, the first one in 1878 when he crossed in the 19ft centreboard sailboat *Nautilus*. The *Nautilus* was specially built for the voyage by Andrews and his younger brother Walter, and the pair left Boston on 7 June 1878 completing the Atlantic crossing in forty-nine days after many adventures. Andrews was not deterred and he built a second boat called *Dark Secret*, only 12ft 9in in length. Attempts were made by the American authorities to stop the proposed voyage but Andrews, now single-handed, sneaked out to sea under the cover of darkness on 17 June 1888. For more than two months Andrews struggled along in this tiny boat but eventually admitted defeat when he was still only little more than halfway across and was picked up by a passing sailing ship.

Even this adventure didn't put him off and in 1891 he was back again, this time with a 15ft boat that he again had built himself. On hearing of Andrew's further attempt, another Boston man, Si Lawlor, decided to make an attempt on the Atlantic crossing, also in a 15ft boat. By the time the press got hold of these two stories they had made the event into a race. Widely advertised by the press, many other boats wanted to enter the race but all were eliminated in a short trial and the pair left Boston on 21 June 1891. Lawlor's boat, the *Sea Serpent*, made the crossing to Coverack in Cornwall in forty-five days, but once again William Andrews had to give up after a capsize and was rescued by a steamer after sixty-one days at sea. Thus Lawlor became the winner of the

William Andrews spent two months sailing *Dark Secret* across the Atlantic before giving up.

first single-handed transatlantic race and also the credit for having made the crossing of the Atlantic in the smallest boat at that time.

Andrews was by now obsessed with the Atlantic crossing and in 1892 he was back again, intent on making the solo crossing in the smallest boat. This time his canvas-covered folding boat was just 14ft 6in long and its construction seems totally inappropriate for such an attempt. Andrews' motive was to cash in on the publicity surrounding the 400th anniversary of the discovery of America by Columbus and he planned to sail from Atlantic City to Spain, but in fact landed in Portugal after eighty-four days at sea, the longest small boat crossing from west to east. This was not a non-stop crossing because Andrews called at the Azores on the way, but eighty-four days at sea in a 14ft 6in sailing boat is a considerable feat of endurance and he deserved credit for this cross-ing. Even after this success he didn't give up and he set out for a fifth time, once again bound from Atlantic City to Spain in a boat called the *Flying Dutchman*. This time he was accompanied by his wife and the boat was a 20ft dory, but the vessel was never seen again and so ended the life of one of the most famous but not one of the most successful of the early small boat Atlantic adventurers.

These early Atlantic small boat sailors were mainly professional seamen of one type or another, but they seem to have had little experience of navigation. Indeed, Si Lawlor's approach to navigating the Atlantic was to simply keep heading in an easterly direction, secure in the knowledge that eventually he must hit land. A few carried sextants that would be used to establish latitude, but a chronometer would hardly stand up to use in a small boat, even if it could be afforded. In many ways, these seamen who ventured out on to the Atlantic were a throwback to the early days of Atlantic crossings when very basic techniques were used for navigation, when the crew endured consider-able hardship and where the outcome of the voyage was by no means certain.

Most of the early boats that either attempted or successfully crossed the Atlantic were either craft designed for life-saving purposes or boats based on working boats of one type or another. The first small boat crossing in what might be termed a yacht was completed in 1911 when Thomas Flemming-Day, the editor of *The Rudder* magazine, sailed his yawl *Sea Bird* across the Atlantic. One of the reasons for making this voyage was to demonstrate Flemming-Day's conviction that small yachts were seaworthy enough to undertake long ocean passages and in this he was highly successful, sailing this 26ft yacht to the Mediterranean. One of the most famous crossings of the Atlantic, however, began in 1895 when Joshua Slocum set out from Nova Scotia in the gaff cutter *Spray*. Slocum crossed to Gibraltar in thirty-three days, having called in at the Azores on the way. This crossing was the start of his famous circumnavigation of the world.

At the other end of the yachting scale was the Kaiser's Cup Race across the Atlantic held in 1905 which attracted ten competitors who fought it out for a gold cup put up by the German Emperor Wilhelm II. Many of the big yachts of the day took part in this race, including the barque *Valhalla* and the brigantine *Utowana*. The smallest boat in the race was the 112 ft schooner *Fleur de Lys*, and another famous boat to participate was *Thistle* which had taken part in the America's Cup competition in 1887. This race will always be remembered for the remarkable performance of the 185 ft schooner *Atlantic* owned by Wilson Marshall. This American vessel won the race convincingly, making the crossing from Sandy Hook to the Lizard in twelve days, four hours to set a new record for sailing ships on the Atlantic that was to last for the next seventy years. The appropriately-named *Atlantic* was a magnificent three-masted schooner, the epitome of the large yachts of her time, and her professional captain Charles Barr took her right up north among the icebergs on the Great Circle route and drove her hard through Atlantic gales, chancing his arm and winning through in a daring and convincing way.

The feats of the yacht *Atlantic* represented the pinnacle of the 'grand era' of yachting. Racing was hard and tough and no quarter was given, but the yachts were also very large and surprisingly comfortable. This approach by the rich to long-distance yachting using professional crews was in direct contrast to the small boat crossings of the Atlantic that had taken place up to the turn of the century. For these small boats the achievement was in just making the crossing and the successes of men like Andrews and Johnson deserve a lot more recognition than they have received. They were pioneers out to prove themselves and their craft, but in the history of Atlantic travel they are largely overshadowed by the big yachts and their big-spending owners. These small sailboat pioneers achieved remarkable feats of seamanship and endurance representing milestones in maritime history.

Thomas Flemming-Day had a lot to answer for when he completed his small yacht crossing of the Atlantic in 1911. He was the first person to show that small yachts could extend their cruising grounds out into the waters of the ocean rather than keep to the coasts and although there wasn't a mad rush to follow in Flemming-Day's footsteps, from this time on we see a steady decline in the big yachts and a slow increase in the small yachts venturing into Atlantic waters. The First World War put a stop to Atlantic cruising in no uncertain manner and was also to a large extent responsible for the decline in the larger yachts. The challengers for the America's Cup still had to sail across the Atlantic but there was a gap of seventeen years between the *Shamrock III* challenge in 1903 and the *Shamrock IV* challenge in 1920. It was not until 1956 that the rule about the challenger sailing across the Atlantic was changed and ushered in the era of the relatively small 12-metre yachts. For their ocean voyages in pursuit of the cup, the beautiful 'J'-class yachts would be fitted with a cruising rig that would be replaced with a racing rig once the yacht had made the crossing. The contrast with the modern, very delicate, highly-tuned yachts that participate in the Cup competition today could not be greater, but the requirement for ocean sailing helped the development of sound seaworthy craft, however much it also played into the hands of the defending nation whose yachts did not have to meet this stringent requirement.

It was many years before yachts ventured out onto the Atlantic after the war. In 1924 the famous French yachtsman, Alain Gerbault, carried out a solo circumnavigation of the world, sailing from Gibraltar in June of that year and taking 101 days for the crossing to New York as the first stage. This 3,200-mile journey was sailed in the 39ft *Firecrest* and the long time for the passage is understandable when you read about the tremendous storms and difficulties that Gerbault went through on his journey. Gerbault was east of Bermuda in an area where reasonable weather might have been expected, but he found himself running in high seas and difficult conditions that developed into a full gale and the boat was taking on water. For six days he carried on in these incredibly difficult circumstances and although the weather moderated for a while, the gales returned with a vengeance with hurricane force winds:

By 10 o'clock the wind had increased to hurricane force. The seas ran short and viciously, their curling crests racing before the thrust of the wind seemed to be torn into little whirlpools before they broke into a lather of soapy foam. These great seas bore down on the little cutter as though they were finally bent on her destruction, but she rose to them and fought her way through them in a way which made me want to sing a poem in her praise. Then in a moment I seemed engulfed in disaster. The incident occurred just after noon with *Firecrest* sailing full and by under a bit of her mainsail and jib. Suddenly I saw towering on my limited horizon a huge wave rearing its curling, snowy crest, so high that it dwarfed all the others I had ever seen. I could hardly believe my eyes. It was a thing of beauty as well as of awe as it came roaring down upon us. Knowing that if I stayed on deck I would meet death by being washed overboard, I had only just time to climb into the rigging and was about halfway to the masthead when it burst upon the *Firecrest* in fury, burying her from my sight under tons of solid water and a lather of foam. The gallant little boat staggered and reeled under the blow until I began to wonder anxiously whether she was going to founder or fight her way to the surface. Slowly she came out of the smother of it and the great wave roared away to leeward. I slid down from my perch in the rigging to discover that it had broken off the outboard part of the bowsprit. Held by the jib stay it lay in a maze of rigging and sail under the lee rail where every sea used it as a battering ram against the planking, thrusting at every blow to stave a hole in the hull.

Gerbault survived this desperate situation despite the despair that took him as he saw the mast shaking loose, the broken bowsprit and the water in the boat. The hurricane finally blew itself out as hurricanes always do, and gradually Gerbault got *Firecrest* back into a sailing condition and eventually made New York under a jury rig. His account above is a vivid description of Atlantic storm conditions in a small boat.

The Bermuda Race covers 600 miles of the North Atlantic and was first held in 1906 when it started at New York. It was revived in 1923 and in the 1936 race participants survived particularly rough seas when a cyclonic low moved up from the Gulf of Mexico, producing conditions only marginally less violent than a full-blooded hurricane. Similar violent conditions were a feature of the 1960 race as well.

The year 1928 was the swansong of the large yachts in another race across the Atlantic Ocean, this time from New York to Spain. The race was for the King of Spain's Cup for the big yachts and the Queen of Spain's Cup for the smaller sailing craft. Among the bigger yachts was *Atlantic*, still active after her record-breaking trip in the 1905 transatlantic race. Another of the large yachts was *Elena* owned by William Bell and skippered by Charlie Barr's brother John. This yacht was sailed by a paid crew numbering thirty-eight and was the winner of the race, showing that size counts on the Atlantic.

A transatlantic race in 1931 saw few yachts over 60ft in length and the winner was the famous Olin Stephens' design *Dorade*. It had come third in the Bermuda Race the previous year and, sailed by the two brothers Olin and Rod Stephens, had won the transatlantic race to Plymouth in England by a margin of two full days over her closest competitor by following the tough but shorter northern route across the Atlantic.

A development of the *Dorade* design by the Stephens brothers, *Stormy Weather* went on to win the 1935 transatlantic race from Newport to Bergen in Norway. This is a distance of over 3,000 miles with the boats tracking to the north of Scotland. This northerly track took the competing boats into the iceberg areas and after taking advice from Grand Banks fishermen, skipper Rod Stephens took an inside route up the east coast of the USA and Canada and then out through the ice fields, a daring route to follow in the thick fog conditions but it gave him victory on corrected time.

Between the wars there was another period of intense small boat activity on the Atlantic. One of the first to follow in the footsteps of William Andrews and Si Lawlor was a German, Franz Romer. He made a quite remarkable voyage crossing the Atlantic in a 21ft canvas-covered canoe. Romer was a captain in the Hamburg Amerika Line and was one of the first of the single-handed Atlantic sailors who set out with a scientific objective, his being to prove that even a tiny fragile craft could survive comfortably in ocean seas. He endured storms, his cooking stove catching fire, and attacks by sharks and flying fish. He and his boat were lost on the return voyage which took place during the hurricane season.

In 1933 the first single-handed voyage from east to west across the Atlantic was achieved by Commander R.D. Graham in the 30ft gaff cutter *Emanuel*. Leaving Bantry Bay in Ireland he completed the 1,765-mile crossing to St. John's in Newfoundland in twenty-four days. Commander Graham followed the northerly route across the Atlantic and met up with the expected fog and icebergs on the Grand Banks but apart from these encounters this was an uneventful journey, a tribute to Commander Graham's seamanship, but one wonders at the wisdom of his setting out in November to make the return passage single-handed. Leaving St. John's he headed south towards Bermuda, but on the way he got caught up in a violent storm:

> I have never seen such a sea before, huge rolling mountains with great valleys between, while every now and then the cross swells would cause a pyramid of water to rise up with almost vertical sides. *Emanuel* was flung about like a cork, swinging broad side on when a steep sea caught her stern. There was nothing to be done. The sea looked so terrifying that I could not bear to look at it and I remained below all day.

Commander Graham finally made Bermuda and thought it wiser to take on board a second man in order to complete the voyage back to Europe.

The year 1933 also saw a famous voyage by Marin-Marie, a Frenchman who sailed to New York from France in the gaff cutter *Winnibelle*. Marin-Marie took the southerly route via the West Indies. Voyages across the Atlantic were still a sufficient rarity at this time for books to be written about the adventure and Marin-Marie went on not only to cross the Atlantic under sail, but also later to cross it under power, following the pattern set by Thomas Flemming-Day just after the turn of the century.

The Second World War put a stop to yachts on the Atlantic apart from four Norwegians fleeing the German occupation. They set out in *King Haakon*, a 38ft seaworthy pilot cutter in July 1940 and sailed the far northern route, landing at St. John's in Newfoundland after forty-one days during which they were at risk from encounters with enemy craft as well as the more normal risks of an Atlantic crossing. After the war there are several accounts of small craft crossings by Eastern Europeans trying to escape Russian persecution.

Transatlantic sailboat racing was resumed in 1950. This contest was scheduled as an extension of the Bermuda Race and open to yachts which had taken part in that competition which then wanted to sail back to England. The British yachts *Samuel Pepys*, *Cohoe* and *Mokoia* were shipped from Britain for the Bermuda Race and were offloaded at Bermuda to get experience of the sea conditions on their way to the start in Newport. On this trip the three yachts got mixed up in an extra-tropical cyclone which made a complete loop over their course and as Adlard Coles, sailing *Cohoe*, describes it in his book *Heavy Weather Sailing*: 'It created a huge swell from two directions and the seas heaped in complete confusion.' Despite their unpleasant experiences in this storm, the three British yachts went on to take part in both the Bermuda and the transatlantic race. They started in July and after fine weather for the first week, got mixed up once again in Atlantic depressions and were soon running in a full storm. Despite broaching to in this storm and losing time, *Cohoe* went on to win on handicap, but *Samuel Pepys* was the first boat home and made the fastest Atlantic crossing ever achieved by a small yacht, taking twenty-one days, four hours to cover the 2,830-mile course.

Yacht designer Colin Mudie sailed his 20ft-long *Sopranino* across the Atlantic in 1951. She was a lightweight centreboard yacht built to demonstrate that small vessels of this type could successfully make long passages. *Sopranino* was little more than an overgrown sailing dinghy and the ocean voyages achieved by this boat were to have a significant impact on future ocean-racing boat design by demonstrating that lightweight construction and seaworthiness could go hand-in-hand.

Some saw the Atlantic challenge as making the crossing in the smallest possible craft. The smallest boat record was nearly broken in 1968 when Hugo Vihlen left Morocco in his 5ft 11in boat. He sailed to within 6 miles of the US coast but adverse winds prevented him landing and he had to be towed the final few miles so did not qualify. Tom McClean made the crossing in a self-built boat measuring just 9ft 9in long in 1982, taking seven weeks for the crossing. His size record was broken three weeks later by Hugo Vihlen in a boat 8in shorter, so McClean used a chainsaw to cut his boat down to 7ft 9in and regained the size record. McClean had something of an obsession with the Atlantic and was back again in 1990, this time in a 37ft boat shaped like a bottle that he had constructed himself. His boat, the *Typhoo Atlantic Challenger*, made the crossing safely and he had another Atlantic adventure when he spent close to six weeks living on Rockall, a rock that stands just 45ft above the wild northern Atlantic located south of Iceland.

In 1993, Vihlen was back sailing a 5ft 6in boat but he was competing with Tom McNally whose boat was 1.5in shorter so he cut 2in off his boat and

Tom McClean's tiny sailboat *Giltspur* in which he crossed the Atlantic.

took 115 days for the crossing, an incredible feat of endurance or, as some might say, stupidity. There is a narrow line between the two!

The concept of a single-handed transatlantic race was developed by two experienced sailors, Francis Chichester and Blondie Hasler with a start scheduled for June 1960. The event was to capture public imagination world-wide and also lead eventually to the development of the modern ocean-racing multihull. When the race was first announced the press billed it as the most sporting event of the century, completely overlooking what had been achieved by some of the pioneers on the Atlantic many years before.

The dilemma facing the four competitors was which route to take. The shortest route, the Great Circle route, could avoid much of the adverse Gulf Stream and pick up the favourable Labrador Current on the far side of the Atlantic, but there were icebergs and fog creating hazards along this route. The more convivial southerly routes are considerably longer in distance but are offered more favourable winds. Then there was the northerly route, longer than the short Great Circle route but along which competitors might expect favourable currents but could be prone to adverse winds.

David Howells took the more southerly route down towards the Azores, while Francis Chichester and David Lewis followed roughly the Great Circle route, with Blondie Hasler going even further to the north. Two weeks out Chichester ran into a violent storm, while Hasler to the north also experi-enced difficult weather. Despite a reasonably fast passage across most of the Atlantic, calms and fog featured in the last days of the race, but finally Chichester passed the Ambrose Light at the entrance to New York after forty days at sea. Hasler came in eight days later and a further eight days behind was Lewis. Among the developments arising from this race was an effective system of self-steering gear and this was to open up the way for a flood of single-handed sailings and the race which was held every four years became an important feature of the sailing calendar. However, there were many pundits who expressed concern about just one man on a boat not being able to keep a good look-out so not being able to conform to the International Regulations for the Prevention of Collision at Sea, which demand the maintenance of a constant look-out.

Doubts had been cast in the first race about the ability of one man to handle a 40ft boat, but in this second race the largest yacht entered, *Pen Duick II*, a 44ft ketch sailed by Éric Tabarly, proved that it was not only possible but also that size told since Tabarly won the race in convincing style, sailing into Newport after just over twenty-seven days at sea. By 1968 the entry list was up to thirty-five and there was a general increase in the size of the competing boats. The largest in the fleet was Éric Tabarly's 67ft aluminium trimaran *Pen Duick IV*, while Alain Gliksman had the largest monohull in the race, a

FRANCIS CHICHESTER
LIMITED

DIRECTORS: FRANCIS CHICHESTER. S.M.CHICHESTER. M.COOPER

9 ST. JAMES'S PLACE, LONDON, S.W. I

TEL: HYDE PARK 0931   GROSVENOR 8196

NAVIGATION   SPECIALISTS
MAP   MAKERS   AND   PUBLISHERS

25th November, 1959

To the News Editor,
(for immediate release).

SINGLEHANDED TRANSATLANTIC RACE 1960

Described by one experienced yachtsman as "The most
sporting event of the century", a transatlantic race for
single-handed sailing boats will start from the South Coast
of England on Saturday, June 11th 1960, and will finish off
Sheepshead Bay, in the approaches to New York, at least a
month later.

The race is open to boats of any nationality, size, or
type provided that they are propelled by the wind alone, and
manned by one person only. The race will be "boat for boat",
without any form of handicapping. The entries may be sponsored,
and boats need not be sailed by their owners.

The race is being run in collaboration with the Slocum
Society, a predominantly American organisation that will look
after the finishing arrangements.   At least four British
yachtsmen are known to be actively preparing to enter, and it
is hoped that many more will come forward in the remaining
seven months.

The British end of the race is at present being organised
by H.G.Hasler and a committee of prospective entrants.   All
enquiries should be made to Francis Chichester, 9 St. James's
Place, London, S.W.1 (Tel. HYDe Park 0931), who is temporarily
acting as Secretary to the Committee.

Add: In originating this race H.G.Hasler hopes that it may
result in simplification of gear and methods of easy handling
which will benefit yachtsmen generally.

The four firm entries to date are - H.G.Hasler,
Francis Chichester, Dr.David H. Lewis and V.N.Howells.

The letter from by Francis Chichester announcing the single-handed transatlantic race.

57-footer. The competition was fierce and full of incident with Tabarly
setting off in the lead but after only thirty-six hours one hull of the trimaran
was damaged in a collision with a ship and he retired. Several other yachts
retired through damage due to bad weather and the monohulls soon led the

Jester, one of the most famous of the single-handed yachts that has taken part in all of the
early races.

The start of a single-handed transatlantic race.

field. Only nineteen of the original thirty-five starters completed the course with the winner being Geoffrey Williams in the 56ft *Sir Thomas Lipton*, but the attrition rate among the competitors with nearly half dropping out started criticism of single-handed sailing.

Potential competitors recognized that size was an important factor as far as speed was concerned in this single-handed race, but no one was really prepared for the arrival of *Vendredi 13*, the 128ft three-masted schooner to be sailed single-handed by Frenchman Jean Yves Terlan. Challenging this enormous monohull were several large multihulls. Fifty-two starters left Plymouth and this year was the year of the multihull with Alain Colas winning in *Pen Duick IV*, clipping five and a half days off the previous record time for the race but with *Vendredi 13* coming in a close second.

If the size of *Vendredi 13* had been thought too large for single-handed sailing in 1972, then the *Club Mediterranee* that Colas brought to the start line for the 1976 race was double her size. She led for much of the race but had to put into St. John's in Newfoundland for repairs, leaving Éric Tabarly and his multihull to win. This was a tough race with more than fifty retirements and two lives lost, leading to more concerns about the safety of single-handed sailing.

The huge *Club Méditerranée* which was sailed single-handed on the Atlantic race.

Now the race was being dominated by multihulls and the size was limited to yachts of 56ft or less in length. Phil Weld brought his *Moxie* across the finishing line in just under eighteen days to knock more than two and a half days off the record set by Alain Colas. Within twenty-four hours of Weld finishing the race, six other boats had crossed the line, all multihulls, and from that point on it was multihulls that dominated future Atlantic races. In 1984 the top multihulls such as *Apricot* and *Elf Aquitaine* now sported wing masts and were truly high-performance racing machines. The outcome of the race was open right up until the last minute and only twenty-one minutes separated the two leading boats at the finish. The record set by Phil Weld was broken by the first thirteen boats in this race, with just two of them being monohulls.

The reduction in the size limit of boats and other restrictions in the 1980 race led to the French organizing their own single-handed race across the Atlantic, the Route du Rhum. This race was first held in 1978 from St.-Malo to Guadeloupe. Open to all-comers, the race 'followed the sun' and was perceived as less demanding but longer than the Plymouth-Newport race. After 4,000 miles of sailing, the first two boats were separated by an incredible ninety seconds with the Canadian Mike Birch in his 38ft trimaran overtaking Michel Malinovsky from France in his large monohull just miles before the finish line. Sadly, Alain Colas sailing *Manureva* (originally named *Pen Duick IV*) disappeared and was never seen again. A similar tragedy occurred on the

1986 Route du Rhum when Loïc Caradec, sailing the massive 85ft trimaran *Royale*, capsized and was drowned.

With the success and obvious following of the single-handed and two-handed transatlantic races there have been many attempts to introduce other races across the ocean, sometimes to commemorate specific events. Such races for fully-manned boats really allow the mighty multihulls to show their paces. Races have been run from the Mediterranean to New York, from Canada to France, and St.-Malo to New Orleans. In 1986 the largest-ever yacht race across the Atlantic attracted more than 200 yachts from 24 nations. This race from the Canary Islands to Barbados over a 2,700-mile route was run under strict rules to ensure that the entrants were genuine amateurs sailing cruising yachts. No damage or major injuries were reported to any of the participants and the race was won by the US entry, the 54ft trimaran *Running Cloud*. This race is perhaps a reaction against the professionalism and sponsorship that has crept surreptitiously into the transoceanic racing scene, where heavy sponsorship is required for the high-performance multihulls. One of the objects of this Atlantic Rally for Cruisers (ARC) race was to bring some 'fun' back into transoceanic racing. The fact that more than 200 yachts could cross the Atlantic safely shows how commonplace this type of cruising has become.

The top echelons of Atlantic racing have increasingly become the domain of the professional. Exotic yachts manned by fully-paid crews and by skippers who, if successful, became national heroes, is something of a throwback to the early days of Atlantic racing when yachts like the *Atlantic* set the pace. The traditional concept of the deep-keeled, finely-tuned conventional yachts has given way to a new breed of multihull ocean racers using the latest technology and exotic construction materials to produce a highly-strung racing machine. Each succeeding Atlantic race, even the single-handed contests, has seen the setting of a new Atlantic sailing record. In 1986 the time was down to just over sixteen days for the east-west crossing and the two-handed races have reduced this time even further. It was inevitable that there would be interest in setting an out-and-out Atlantic sailing record from some of the race competitors on their return leg back to Europe when the prevailing winds and currents should give the optimum conditions for a fast crossing and this set the scene for some remarkable performances.

Chapter Seven

Rowing, Rafts and Unconventional Craft

The role of the Atlantic Ocean as an arena for human endeavour and for the evaluation of new concepts is probably seen most clearly in the wide assortment of strange and unconventional craft that have attempted to cross it. As we have seen in the last chapter, some of the early sailboats were unconventional in the rigs they carried and it was also the proving ground for new types of life-saving craft. With sailing at least you had the wind to help but with rowing it was all hard manual work to make progress. Rowing the Atlantic must be a particularly personal endeavour, pitting one's own strength against the ocean, but some of the crossings in rafts and other assorted craft have occurred under the guise of scientific expeditions. Although some of the more adventurous crossings have been more in the nature of stunts geared to generate maximum publicity for the individuals involved, there has usually been an element of seriousness underlying many of these projects, certainly in the eyes of the participants. In many cases, however, enthusiasm has outweighed expertise. I was tempted to label these Atlantic crossings the 'freaks' but this would do many of the genuinely serious attempts an injustice, and indeed the collection of voyages listed here demonstrates the extent to which human beings will undergo long periods of suffering in order to prove their own capabilities or their point of view. What they all have in common is the use of the Atlantic as the ultimate marine and human testing ground.

The idea of rowing a boat across the Atlantic still sounds like an incredible feat and back in 1897 it must have sounded even crazier. However, it should be remembered that at that time rowing was widely used for propelling small craft in harbours and rivers. Out on the Grand Banks of Newfoundland rowing boats were used by the fishermen in the open ocean and they often made long and epic voyages back to shore when they lost touch with their mother ships in fog. Equally it was a highly dangerous occupation, but it was this fishing background that spawned the early small boat crossings of the Atlantic under sail and was also the experience behind the first recorded attempt at rowing the Atlantic.

George Harbo and Frank Samuelson were experienced fishermen and they used a little 18ft boat for their Atlantic row. Built as a double-ended whaler of clinker construction, there were watertight boxes at each end to keep it afloat even if it filled with water. Otherwise the boat was a conventional open boat of the period. It was equipped with five pairs of oars, food and water, very basic navigation equipment and very little else, not even somewhere dedicated to sleep. Heavily loaded, the boat had a freeboard of just 8in when they set out from New York on 6 June 1897 which would be a frighteningly small amount even in moderate seas, let alone out on the Atlantic.

This was one of the first sponsored rows of the Atlantic with the boat named *Richard K. Fox* after the editor of the New York newspaper that was sponsoring the crossing. The crew rowed day and night with the two men taking turns to sleep during the night. A month out from New York the boat was capsized by a huge breaking sea, throwing both men into the water. They hung on to handgrips built into the keel and managed to right the boat and climb back on board. During this capsize they lost a fair amount of their equipment, but they were able to pick up more provisions and water from a passing sailing ship and eventually made an accurate landfall after an otherwise uneventful crossing. They arrived in the Scilly Isles off the south-west English coast after fifty-five days, averaging 56 miles a day. Even though they had had favourable winds and currents that would have helped considerably, this first row across the Atlantic is an amazing feat of seamanship and endurance and deserves much more credit than history has accorded it.

Harbo and Samuelson rowed the Atlantic in this tiny boat in fifty-five days, enduring a capsize on the way.

Fourteen years later Joseph Naylor announced that he would attempt a solo rowing attempt but no record exists of the attempt ever having been made. It was another seventy years before a further rowing attempt was made when British sailor David Johnstone commissioned a specially-designed boat from naval architect Colin Mudie. Mudie already had experience of the Atlantic having sailed across in his lightweight 20ft *Sopranino* in 1951 and he was also one of the first people to complete an Atlantic journey partly by air and partly by water. This last feat was achieved when he attempted a balloon crossing of the Atlantic from the Canary Islands in 1958. The balloon came down with 1,500 miles still to go, but the gondola of the balloon had been designed as a boat and the four-man crew continued the journey to Barbados under sail to complete one of the most unusual Atlantic crossings.

Johnstone's boat, the 15ft 6in *Puffin*, was designed with a large part of the boat enclosed to provide protection for the crew and equipment, and the rowing cockpit was carefully planned to give maximum comfort during long periods of rowing. Johnstone's crew was a fellow journalist, John Hoare, and while they were finalizing plans for a departure in 1966, another Atlantic rowing attempt was being developed. Inevitably, with two attempts to row the Atlantic going on at the same time, the media hailed it as a race, changing the whole approach to the event. The second pair in this Atlantic rowing 'race' comprised John Ridgway and Chay Blyth, both members of the Parachute Regiment and perhaps better prepared mentally for the ordeal. The boat they chose was a 20ft Yorkshire dory with raised enclosed compartments at each end to give buoyancy. The boat was strengthened and improved for its Atlantic crossing and was patriotically named *English Rose III*.

Puffin's departure point, Virginia Beach, was a lot further south than that of *English Rose III* which set out from Cape Cod. This southerly departure point was probably a mistake on the part of the two journalists, for it not only considerably increased the distance they had to travel but made it more difficult to get out into the Gulf Stream to gain any benefit from the current. *Puffin* was eventually found nearly five months after her departure, some 800 miles east of Newfoundland, upside-down and heavily encrusted with barnacles. There was no sign of her crew but the log found on board had close to 100 days of entries. It is thought that the boat was overwhelmed by a hurricane that passed through the area. *English Rose III* set out later and experienced her fair share of gale force winds across the northern part of the Atlantic and landfall was made on the west coast of Ireland after ninety-two days at sea. At one stage the crew was running desperately short of food but managed to get extra supplies from a passing ship. Ridgway and Blyth became the first people to row the Atlantic for nearly seventy years but they took nearly forty days

Puffin, the boat in which Johnson and Hoare attempted to row the Atlantic but in which they lost their lives. (*Author*)

longer than Harbo and Samuelson and the crossing was over a shorter route, which just serves to highlight the achievement of those early rowers.

Another epic long-distance rower was not so fortunate. Bob Willis made two successful crossings of the Pacific under oars, but three times he set out to row the Atlantic and twice he was picked up in mid-ocean. On his third attempt Willis was lost and his boat was found empty ninety days after he set out.

However, these losses didn't deter others and the single-handed human-powered crossing remained to be done. The next attempt was made in 1969 when John Fairfax had a 22ft boat designed by the celebrated designer Uffa Fox which was a self-righting design that set the pattern for all future Atlantic rowing attempts. It also featured a self-draining cockpit and a sliding rowing seat was incorporated to improve rowing efficiency. This boat was one of the best-designed craft ever used on an Atlantic rowing attempt. Fairfax planned to row the Atlantic travelling from east to west and had the boat shipped to the Canary Islands from where he set out for his Atlantic row on the southerly route across the ocean. There was, of course, less chance of strong winds on this southerly route and the warmer temperatures would help, but it took Fairfax 180 lonely days to make the crossing from the Canary Islands to Fort Lauderdale in Florida, which probably ranks as one of the longest of all Atlantic crossings.

This same southerly route was followed later by Sidney Genders when he rowed the Atlantic in 1970. However, unlike Fairfax, Genders started out from Cornwall in England and rowed from there to the Canary Islands, continuing on from the Canaries to Antigua in the West Indies and thence on to Miami.

In the 1960s and early 1970s the Atlantic became the venue for a wide variety of daring feats and publicity stunts. A 20ft pontoon with a single outboard motor set off from London for the USA but did not make it out of the Thames estuary. A wartime amphibious vehicle set off on a similar voyage but sank off Dover. These less than serious attempts echoed attempts in the 1930s to cross the Atlantic in a huge rubber ball and another one using two large barrels lashed together!

More seriously, Tom MacLean set out in 1969 to be the first person to row solo across the Atlantic from west to east. He chose the shortest possible distance across, leaving St. John's in Newfoundland and arriving in Ireland seventy days later. The boat used by MacLean was a 20ft Yorkshire dory very similar to that used by Ridgway and Blyth. He made another attempt the following year and this time set a record time for the crossing under oars. He was followed by several attempts using the more benign southern route and now there is a rowing race across the Atlantic that takes place every year rowing from the Canary Islands to Antigua, a distance of 3,000 miles. Sponsored by Talisker Whisky, this race attracts around twenty teams each year, the boats are equipped with a good level of safety equipment and escort boats are provided. This makes rowing the Atlantic look almost like a routine cruise and the aim has become to make the fastest time rather than just achieve the crossing. However, the northern route still offers the much greater challenge for rowers.

The concept of a rowing race across the Atlantic was conceived by Chay Blyth in 1997 with Talisker taking over the project later. With the number of teams making this crossing now, it is not a question of just rowing across but the challenge is to make the fastest crossing with the record currently standing at thirty-two days, which is fast for a 3,000 mile crossing. Boats attempting the record may have up to eight-man crews.

The Atlantic has seen a number of accidental and some remarkable feats of survival. One such in a small rowing boat involved two of the crew of the British tramp steamer *Anglo Saxon*, which was torpedoed in mid-Atlantic in 1940. The nearest land was the Canary Islands 1,000 miles to the east, but the longer distance to the land to the west was chosen as the direction to steer because of the favourable currents. There were seven men in the wooden jolly boat when their ship was sunk, but only two survived the harrowing seventy days at sea in this 18ft boat. An even longer period of survival followed another sinking during the Second World War. The SS *Ben Loman* was torpedoed in the Atlantic 750 miles off the Azores. One of the Chinese stewards, Poon Lim, spent 133 days in a ship's lifeboat before being picked up. The heavy wartime toll on shipping during the Second World War meant that many crews were forced to take to their lifeboats and so rowing on the Atlantic became quite commonplace until rescue came, even though most ship's lifeboats are not the easiest of boats to row.

There have been several attempts to cross the Atlantic by raft, although the definition of a raft is a little vague. It could be argued that the *Nonpareil*, the inflatable life-saving device that crossed the Atlantic back in 1867 was a raft, and indeed it was described by its makers as a 'life-saving raft', but this craft was equipped with two masts and a good sailing rig whereas a raft is more usually thought of as something that drifts rather than sails. One of the first to look at a raft crossing of the Atlantic was the Canadian, Henri Beaudout. He admits to wanting to make this attempt as a means of bringing some adventure into his life and the first raft he built, sailed by a three-man crew, left Montreal in 1954 only to be wrecked on the Newfoundland coast before getting out into the Atlantic. It had taken the crew sixty-six days of drifting just to get to Newfoundland but, undeterred, a second raft was built in 1956 comprising logs lashed together to form the 'hull' and a canvas-covered cabin built on the deck provided the home for the crew. A bipod mast was erected to carry a very basic square sail. This time the crew had learned their lesson and *L'Égaré II* set out from Halifax, Nova Scotia straight out into the Atlantic. They arrived off the Lizard in England eighty-seven days later. *L'Égaré II* encountered the usual North Atlantic storms including winds recorded at 50 knots but the log raft managed to weather these.

Thor Heyerdahl achieved fame with his voyage across the Pacific on the raft *Kon-Tiki*. Obsessed with trying to demonstrate the movement of early civilizations around the world, he later set out to show that there could have been a sea link between the ancient Egyptians and the early civilizations in Peru and Mexico. Heyerdahl identified what he perceived as similar advances in each society, such as the building of pyramids. The papyrus boats used by both these early empires also had a strong similarity and Heyerdahl built the papyrus raft *Ra* in an attempt to demonstrate that a seaborne link could have been feasible centuries earlier. A great deal of research was necessary to establish the form and character of these early boats, and it was an even harder task to find people still capable of building them. The first raft of this type almost succeeded in making the Atlantic crossing but was breaking up as it made the approach to the Caribbean.

Later Heyerdahl built a second raft, *Ra II*, 39ft long and 16ft wide. The papyrus mattress from which this boat was constructed was 6ft thick with raised ends. Above this a 13 ft × 9 ft cabin was constructed to provide shelter for the crew. The raft carried a bipod mast on which a square sail was rigged and both *Ra* voyages followed the favourable wind and current route down to the Canary Islands and then out across the Atlantic to the Caribbean. At times the raft would travel at over 3 knots with favourable winds and currents and on the second crossing the crew experienced some big seas which the raft negotiated very well. *Ra II* finally made Barbados after a 3,270-mile journey, having taken fifty-seven days. While this was a considerable achievement, I am not convinced that it settles the question of whether such a voyage could have been made all those years ago. It is easy to accept that a raft such as *Ra* could have been picked up by the winds and currents and blown across the Atlantic on this route with the crew being unable to make progress back to the land from where they started. However, would such a boat have been equipped with provisions to enable the crew to survive on such a crossing, and would the crew of such a boat have been of the calibre to establish a matching civilization on the other side of the ocean? To both questions the answer would appear to be no, and it is hard to imagine a full-scale expedition being mounted from Egypt to find a new land across the ocean. Even if such a crossing had been achieved, it only seems possible for the detailed technology of a civilization to be transferred across the oceans if it was possible also to make the return journey to inform others of the discovery. This appears to be the weak link in Heyerdahl's argument that a sea link existed, but it does not detract from the unique achievement of the crew of *Ra* and *Ra II*.

A similar type of voyage was undertaken in 1976–77 by Tim Severin. He set out to demonstrate that the Irish monk Saint Brendan might have been one of the first discoverers of America when he made his epic voyages in Atlantic waters. As far as research can identify, the early Brendan voyages did not encompass the coast of America, but Saint Brendan almost certainly reached Iceland and the Azores. The *Brendan* boat built by Tim Severin to try to follow the route of the sixth-century Irish monk was constructed in traditional Celtic style with a light wooden frame covered by animal skins. This comparatively light craft had a square sail hoisted on a single pole mast and was a surprisingly efficient sailing craft. Severin took the northerly route from Ireland to the Shetland Isles and then on to the Faroes and across to Iceland, then Greenland before finally making his North American landfall at Newfoundland. Perhaps even more definitely than the *Ra* voyages, this replica craft proved itself capable of making an Atlantic crossing, but of course this cannot prove that the same crossing was necessarily enacted back in the sixth century.

In 1963 an Atlantic crossing was made on the southerly route from the Azores to Guadeloupe in the West Indies by a Frenchman, René Lescombes.

His 25ft-long raft was equipped with a cutter rig and although it succeeded in making the Atlantic crossing, the craft and crew were subsequently lost at sea.

Ten years later an unusual raft voyage was enacted across the Atlantic. The voyage, aboard a strongly-built steel raft, was designed to study human behaviour in a closed environment. Five couples boarded the *Acali* which set out from the Canary Islands on 12 May 1973 and after a variety of storms and other adventures, they finally made landfall on the Mexican coastline on 20 September after a total of 101 days isolated at sea. This scientific experiment was carried out under the auspices of the Instituto de Investigaciones and Antropologicas in Mexico but the press degraded the whole affair by calling it the 'Mexican Love Raft'. This raft had been designed by Colin Mudie using his 'Atlantic' experience and the fact that it made the crossing successfully is a tribute to his design. Once again, sail was used to propel the raft and this was one of the few crossings of the Atlantic by this southerly route that did not stop at the barrier of islands forming the West Indies but carried on right through to the Central American mainland.

Two years later Dr Santiago Genoves, who masterminded the *Acali* experiments, conceived the idea of a further experimental raft designed with the intention of crossing the Atlantic under water. The raft designed for this had a clear plastic accommodation chamber located beneath the waterline. Once again this raft was designed by Colin Mudie and the experiment involved the study of an individual's reaction when continually surrounded by water. The whole concept was, to say the least, far-fetched and it was probably fortuitous that the raft built for this project was dropped and destroyed while it was being unloaded from the ship that transported it to the Canary Islands for the start of the voyage, thus ending the experiment rather abruptly.

One of the most famous scientific experiments to be carried out on the Atlantic was Dr Alain Bombard's voyage across the Atlantic in a small inflatable boat. Bombard sought to demonstrate in a highly practical way his theory that a shipwrecked sailor could live for long periods off what the ocean could produce. Carrying no stores on board, Bombard drank limited amounts of sea water, tests having shown that sea water could safely be drunk in small quantities, and fish were his main source of food. Bombard's crossing ranks as an epic of survival existing on what was available from the ocean for sixty-five days. This crossing was made in a fairly standard Zodiac inflatable just 15ft in length and the boat survived the crossing with very few problems. The inflatable, called *L'Hérétique*, was equipped with a small mast and sail so that Bombard could take advantage of the prevailing winds to boost his speed and

The raft that was designed to drift across the Atlantic with its crew underwater but was dropped by a crane before starting.

The small inflatable in which Dr Bombard drifted across the Atlantic.

the time taken is a very creditable performance. Bombard's crossing was the first in an inflatable boat since the voyage of the *Nonpareil* nearly a century earlier.

In 1978 an Irishman set out from Halifax in Nova Scotia in an attempt to cross the Atlantic in an inflatable boat powered by an outboard motor and also equipped with a sail. Enda O'Coineen left harbour very quietly, fearing that if his intentions were known the coast guard would stop him leaving. This first crossing very nearly ended in disaster when the boat was capsized just a few hundred miles off the west coast of Ireland. O'Coineen had spent two days lashed to the bottom of the capsized boat and he was near to death

The powerful ocean-going tug *Oceanic* heads to the rescue of a ship in storm conditions.

The size of storm waves can be judged from this 40ft pilot boat heading into storm waves. (*Safehaven*)

An offshore service vessel heading into hurricane seas. (*Bourbon*)

A replica of Columbus's flagship the *Santa Maria*.

A typical early Atlantic sailing packet carrying cargo and passengers.

Shipwreck was a constant hazard to the sailing packet ships.

An American advertisement for the Cunard Line Atlantic steamers.

An artist's impression of the German liner *Columbus* for an advertisement.

The SS *United States*, the last of the true Atlantic liners.

The tiny *City of Ragusa* that made the first two-way crossing of the Atlantic in a small sailing boat.

A modern crew rowing in the Atlantic rowing race in trade wind seas. (*Talisker Whisky*)

Thor Heyerdahl's unlikely-looking raft *Ra II* in which he crossed the Atlantic.

Virgin Atlantic Challenger sinking in the Atlantic just 138 miles from the finish line. (*Author*)

Al Grover completed the first outboard motor-powered Atlantic crossing in this 26-footer.

Azimut Atlantic Challenger at speed, powered by its four CRM engines. (*Azimut*)

Destriero, which achieved the fastest-ever crossing of the Atlantic, averaging 53 knots.

The catamaran *Virgin Atlantic Challenger* that sank just 138 miles from the finish line.

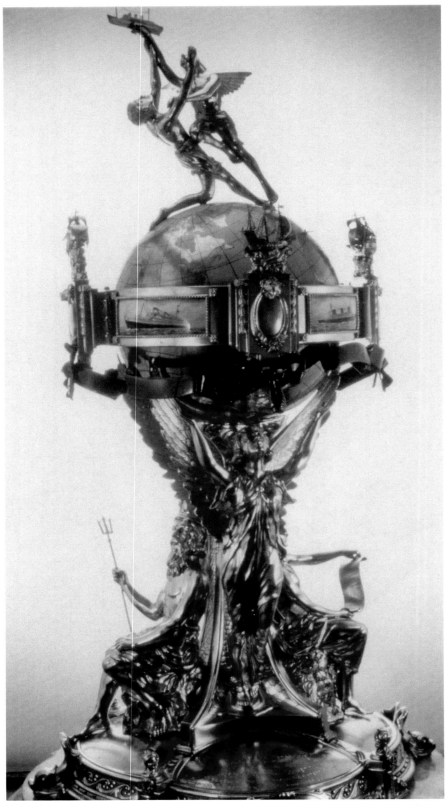

The magnificent Hales Trophy that was awarded to the fastest ship on the Atlantic.

The French trimaran *Banque Populaire* that currently holds the Atlantic sailing record.

Prototype of a powerboat being developed to break the Atlantic record under test in the open sea.

Meeting a rogue wave with its near-vertical wall of water.

The US Coast Guard Ice Patrol monitors the icebergs in the North Atlantic.

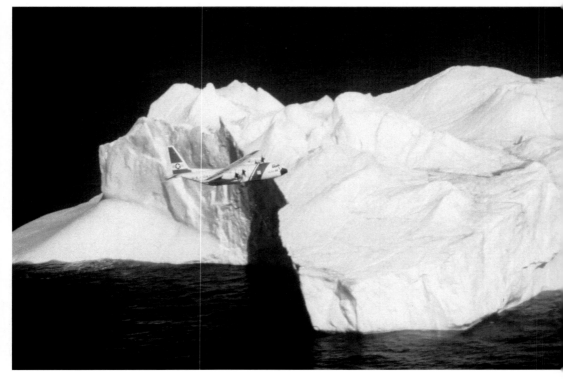

The view from the bridge of *Polar Star* when a large wave is approaching.

The tracks of hurricanes in one year on the North Atlantic, showing the varied route of these storms.

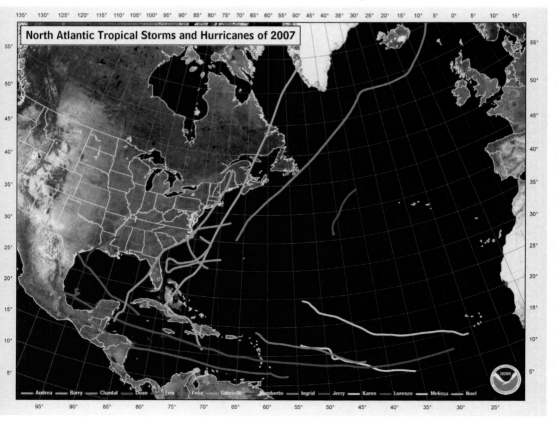

North Atlantic Tropical Storms and Hurricanes of 2007

Andrea   Barry   Chantal   Dean   Erin   Felix   Gabrielle   Humberto   Ingrid   Jerry   Karen   Lorenzo   Melissa   Noel

The wreck of the *Amoco Cadiz* spewing oil that ended up on the French coastline.

A rendering of a fast sailing trimaran that is being developed to sail across the Atlantic unmanned.

The view of massive storm waves from a small boat.

Container cargoes, even on the largest ships, are always at risk in storm conditions.

Modern ships rely extensively on electronics for navigation and safety but the Atlantic still remains a challenge.

when he was finally rescued by a NATO warship that was out on exercise in the area. O'Coineen had spent seventy-nine days in the boat and vowed that he was finished with the Atlantic and inflatable boats forever after this trip. However, he was not very happy at being remembered as the man who nearly made it across and he scheduled a second attempt to be made in 1985. The original voyage had a partly serious purpose to it, since it was intended to assist the development of a sailing life-raft that would allow survivors from a shipwreck to make progress towards land and safety. It also looked at the problems of self-sufficiency and survival at sea. O'Coineen had worked with a life-raft company developing survival equipment before this attempt but his second crossing in 1985 was intended, he said, purely to set the record straight and to get the Atlantic out of his system.

On this second attempt, O'Coineen selected a rigid inflatable for the job. Like Bombard's inflatable it was just 15ft in length and was equipped with a mast and sails as well as two outboard motors. After his earlier experience on the Atlantic, this boat was fitted with self-righting equipment in the form of an airbag on a frame over the stern, which could be inflated if the boat capsized. After leaving Halifax O'Coineen encountered the tail end of Hurricane Anna but he fought his way into St. John's in Newfoundland to fill up with fuel for the Atlantic crossing. The idea was to burn off most of the fuel during the first half of the passage to get through the Labrador Current and out into the Gulf Stream and from there on the sails and the current would carry the boat towards Ireland. Four stormy days out from St. John's the boat bumped into an iceberg. Another storm capsized the boat but fortunately the self-righting gear worked and O'Coineen climbed back on board, shaken and exhausted. Storm followed storm for ten days and finally, after twenty-eight days, O'Coineen made landfall in Ireland, the first rigid inflatable to cross the Atlantic.

In this look at the more unusual craft that have crossed the Atlantic, we can't miss out the windsurfers who have made the passage. In 1982 Pascal Marty made a crossing on a windsurfer from Dakar in Africa to the West Indies. On this crossing Marty sailed his windsurfer all day but was taken on board an accompanying 50ft yacht at night, where he ate and slept ready for the next day's sail. It is a remarkable effort, although having the luxury and comfort of a yacht close by all the time must certainly have made things a lot easier and, of course, it takes much of the risk out of the attempt. It was also the French who made the first non-stop crossing by windsurfer. This crossing was made in a specially-prepared tandem windsurfer that was built up so that minimal accommodation could be fitted into the hull. The crew took it in turns to squeeze through the small hatch in order to sleep and this remarkable

The two-man windsurfer *Liberté* which was sailed across the Atlantic.

crossing has to rank as one of the most extreme Atlantic crossings but you might wonder just what it proved.

Sponsorship and attendant publicity is now becoming a strong motive for carrying out unusual voyages and there will always be people whose enthusiasm will outweigh their expertise or natural caution in undertaking such voyages. This motive has almost certainly lain behind some of the attempts to cross the Atlantic in tiny sailing boats. After the enthusiasm for small sailing boats towards the end of the last century, the next small boat attempt was in 1934 when Al Lastinger set out from Florida in a 10ft sailboat. With the boat leaking badly, he only lasted a few days before he was rescued, but he set out again four years later in an 18ft vessel without achieving any more success.

In 1955 Hanns Lindemann made an Atlantic crossing from the Canary Islands to the West Indies in a 17ft collapsible kayak, *Liberia II*. This tiny craft had a small sail to help it on its way and the crossing took sixty-five days over the 3,000-mile route, thus emulating Captain Romer's remarkable feat back in 1928, although Lindemann arrived in a much better physical condition than his predecessor.

The 1960s saw several attempts to cross the Atlantic in the smallest possible sailing boat with *Sea Egg* making the crossing in 1964. This 12ft sloop was shaped as its name suggests and was refused entry in the 1964 transatlantic race because of its size. The owner John Riding decided to sail across the Atlantic anyway, and after calling at Spain and the Azores went on to

Bermuda and then Panama in this tiny craft. The west-east record for the smallest boat had been held by Si Lawlor since his first single-handed crossing of the Atlantic in 1891 and his size record was not beaten until 1965 when an American, Robert Manry, sailed from Falmouth, USA to Falmouth, England in seventy-eight days. Manry's boat was the *Tinkerbelle* which was just 13ft in length. Boats were getting smaller and smaller and *Giltspur*, 9ft 9in in length, and *Winds Will* at 9ft in length also sailed across the Atlantic but the record for the smallest has to go to *April Fool* sailed by the American Hugo Vihlen from Casablanca to Fort Lauderdale in 1968. This amazing boat was just under 6ft in length, barely long enough to sleep full-length, and Vihlen took eighty-five days for the 3,000-mile crossing, averaging just 1.4 knots.

It is hard to imagine such a record for small sizes being beaten, simply because of the sheer difficulty of living and sleeping in such a small space. However, in their quest for the daring and difficult, men do many strange things and no doubt this record will eventually be broken but to what point it is not easy to see. While many of the unusual trips across the Atlantic may have been done for the very private reason of proving something to the person concerned, living in totally cramped conditions on a tiny boat seems like a particularly odd form of masochism and one can really only feel that some Atlantic crossings are done for the worst type of publicity. There is nothing to be gained technically from such an exercise, but perhaps we shouldn't be too

Robert Manry at Falmouth, UK at the end of his transatlantic sailing trip.

harsh on such attempts because with so many things now having been achieved on the Atlantic it is harder and harder to find new challenges that stretch the imagination and the physical ability of the participants. People will always find new and even more difficult ways to make the Atlantic crossing and it is perhaps a tribute to the advances in modern boat technology that crossings by boats under 30ft are now routine rather than exceptional. I don't think anyone has crossed in a pedalo yet, so there is a new possibility to try.

Chapter Eight

Motor Boats take to the Atlantic

It took nearly fifty years for the steam engine to become an accepted and reliable power unit for ships but even then ships were challenged to carry enough coal to make the Atlantic crossing. Using steam power for propulsion only worked over longer distances for larger ships because of the amount of coal needed. So for small boats wanting to cross the Atlantic under power they had to wait for the development of the internal combustion engine. For this type of engine using diesel, petrol or kerosene as a fuel the development period was much shorter because engineering experience was already well developed. It was just ten years from one first internal combustion engine being fitted into a boat before the idea of crossing the Atlantic with a boat powered by such an engine was mooted. As had happened with steam engines though, there was also the problem of how to carry enough fuel.

The first boat to attempt an Atlantic crossing with an internal combustion engine was the *Abiel Abbot Low* in 1902. The man behind the project was an American, William Newman, and the purpose of his proposed crossing was to demonstrate that the newly-developed small internal combustion engines were up to the task, and what better testing ground than the Atlantic? The *Abiel Abbot Low* had a length of 37ft 6in and the paraffin-fuelled engine was a small 10 hp single cylinder unit with a capacity of just 150cc, which would be little more than a moped engine today. She was also equipped with two masts and sails as happened with early steam but the promoters of the voyage claimed that the sails were only intended to act as steadying sails to reduce the rolling and not for propulsion! This is a rather ingenuous response when you consider the prevailing westerly winds on the Atlantic that would have allowed the sails to be a considerable help.

The *Abiel Abbot Low* was loaded up with 660 gallons of paraffin in the tanks and another 70 gallons were stowed in 1-gallon cans in the engine compartment. In case of any breakdown of the engine a complete spare engine was carried on board in spare parts, but little could be done about the transmission and propeller should they have failed. William Newman and his 16-year-old son sailed from New York and for the first six days they enjoyed good weather and covered 150 miles per day with the engine running smoothly. Then a blocked carburettor jet brought it to a halt but that problem was soon

The *Abeil Abbot Low* in Falmouth after her pioneering Atlantic crossing under power.

solved and they were on their way again. Later the same day, the engine stopped again with a hot bearing which again was soon sorted. Then the weather changed and the boat rode hove-to using a sea anchor for two days and in addition to the bad weather their problems really began in earnest. There were leaks in the fuel tanks that not only reduced the fuel available but also created a fire hazard. They were losing more than 9 gallons a day from the tanks which found its way into the bilges from where it was then collected and poured back into the tanks.

After ten days of this, the Newmans were in a very bad state with the whole boat and all their clothing and bedding saturated in paraffin, but the engine kept running. After thirty-seven days at sea and amid continuing bad weather and difficult seas, the Scilly Islands were sighted off the English coast and at 6.00 pm that evening the *Abiel Abbot Low* tied up in Falmouth harbour. Although the crew was exhausted, the engine was still running well having been running for a total of 613 hours out of the 861 hours spent at sea. During this time the engine had consumed just under half a gallon of paraffin an hour giving ample reserves and an average speed of 5 knots for the crossing, a quite remarkable performance in the face of adversity.

The next crossing by a boat with an internal combustion engine took place a year later almost to the day. However, the engine of the *Gjoa* was installed as an auxiliary engine with sail installed as the primary means of propulsion. The

William Newman and his son at the helm of the *Abeil Abbot Low*.

Gjoa sailed from Norway in 1903 under the command of Captain Amundsen and as well as crossing the Atlantic by the northern route she also completed the North West Passage and ended the voyage in San Francisco. The engine was a Dan two-cylinder unit running on heavy oil to give a speed of 4 knots to this 69ft vessel.

The next true motor boat crossing of the Atlantic was carried out to demonstrate that the 12 hp two-cylinder Scripps petrol engine could perform happily over long distances. Similar in size to the *Abiel Abbot Low*, the *Detroit* was built for William E. Scripps who owned the Scripps Motor Company. He gave the job of skippering the boat to the experienced Thomas Flemming-Day who had crossed the Atlantic under sail the previous year. As the editor of *The Rudder* magazine, Flemming-Day could get a lot of publicity for the project which was the name of the game as far as this engine manufacturer was concerned.

The Scripps engine was fuelled by petrol that was carried in five cylindrical steel tanks inside the hull giving a total capacity of 1,000 gallons and in addition there were two further 100-gallon tanks mounted on each side of the deck. A further 100 gallons were carried in 5-gallon cans stowed about the boat. Surprisingly there was a distinct lack of engineering experience reported among the four-man crew and again auxiliary sails were fitted.

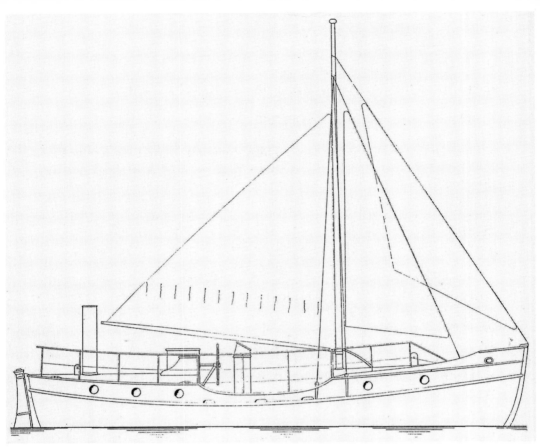

Outboard profile of the *Detroit* that crossed the Atlantic in 1912.

The *Detroit* left New York in 1912 and out in the open sea the crew had trouble with the very heavy rolling of the boat, suggesting that the sails were not doing much of a job in steadying the rolling. Then the inside ballast on the boat shifted during a heavy roll and it became evident that the preparations for this voyage were less than perfect. Nine days out on the crossing the hull began to leak but the engine-driven bilge pump managed to keep this leak under control. Crew morale was low with the constant rolling of the boat, the fact that they had to stand outside to steer in all weathers and because of the loud and continuous noise from the unsilenced exhaust. After twenty-three days at sea they finally made landfall on the Irish coast and arrived in Queenstown to a great reception.

The poorly-prepared *Detroit* was the first petrol-engined boat to cross the Atlantic and was also the smallest boat to date to make the crossing under power. She was fitted with what were called stabilizing sails to reduce the rolling which did not prove very effective but again must have helped progress in the following winds. It seems that no one had the confidence yet to put their trust in the reliability of the engines, thus making auxiliary sails completely unnecessary.

Although the *Abiel Abbot Low* and the *Detroit* were the pioneers as far as Atlantic powerboat crossings are concerned, by 1904 there were proposals for a transatlantic race for motor boats. Thirty-four entries had been received for this race and among these was a 65ft vessel with twin 150 hp engines built by the British Napier Company and another 65ft craft with twin Mercedes engines. Despite the excitement and enthusiasm for the race it was never held, and as far as is known, none of the craft that were being developed to compete in it ever crossed the Atlantic. However, the boat being built by the Napier Company was very advanced for its day and its designer, the famous S.F. Edge, expected his cruiser to cross the Atlantic at a speed of 17 knots to take just seven days for the crossing, a speed almost equal to that of the Atlantic liners of the time but it never made the attempt.

After the initial enthusiasm from pioneers with small engines and sails the interest in Atlantic motor boat crossings waned considerably, although in 1912 a motorboat race was run from New York to Bermuda. This race was held annually for several years after this date but eventually interest in that also faded and it was another twenty-five years before Atlantic motor boat fever started up again.

In Britain, Betty Carstairs had a boat built to make not only a powered crossing of the Atlantic but to set a new record, challenging the Atlantic liners. The plan developed by the builder of this boat, Sam Saunders, was to make a 3,000-mile crossing from Cowes to New York in ninety hours, maintaining an average speed of 45 knots! Saunders designed a 78ft hull with a beam of 15ft 6in that was to be powered by no fewer than four Napier Lion engines developing a total of 3,600 hp. The plan was to run these in pairs alternately, stopping and starting them every hour.

The *Jack Stripes*, as the boat was known, had many similarities to modern powerboat designs. The bow was very fine, designed to cut through the waves rather than ride over them, and four steps were incorporated into the underwater surfaces. *Jack Stripes* was completed in 1928 but never attained her hoped-for speed on trials and was eventually re-engined and used as a cruising boat. She was perhaps some fifty years ahead of her time in both size and power which in many ways comes close to the specification of *Virgin Atlantic Challenger II* which set a new Atlantic record in 1986.

The next record of a motor boat actually crossing the Atlantic comes in 1937 when Marin-Marie made the journey in the 42ft *Arielle* from New York to Le Havre. Marin-Marie had already sailed the Atlantic single-handed in 1933 but with this motor boat crossing he set several new records, including the first single-handed crossing by motor boat and also the fastest crossing of the Atlantic by motor boat. *Arielle* had a single mast on which an emergency or steadying sail could be rigged and was also equipped with a very primitive type of autopilot so that the boat could keep going day and night even as the helmsman slept. Unlike his sailboat crossing, Marin-Marie's voyage across the Atlantic by motor boat was remarkably uneventful and this is probably why it received very little publicity. When projects go as planned there is no exciting story and it seems there has to be a disaster or near-disaster in order to capture the public's imagination and gain publicity.

In 1939, the first motor boat crossing from east to west was made in the 31ft *Eckero*. The owner, Uno Ekblom, was unable to obtain a US visa and so could not to buy a steamship ticket; therefore, he decided to make the crossing in his motor boat which seems a rather extreme approach. The *Eckero* was fitted with a single-cylinder 10hp diesel engine and she first made the trip from the Baltic to England before departing on the Atlantic crossing from Falmouth in 1938. The first refuelling stop was made in the Azores and from there the *Eckero* set off for Bermuda, 1,800 miles away. The final leg was from Bermuda to New York, arriving there in a total of thirty-four days for the 3,750-mile voyage.

Obviously the Second World War stopped Atlantic crossings by boat but in 1955 the 52ft converted lifeboat *Aries* left England and made a double crossing of the Atlantic. On this, the first double voyage by a motor boat, bad weather was experienced in both directions but the solid lifeboat design enabled the boat to motor this through without problems and both engines and boat performed as required.

As engines became more reliable and technology improved, crossing the Atlantic by powerboat was becoming more common and some voyages were used to promote both the boats and the engines. In 1958 a tiny 22ft motor boat powered by twin outboards took on the Atlantic in a unique approach to Atlantic crossings. The boat *Coronet Explorer* was a standard fibreglass design produced by Coronet Boats in Denmark and the owner of the company, Aole Botved, was accompanied by American Jim Wynne, a boat designer who was to achieve fame in nautical circles by inventing the first modern stern-drive propulsion unit. For the 1958 crossing the *Coronet Explorer* was powered by twin 50hp Johnson outboards, and the plan was to make the Atlantic crossing in company with a freighter the *Clary Thorden* from which the diminutive boat could receive fuel twice a day. This meant that the *Coronet Explorer* had to keep up with the freighter whatever the weather, which was not inclined to delay its voyage unnecessarily although the freighter was only running at between 12 and 15 knots.

The *Coronet Explorer* set out from Copenhagen, heading north-about round the top of Scotland. In the passage between the Orkney and Shetland Islands, bad weather was encountered and the tiny boat experienced such a rough ride that eventually she had to be lifted on board the freighter until the weather eased many hours later. The boat was then put back into the water and the voyage continued. The engines suffered continual problems from spark plug fouling, but the voyage continued until once again bad weather off the coast of Nova Scotia meant that *Coronet Explorer* was lifted aboard the freighter. Approaching the US coast the boat was put back into the water and finally after ten days, sixteen hours, eighteen minutes, the *Coronet Explorer* arrived in Newport. This was the first outboard power crossing and certainly the smallest motor boat, but with around 50 miles of the crossing being spent on board the accompanying ship it was less than a true Atlantic crossing and fuel was readily available as required from the freighter.

Like some sailboats before her, the *Dana Rescuer* was a new lifeboat concept and the builders decided to make an Atlantic crossing to prove the concept. This small 23-footer constructed from metal took the southerly route, stopping off at islands before completing a thirty-three-day passage to Panama. The *Dana Rescuer* was powered by a Perkins 46 hp diesel engine and is reputed to have had a range of 4,000 miles at an average speed of 6 knots, although this extensive range was never put to the test and she was also fitted with sails. Apart from those very early crossings, no motor boat had made a non-stop crossing of the Atlantic.

In 1977 a 50-year-old American, Alan Cargile, planned to make an Atlantic crossing in a powerboat to commemorate the fiftieth anniversary of the air-craft crossing by the *Spirit of St. Louis*. For this trip he selected a 30ft Great Lakes cruiser, which certainly looked most unsuitable for ocean crossings with its large areas of glass and its shallow draft. The *Spirit of Nashville* was powered by a single Volvo Penta diesel engine coupled to stern-drive propul-sion and was more of a houseboat than an ocean-going vessel. When Cargile left New York with two companions on 16 July 1977, the boat was loaded with nearly 4 tons of fuel and speed was kept down to about 6 knots to mini-mize fuel consumption. After five days, having covered about 1,100 miles, the *Spirit of Nashville* ran into a storm with waves reported to be over 30ft in height. Lying to a sea anchor and keeping the engine in reverse, they managed to survive this storm, but the radio had been put out of action and they went into St. John's in Newfoundland for repairs.

After five days they set out again and encountered another storm which again put the radio out of action, but this time they carried on and arrived at Le Havre on 14 August, having taken thirty-one days for the crossing. The engine had run non-stop for 695 hours to give a fuel consumption of 2.13 gallons per hour. This was proof of the capabilities of modern small boat diesel engines and Volvo Penta received a great deal of positive publicity from the voyage despite the boat being the most unseaworthy design for operating on the Atlantic.

Rival marine diesel engine manufacturer BMW recognized the value of Atlantic crossings in promoting its products and agreed to support an Atlantic double crossing planned by a French boat-builder, META. The boat for this event, the *Voyageur 47*, was a modern sailing yacht type hull, 47ft long, designed to offer minimum water resistance and thus minimize the power necessary to propel her through the water. She was fitted with fuel tanks to give a total capacity of 1,850 gallons for the Atlantic crossing and the two BMW D50-2 diesels each produced 45 hp. The top speed was 9.5 knots and an economical cruising speed was 7.2 knots. The route chosen for this crossing was from Lyon on the River Rhône, where the boat was built, direct to New York. This east-west non-stop crossing was claimed to be the first to be made by a small powerboat with *Voyageur* covering 4,800 nautical miles in just 720 hours and using 1,320 gallons of fuel. It ranks as one of the most fuel-efficient and probably the longest non-stop voyage ever made by a powerboat and *Voyageur* also made the return crossing of the Atlantic later.

Although powerboats now make Atlantic crossings each year, such a passage will always require a degree of planning. Using the optimum route with island stopping-points, there are still at least 1,200 miles to cover without refuelling. An Atlantic crossing by motor boat at slow speed is not a difficult proposition any longer, although there will always remain the weather to contend with and any motor boat attempting the passage must be completely seaworthy.

However, 'seaworthy' is hardly a word that could be used to describe *Half Safe*. This wartime-built amphibious craft was designed for military river crossings in fine conditions. American Ben Carlin and his wife set out to cross the Atlantic in this vessel and, quite amazingly, succeeded! As Ben Carlin describes it: 'These Ford amphibious quarter-ton trucks proved almost useless in military service. With a freeboard of just 15inches when unladen, they were easily swamped in all but the calmest of inland waters.' Carlin was not a man to be easily put off and he converted the craft by building a cabin on the top, creating bow and belly fuel tanks and generally adapting the craft in every way he could to make it more suitable for an ocean crossing, including raising the freeboard. The couple sailed from Halifax in Nova Scotia in 1950 and after stopping in the Azores and Canary Islands, *Half Safe* made a landfall at Cape Juby on the African coast and then continued the voyage by land up into Europe. *Half Safe* survived some extremely bad weather that was severe enough to test far more seaworthy craft and also experienced mechanical and fuel troubles, but Ben and Elinore Carlin triumphed despite all the doubters.

Half Safe, the wartime amphibian in which the Carlins crossed the Atlantic.

Advances in technology had made crossing the Atlantic at low speeds almost routine but the possibility of crossing the Atlantic at high planing speeds was being considered. Was it possible for a small fast boat to cross the Atlantic at high speed and perhaps make the crossing at an even higher speed than the Atlantic liners? Certainly with the possibility of crossing the Atlantic in perhaps three days, it meant that the crossing could be timed to take advantage of a spell of fine weather. Weather forecasting had advanced to the point where it could be predicted with a considerable degree of accuracy over the whole route for a three-day voyage, but even when it is in a comparatively calm mood the Atlantic Ocean can throw up some uncomfortable seas for a boat travelling at 40 knots or more. High-speed boats are very sensitive to even small waves, which can make for an uncomfortable and possibly damaging ride. The Atlantic does not give up its secrets easily, but there were teams now looking seriously at challenging the Atlantic liners for the Blue Riband. The absolute Atlantic speed record had stayed constant for too many years in the hands of the SS *United States*, and with the Atlantic liners never being likely to attain high speeds for a record crossing again, several people started to look very seriously at their chances of taking the record with a variety of schemes. The Atlantic had been crossed by a wide variety of boats and ships but a high-speed small boat crossing remained one of the last big challenges on the Atlantic. By 1984 the Atlantic had not even been crossed by a power-boat at planing speeds which start at around 18 knots, let alone reached the magic 40-knot average figure for a new record. There was a lot of work to be done but the challenge was there and it was not long before it was taken up.

Chapter Nine

New Atlantic Records

In the 1970s it was no longer a matter of just crossing the Atlantic or being the smallest or most extreme because the focus was now on being the fastest with interest in Atlantic records under both power and sail. With the sailboat racing across the Atlantic setting new records for the east to west crossing it was inevitable that the top yachts would try to go even faster on the return voyage when they had more favourable winds and when they were heading home anyway. In France sailing had become big business with the top yachtsmen able to get generous sponsorship and while this tended to be focused on the racing, there was a bonus for the sponsors if the yacht could get more publicity by setting a record on the return voyage.

After Alain Colas won the 1972 single-handed Atlantic race in *Pen Duick IV* with a new record in the east-west direction of twenty days, thirteen hours, he made a record attempt on his return to France but could only achieve a crossing in nineteen days, even with a full crew on board. This was a long way outside the record of just over twelve days set nearly seventy years earlier by the yacht *Atlantic*. This remarkable time under sail set by *Atlantic* was the benchmark and was proving hard to beat. The year 1977 saw two attempts; the first by Huey Long in his beautiful 25-metre maxi yacht *Ondine* and for this attempt *Ondine* followed a northerly route just skirting the ice floes off Newfoundland and Greenland. Right up until the ninth day of the crossing she was ahead of the record schedule but then came four days of light winds and even calms and *Ondine* was two days behind with the record well out of reach. The second attempt was made by *Great Britain II*, a 24.25-metre trimaran, and she came very close with a time of thirteen days, one hour. Weather forecasting was the challenge here and forecasts were fine for the first five days or so but after that the accuracy deteriorated and it became a matter of luck whether the winds would be favourable for a record. With modern record-breaking under both power and sail, getting the weather right for the crossing is the key to success and the top forecasters are worth their weight in gold.

Part of the incentive for these Atlantic sailing record attempts was a trophy donated by the *Sunday Times* newspaper, and a prize of £10,000 to the first boat to beat the record set by the *Atlantic* in 1905. It was clearly not going to

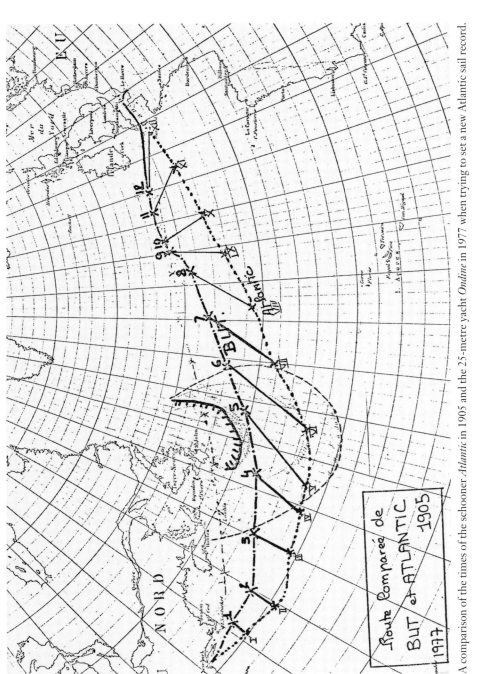

A comparison of the times of the schooner *Atlantic* in 1905 and the 25-metre yacht *Ondine* in 1977 when trying to set a new Atlantic sail record.

be an easy record to break but in 1980 a very determined effort was made during the Atlantic Challenge Cup Race, a race for fully-crewed yachts from New York to the Lizard and then on to Brest. The official distance for the Atlantic sailing record is from New York to the Lizard and this race was carefully timed to take place after the finish of the 1980 single-handed race when many of the top European boats would be in America and have to make the return journey anyway.

The 60ft-long trimaran *Paul Ricard* was one of the first of the multihull sailboats to be fitted with hydrofoils to lift the hull out of the water and so reduce the resistance. Sailed by Éric Tabarly, she made the crossing in five hours over ten days to finally break the seventy-five-year-old record. Tabarly was fortunate with his winds and his fastest daily average speed was 16.1 knots, which in those days was fast for a sailboat.

By 1980 ocean sailing and racing had really captured the imagination of the French and large, powerful multihulls were being built under the incentive of very strong sponsorship. Marc Pajot sailing *Elf Aquitaine* made an attempt on the record following the two-handed transatlantic race in 1981 and he clipped nearly nineteen hours off Tabarly's record with a time of nine days, ten hours and six and a half minutes. Pajot picked up a 100,000-franc prize for this attempt and sparked off a whole series of Atlantic record attempts that brought the record down further and further.

The year 1983 saw *Club Mediterranee*, the huge 72-metre monohull that had dominated the 1976 single-handed race, back on the Atlantic again under the name of *La Vie Claire*. Skippered by Philippe Morinay and with a sixteen-man crew, this huge yacht made her attempt at the sailing record in February when strong winds could be anticipated. After nine days of hard sailing she was just 145 miles from the Lizard and on schedule for a new record when the wind died and the attempt failed. That demonstrated just how close the weather margins can be for a sailing record attempt. Not to be put off, Patrick Morvan took his 60ft catamaran *Jet Services* to a new Atlantic sailing record in 1984 that knocked nearly eighteen hours off Marc Pajot's time in almost perfect sailing conditions over the whole route. It seemed that nothing could stop these flying multihulls on the Atlantic and that the days of the monohulls were numbered, despite their superior seaworthiness.

In 1986 it was virtually a race across the Atlantic for the record when two 85ft multihulls set out on the same day. *Charente Maritime II* and *Royale* followed different routes from the start in New York with *Royale* taking a more northerly route where she found consistent winds from the right direction. Covering more than 300 miles in every twenty-four-hour period, *Royale*, skippered by Loïc Caradec, passed the Lizard Lighthouse with a time of seven days, twenty-one hours and five minutes, averaging 16.29 knots. After we had

The French catamaran *Royale* after her record-breaking Atlantic sail.

set the new Atlantic record under power in *Virgin Atlantic Challenger II* that same year, we met up with *Royale* in Southampton and I got the chance to sail in her. The sensation of travelling at 26 knots under sail was so much more exciting than travelling at twice that speed under power.

Consistent winds from the right direction are vital for the setting of fast times on the Atlantic. The multihulls need winds abeam or just slightly abaft the beam rather than following winds to give them maximum speed. *Royale* sported a huge wing mast the size of a jumbo jet wing, and both wing mast and hull were constructed from exotic composites to give the lightest weight and the highest strength combination. It is sad that both *Royale* and her skipper were lost in an Atlantic race at the end of 1986, but this loss serves to demonstrate the risks involved in sailing huge multihulls and the fact that you can never relax where the Atlantic is concerned. However, his record stands as a fitting memorial to Caradec, a fine seaman in the Atlantic tradition.

The faster these big multihulls went, the better the potential for getting the right weather. Weather forecasting can be fairly accurate up to five days ahead but after that the accuracy and particularly the timing of changes can start to deteriorate. With these yachts crossing the Atlantic in seven days they have a much better idea of what the weather will do over the period of their record

Elf Aquitaine with her massive sails necessary to maintain speed over the 3,000 miles of the Atlantic.

attempt than the earlier yachts that were taking ten days or longer. Also with the passage of time the quality of the weather forecasts has improved considerably so that when a yacht sets out from New York they could be pretty comfortable that they would get the weather conditions that were forecast. I have been the 'weatherman' on several Atlantic power record attempts and have been well aware of the improvements that have taken place since I first started back in 1985.

The summer of 1987 saw another French multihull making an attempt on the Atlantic sailing record. This time it was Philippe Poupon who left New York early in June and just seven days, twelve hours and fifty minutes later he was passing the Lizard Lighthouse with a new record. Poupon was sailing the giant multihull *Fleury Michon* and took eight and a quarter hours off the record set by *Royale*, averaging 17.28 knots for the crossing. The best day's run was 520 miles to set a new twenty-four-hour sailing record at an average speed of 21.7 knots.

I was invited to be navigator and weatherman on a British project to break the record by the experienced skipper Peter Phillips in *Chaffeteaux Challenger*. The boat was an 80ft-long catamaran and while we set out from New York on the promise of a good forecast for the winds we wanted, we got slightly out of step with this forecast which led to much slower progress than expected and a near-disaster rescue in mid-Atlantic. We were overtaken by a major storm with winds close to 100mph and I recall one occasion when the boat nose-dived into a wave and I was up to my waist in water standing by the mast. The boat surfaced again but the stress on the hull was becoming too much and soon cracks appeared in the port hull. Concerned that the boat could break in two, we sent out a distress signal and rather than risk being rescued in the dark we decided to wait till dawn. A 900ft-long container ship appeared over the horizon and with great seamanship parked alongside us. That was fine, but we still had to get onto their deck which was 40ft above sea level. We drifted down the side of the ship, the mast came down and we ended up under the stern with the ship's 28ft-diameter propeller slicing bits off our bow! Then the ship sat on us and pushed us under water but we popped out of the stern with none of the seven-man crew hurt. It took a few hours to discuss the next step which proved successful and we were finally rescued and taken back to the US. To me, this experience demonstrated just how difficult rescue can be in the open ocean and how ill-equipped modern ships are to rescue casualties. As the captain of the ship said, 'I was not going to put my crew at risk by launching a lifeboat to come to your rescue.'

So we didn't join the list of record-breakers but three more record attempts saw the time drop to just over six and a half days with French multihulls again leading the way. This left the record in the hands of Serge Madec with a time

A container ship coming to our rescue in *Chaffeteaux Challenger*. (*Author*)

of six days and thirteen hours set in 1990 and then two years later American Steve Fosset challenged this French domination of the Atlantic with a remarkable new Atlantic record. Fosset was a wealthy American who undertook a number of adventures but his average speed of close to 26 knots across the Atlantic under sail was one of his finest achievements, taking nearly two days off the previous record time.

It was more than five years before the French could retaliate and in 2006 Bruno Peyron sailing *Orange II* reduced Fosset's time by just under ten hours, averaging 28 knots. Now the target was to be the first to sail across the Atlantic averaging 30 knots. Few sailors have ever sailed at 30 knots, let alone maintained this speed for 3,000 miles, yet Franck Cammas almost achieved this in 2007 when he took *Groupama 3* across the Lizard finish line in a shade over four days, averaging 29.26 knots. *Groupama 3* was a 103ft-long trimaran, a massive brute of a sailboat, and it must take a lot of courage to power a yacht of this size in the dark in Atlantic seas.

Groupama 3 was big but it was an even larger trimaran that not only broke the record but was the first to top 30 knots for the crossing. *Banque Populaire* was the largest performance trimaran ever built with a length of 130ft. Skippered by Pascal Bidégorry, she set the remarkable time of three days, fifteen hours and twenty-six minutes across the Atlantic in 2009 which is an average speed of a shade under 33 knots and in a time that was only a few hours under the time taken by the SS *United States* on her record-breaking

Blue Riband run. It is hard to picture this record being broken but that has been said about many previous records. Sailboat record-breaking depends very heavily on getting the right weather for the attempt and you can wait in New York for just the right conditions. Weather forecasting for this type of record is now a science rather than intelligent guesswork and it is possible to get an accurate picture of what the wind will be doing over the whole of the Atlantic route, which is one of the reasons that the sailing record has seen such a significant increase in the sustained speeds in the past decade.

A century ago any small boat crossing of the Atlantic was a remarkable event and the achievement was in simply completing the crossing. Today a cruise across the Atlantic under sail passes almost unnoticed, although for the individuals concerned it is no less a challenging and exciting experience, particularly if done single-handed. The finely-tuned multihulls that now set the sailing pace on the Atlantic appear to represent the peak of technological sailing achievement in much the same way as the last of the Atlantic liners represented the peak of marine technology in their time. Both have taken risks to achieve their high speeds and some have paid the price.

By 1977 the SS *United States* had held the out-and-out speed record for the Atlantic for twenty-five years and just like the sailboat record teams there were people wondering if the speed record of this ship could be beaten. Obviously it was not going to be done by building a new liner because the cost would have been very high and the ship uneconomic to operate in the prevailing climate. Transatlantic ships had been replaced by slower cruise ships that were ambling across the Atlantic at speeds between 20 and 25 knots. However, could a small boat be the solution for a fast crossing, perhaps by refuelling on the way? By this time offshore powerboat racing was a well-developed sport to the degree that boats were capable of reliable speeds over 60 knots and in 1974 Bob Magoon had set a record for a run up the eastern seaboard of the United States from Miami to New York at an average speed of 55.4 mph in a 40ft boat powered by a pair of 450 hp petrol engines. Could such a boat make the Atlantic crossing?

Magoon thought it could and with the help of Roger Penske and sponsorship by Citicorp, the *Citicorp Traveller* project was born. The boat, a 36ft deep V-hull racing boat, was powered by four 200 hp Mercury outboard motors. The hull was a well-proven design and it had tanks to hold 1,610 US gallons of fuel. She was a tiny boat to take on the Atlantic but the figures suggested that it could be done if the crew could stand the pace.

Magoon chose the southern route from Spain out to the Azores where two refuelling stops would be made on the islands before heading out into the Atlantic for the third and final stop which would be from a ship placed there for the job. Aircraft would monitor the voyage as much as possible, flying

Citycorp Traveller was a tiny powerboat to take on the Atlantic.

overhead and acting as a communications link and it was planned to make the crossing in just three days. There was nowhere to sleep comfortably on board and the crew was accommodated in individual padded compartments in the cockpit. A small wheelhouse gave some protection from the elements but it would be a hard, tough ride over the three days.

Once a suitable weather forecast had been received, the *Citicorp Traveller* set out for the Azores but the crew found they were burning more fuel than expected and when they did the sums they realized they did not have enough to get to the Azores. After being towed by a passing ship for a while they finally made it to the first of the Azores refuelling stops but by being towed they would not qualify for the record so the attempt was abandoned. Not carrying enough fuel seems such a basic mistake to make but in the open seas a powerboat will burn more fuel than it will in calmer conditions.

Magoon did not give up easily and the following year he was back with a larger 45ft boat, this time powered by six outboards. Fuel capacity was increased to 2,500 US gallons and the same route and refuelling stops would be followed. However, trouble with getting all six outboards that were strung across the transom of the boat working together became a problem with the two outer engines having difficulty in keeping their propellers in the water, leading to the project being abandoned for that year. The following year the outboards were replaced with a pair of powerful 1,100 hp diesels. With a potential speed of 70 mph when light on fuel and 50 mph when fully loaded, the boat had the potential for a new record but this time no sponsor could be found to support the project financially so the record set by the SS *Unites States* remained unscathed.

Magoon's record attempt had led to others thinking how they could break the Atlantic record with a small powerboat. It began to look like a feasible proposition, at least from a technical point of view if the refuelling stops could be sorted out. I got involved when I got a phone call from Ted Toleman who I knew from both his and my involvement in offshore powerboat racing and with his Formula 1 racing car team. We met at a hotel in Essex for lunch and Ted said, 'We plan to make an attempt on the Atlantic record, will you be the navigator?' That was the start of two years of life-changing events that finally led to a new record for the fastest-ever crossing of the Atlantic.

Toleman owned Cougar Marine, a boatyard that specialized in high-performance catamarans for both military and leisure use. The plan was to build a 65ft-long aluminium catamaran powered by two 2,000 hp MTU diesels and propelled by newly-developed surface-piercing propellers. The

The catamaran *Virgin Atlantic Challenger* on trials.

project looked feasible on paper but when we took the boat out on trials for the first time it would only do 8 knots! The calculations showed that a speed of over 50 knots should have been possible and it took us a few days to sort out the new type of propeller and get that boat moving as it should. Now we had the performance that was predicted and we could start making our plans. Richard Branson joined the project only a short time before departure with sponsorship from his newly-formed Virgin Atlantic airline.

The boat was shipped to New York and we waited there for six weeks before we got the weather forecast we were looking for. Fast powerboats like *Virgin Atlantic Challenger* need calm seas to maintain their high speeds and it was a challenge to find the conditions we needed over 3,000 miles of ocean. When the weather did turn favourable we knew it was still going to be a rough ride because the ocean is never calm for a fast boat, but we set off from New York in the early hours of the morning on this great adventure with the world watching our progress. On board were Richard Branson, Ted Toleman, Chay Blyth, myself as navigator, Eckie Rastig as engineer, Steve Ridgway from Cougar Marine and three Royal Marines who came along for the ride. It was crowded and most of the time there was little to do except suffer from the continuous pounding in the waves. We took a risk by heading across the Nantucket Shoals that had been the graveyard of so many ships crossing the Atlantic rather than skirting round them, which saved us 50 miles of distance; shortly afterwards we hit the first of the fog.

The route and the challenges of an Atlantic record attempt.

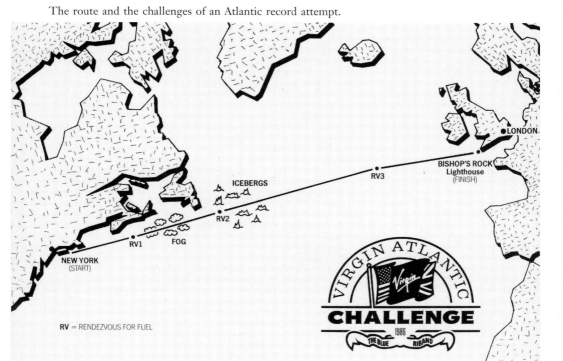

Virgin Atlantic Challenger passes the Ambrose Light at the start of her Atlantic record attempt.

The fog was to persist for the next 800 miles but we got to our first refuelling stop off Halifax, Nova Scotia on schedule, despite the thick fog. This went according to plan, we thought, and the course was set for Cape Race on the south-east corner of Newfoundland. This was where we encountered the first icebergs and it was a weird feeling running at 50 knots skirting around these huge lumps of ice. The bergs themselves show well on the radar but my worry was the small bits of ice, the growlers and the bergy bits that clutter around the base of the iceberg. They could do us serious damage if we hit one at speed. I had done a lot of research about icebergs in anticipation and I realized that these small bits of ice all tend to gather windward of the main berg which of course is going downwind faster than the smaller stuff because those small bits are not affected by the wind. So by passing to leeward of the berg we were in safer waters but we did not want to get too close anyway. It was a tense time running in the dark and glued to the radar to work out the safe route.

Our next refuelling stop was on the Grand Banks and now we discovered that at the previous refuelling stop the tanks had not been fully topped up because the fuelling had been stopped when foam started to come out of the filler rather than the fuel itself so we were many gallons short. We made it to the refuelling ship only when it steamed towards us but that meant now it

The author at the navigation station on *Virgin Atlantic Challenger*.

would be further to the next refuelling stop way out in mid-Atlantic. That ship also started to steam towards us to reduce the distance we had to travel but even then we realized that we were not going to make it. A passing ship stopped to lower four drums of fuel down onto our deck so we could pump it into the tanks and off we went again. Once refuelled from our scheduled stop we were then on track to make the final leg all the way to the traditional finish line at the Bishop Rock lighthouse. It had been a rough, harsh ride the whole way and it became obvious that this small catamaran was not the right boat to take on the Atlantic and for that last 1,000 miles the various delays meant that the weather turned against us and it was a rough and tough ride towards the finish line.

Just 130 miles from the finish there was a big bang as we hit yet another wave. Water started to flood into the starboard hull which had split and it quickly became obvious that we were sinking! I was at the radio sending out the distress message that became what is probably the most famous distress message since the *Titanic*! The world was watching our progress and we were the lead item on the 6 o'clock TV news, only to have the news bulletin end by saying that we were sinking. I had not received a response to the distress signal so when we abandoned ship into the two life-rafts we did not know if rescue was coming. It was dusk and there was the prospect of a night at sea in the flimsy life-rafts but then an aeroplane flew overhead and we knew help was on its way.

We were picked up by the cargo ship *Geest Bay* and then taken off by helicopter and landed on the Scilly Isles still in time for the record but you have to make the whole trip on the water. However, we were already planning how we would make another attempt the following year. Within three months *Virgin Atlantic Challenger II* was under construction. Working with Richard Branson certainly got things moving quickly.

This time we went for a more conventional design with the team of Sonny Levi and Peter Birkett producing a long sleek deep V-monohull. Our team was much smaller and more experienced with Chris Witty as the project leader, myself as navigator again, plus Birkett and Eckie Rastig as designer and engineer. You can get things done quickly with a small team and by late spring 1986 we had the boat on the water and I had the privilege of taking the boat out on its first sea trials where it did 52 knots over the measured mile at the first attempt. With some tuning of the engines and propellers we took that speed up to 55 knots and the boat was shipped to America ready for the right weather to make the record attempt.

The last we saw of *Virgin Atlantic Challenger* while sitting in the life-raft awaiting rescue.

Richard Branson and Chay Blyth in the life-raft awaiting rescue after *Virgin Atlantic Challenger* sank.

This time the wait was short and with Branson, Blyth and Steve Ridgway completing the team we set out from New York at the end of June. At 200 miles out of New York we again took the short cut across the Nantucket Shoals and again the fog came down on the way to the first refuelling stop at Halifax. It was beginning to look like a re-run of the previous year's attempt and the refuelling passed off without incident. Now we set off for the Grand Banks and the icebergs with hope in our hearts and thick fog restricting visibility. We were ahead of schedule and running well but the Grand Banks refuelling ship got its tanks mixed up and they gave us 8 tons of water and 4 tons of fuel.

Diesel engines do not run on water and we spent ten hours getting rid of the mess and taking on good fuel. With this delay we assumed that the record was now beyond our grasp and we were prepared to head back to Newfoundland and think about the next step. However, our weather window had been tight and coming up behind us was a massive storm that effectively blocked any possibility of heading back without serious risk. So we decided to run before the storm and head out into the Atlantic with the engines stopping at frequent intervals as some residual water came through the system. With the help of an air drop of extra fuel filters we carried on but we were now out of step with our weather window and it was a rough ride. The Irish navy was an efficient refuelling stop in mid-Atlantic, serving Irish stew as well as diesel oil, and now we could see the finish line looming ahead and we might just be in time for a new record if we could keep going.

That last night at sea was horrendous, the whole boat flying out of the water as we kept the pressure on and the conditions deteriorated. After being awake for three days and three nights we were beyond caring and so, exhausted and battered, we eventually fought our way through the rough patch and into better conditions for the last 200 miles. What a feeling it was to power cross the Bishop Rock finish line just two hours inside the record of the SS *United States* to become national heroes. Our finish was exactly at half-time in the World Cup football final where our success was announced to the biggest TV audience ever. Prime Minister Margaret Thatcher came for a ride in the boat up the River Thames and we seemed to spend our time with television cameras in our faces. It was a magical time but looking back makes me realize that you challenge the Atlantic at your peril and there are real risks out there travelling at high speed.

The Virgin success led others to think about record attempts. The Italian Azimut team designed and built a boat to attempt a record crossing of the Atlantic without refuelling. The *Azimut Atlantic Challenger* was a remarkable design just 85ft in length so 10ft longer than *Virgin Atlantic* but this 40-ton boat was capable of carrying 80 tons of fuel, just enough to make the Atlantic crossing non-stop. With four diesel engines producing 8,000 hp she was capable of 30 knots when fully loaded and 55 knots after much of the fuel had been used up, a combination that was enough to set a new record. This was an all-Italian project except for me when I was signed up as weatherman and navigator. Paulo Vitelli, the boss of Azimut which is a leading Italian yacht-builder, was asked why he had a British navigator on this all-Italian project at the launch press conference and just said, 'Because he is the best.' After that I simply could not afford to make any mistakes.

At the same time an American team was working on a project to significantly beat the refuelling record we had set with *Virgin Atlantic*. *Gentry Eagle* was 115ft long and powered by two diesels and a gas turbine to give her a top speed of close to 60 knots. *Gentry Eagle* planned to follow the path set by *Virgin Atlantic* and both she and *Azimut Atlantic Challenger* left New York on the same day, taking advantage of the same promising weather forecast. This forecast turned out to be much too optimistic and the bad weather that both record-breakers found out in the Atlantic forced both boats to turn back and end up in St. John's, Newfoundland. *Azimut Atlantic Challenger* returned to New York but never attempted the record again, while *Gentry Eagle* set out the following year and took the record speed to a massive 45 knots. The engine installation on *Gentry Eagle* worked well with the vessel running with just the two diesels when the conditions demanded a slower speed and then

Virgin Atlantic Challenger II approaching the Bishop Rock Lighthouse at the end of her Atlantic record run.

The crew of *Virgin Atlantic Challenger II* with Prime Minister Margaret Thatcher.

the 5,000 hp gas turbine was switched in when calmer conditions prevailed to increase the speed close to 60 knots. It is interesting to think that *Virgin Atlantic Challenger* could have made the crossing at a similar average speed if there had not been the delay of ten hours caused by the water in the fuel at the Grand Banks refuelling. It was amazing that we actually set a new record with such a delay and taking into account that our crossing had got seriously out of step with the planned weather window. *Gentry Eagle* made the record crossing look easy with no dramas on the way but if you do that you do not get much publicity. At least *Virgin Atlantic Challenger II* won the publicity stakes which was the name of the game as far as sponsor Richard Branson was concerned and now even thirty years later people still remember it.

The next record attempt on the Atlantic was a very quiet affair in terms of publicity, even though the vessel designed and built for the job was one of the most dramatic ever created. *Destriero* was another Italian project and this one was largely sponsored by the Aga Khan. The plan was to build a ship to break the record and then convert it into a performance super yacht after the event. The size and scale of *Destriero* were impressive by any standards and in many ways they reflected the ethos of the Atlantic liners that were designed to take

Gentry Eagle on trials before being shipped to the US for her Atlantic record attempt.

existing technology to the limits. There was nothing subtle about *Destriero* and with a length of 68 metres she looked every inch a record-breaker with her sleek lines and impressive size. However, the most impressive part was hidden from view and inside she was powered by three 20,000 hp gas turbines that were the equivalent of three jumbo jet engines. These were coupled to water jet propulsion that was a favourite propulsion system on the new generation of fast ferries entering the market and her top speed was 65 knots. Up on the bridge there was the luxury of reclining seats for the crew and a vast array of electronics for communications and navigation.

In 1992 *Destriero* set out from Gibraltar to cross to New York and achieved a record time for the east to west crossing but it was on her crossing from New York to the Bishop Rock Lighthouse that she made the fastest-ever crossing of the Atlantic, taking just under two and a half days from New York to the Bishop Rock. Not only did she achieve the fastest-ever crossing but she also holds the record for the fastest two-way aggregate time across the Atlantic. Her average speed for the record crossing was 53 knots, a record speed that is going to be very hard to beat, and when she left New York she was carrying 700 tons of fuel which was being burnt up at the rate of 10 tons per hour by the thirsty gas turbines. I was doing the weather routing for *Destriero* and the designers of the vessel stipulated that when she was running at full speed the waves must be no more than 6ft high. The hull was not strong enough to withstand the pounding of waves any larger than that. Waves of 6ft or less comprise what might be termed a calm day on the Atlantic and finding such benign conditions over 3,000 miles of ocean was a real challenge. My solution was to find a weather pattern where there was a relatively stationary large low-pressure area dominating the North Atlantic and then route *Destriero* around the southern edge of this. By angling their course edging to the north into the low pressure they could run until they encountered waves close to 6ft and then level off heading in a more easterly direction as they made their way around the southern edge of the low pressure. This worked well apart from a small depression forming off Spain and heading north to join its big brother in the North Atlantic, but we got *Destriero* through the gap just before the weather door shut firmly behind them. Because the Italians were nervous of failure they did not announce that they were making the record attempt beforehand and were left wondering why they did not get much publicity when they arrived in Plymouth after their high-speed crossing. It needs drama and excitement to get publicity and the *Destriero* crossing did not have either, thus making it appear almost routine.

The *Destriero* voyage was a good example of how important the weather, or rather the sea conditions created by the weather, is when you want to cross the Atlantic at high speed. It would be wonderful to think that a new generation of high-speed vessels could make the crossing and be immune to the weather but that looks a long way off. Also with the current focus on 'green' shipping we are very unlikely to see the likes of the fuel-hungry *Destriero* again on the Atlantic and she probably represents the end of an era of Atlantic records by smaller private vessels.

None of these 'private' and sponsored Atlantic record attempts qualified for the Hales Trophy which is only awarded to vessels making the fastest crossing and having some commercial function such as being a passenger-carrier. Following its award to the SS *United States*, this magnificent trophy was on display in the US Merchant Marine Museum. However, the trustees who had administered the trophy were all dead so there was no one to award the trophy to any new contender. It was Richard Branson who funded the legal process to set up a new board of trustees and so by 1988 the trophy could be awarded again, but with Atlantic passenger ships now operating at modest speeds there did not appear to be any potential contenders.

However, by this time a new type of passenger vessel was appearing on the seas and the large fast ferry era was born. The market for these ferries was dominated by the wave-piercers built in Australia and when the British company Hoverspeed, who operated ferries across the English Channel, bought one of these advanced ferries it was delivered from Australia by sea across the Pacific and then the Atlantic. The boss of Hoverspeed, James Sterling, thought that this offered a good chance for getting publicity by diverting the ferry to New York and making the Atlantic crossing in record time. *Hoverspeed Great Britain* duly arrived in New York and filled up with fuel for the 3,000-mile crossing. No passengers were carried but the Hales Trophy Trustees agreed that because it was a passenger ship it did qualify for the award.

Hoverspeed Great Britain set out in June 1990 and had an uneventful non-stop crossing, taking three days, eight hours for the 3,000-mile journey to average 36.6 knots which was just a shade faster than *Virgin Atlantic Challenger II*. I was asked to work with the Hoverspeed team and did the weather routing and was at Falmouth when she arrived triumphant after the crossing. Again it was a low-key project and lacked excitement and so did not get a lot of publicity apart from being awarded the fabulous Hales Trophy, the first time it had been awarded for nearly forty years.

Other European ferry operators were buying the wave-piercer ferries and the designs of these ferries had grown in size and power. Mediterranean operators Buquebus España decided to make an attempt on the Atlantic record in 1998 taking a route from New York to Tarifa in Spain, close to Gibraltar, which is one of the approved routes. This is a longer route so their time was a couple of hours longer than *Hoverspeed Great Britain* but it is

Hoverspeed Great Britain approaches the Bishop Rock Lighthouse at the end of her Atlantic record run.

average speed that counts and *Catalonia* averaged close to 39 knots and so was the next ship to be awarded the Hales Trophy.

Her reign as the Atlantic record-holder was short-lived and Scandinavian ferry company Scandlines made a record attempt just a month after *Catalonia*, following the traditional route from New York to the Bishop Rock. *Cat-Link V* was the latest manifestation of the Incat wave-piercers, a 91-metre version powered by four big diesel engines of 7,080 kW each that were coupled to water jets; this was about half the power of *Destriero*.

After taking on more than 500 tons of fuel and provisions, *Cat-Link V* set sail with a VIP send-off from New York Harbour. Her official starting-line was the Nantucket Light some 200 miles east of New York which she passed running at 40 knots with her heavy load of fuel. After steaming for twelve hours *Cat-Link V* had averaged 38.6 knots and by the next morning the ship's speed was up to 43 knots as the fuel was being burned off. *Cat-Link V* then received a MAYDAY message from Rescue Control Centre, Halifax, advising all shipping to keep a sharp look-out for a ditched single-engine aircraft whose last reported position given about forty hours previously was nearby. Captain Claus Kristensen on board *Cat-Link V* reported his current position and notified RCC Halifax that he was proceeding to the last reported position as he was obliged to do under international conventions.

Two hours later a rescue plane circling overhead advised of debris some 30 nautical miles behind. *Cat-Link V* was asked to turn around back towards New York and proceeded immediately to the area. After an hour the *Cat-Link V* crew sighted the smoke flare dropped by the aircraft and then the debris. Crew member Soren Kristensen donned an immersion suit and went over the side to recover a block of foam and a long plastic cylinder. They also recovered a fishing buoy about a mile away but none of the debris related to the missing plane. Eventually *Cat-Link V* resumed her course and the record attempt. The weather was deteriorating and so was the ship's speed which was now down to 40.5 knots. However, with just 130 miles to go she was back up to full speed of over 47 knots and the record was still in sight. Finally *Cat-Link V* crossed the Bishop Rock finish line to set a new Hales Trophy record, the first to reach over 40 knots across the Atlantic. The Hales Trophy Trustees adjusted the distance travelled to take into account the time spent on the search operation and *Cat-Link V* was credited with an average speed of 41.3 knots for the crossing, a record that still stands for the Hales Trophy but more than 10 knots slower than *Destriero*'s record-breaking speed.

Cat-Link V could carry 900 passengers and 240 cars and has been in regular service ever since her record crossing. When we made our Atlantic crossing in *Virgin Atlantic Challenger*, the main man behind the project was Steve Ridgway who ran Cougar Marine. Steve later became the head of the Virgin

Cat-Link V, shown here after a change in ownership, still holds the Hales Trophy for the fastest Atlantic crossing by a commercial vessel.

Atlantic airline and since retiring from that position has become the chairman of Scandlines where he can now see the Hales Trophy sitting in the office where he works. They would not give it to us when we set a new Atlantic record in *Virgin Atlantic Challenger* because we were not a passenger ship but now Steve has found a back-door route to the Hales Trophy!

While we have talked here mainly about the successes in setting new Atlantic records, there have been many who have had ideas and concepts to challenge for records. Some have fallen by the wayside for technical reasons but they mainly fail because of the huge sums of money required to mount any sort of challenge these days. While there have been many exotic or even advanced designs for breaking records under both power and sail, the Atlantic does not take any prisoners when it comes to travelling fast across the ocean. Even when you get the weather on your side, the Atlantic is a formidable challenge and modern technology does not offer many solutions and in my opinion it tends to be the tried and tested technology that offers the best solutions.

A French team actually built a boat to attempt the record without refuelling in 1990 not long after *Azimut Atlantic Challenger* failed in her attempt. *Jet Ruban Bleu* was a 26-metre-long deep V-monohull that was built at Multiplast with a single 3,000 hp diesel engine. Capable of carrying 36 tons of fuel, this long thin boat certainly looked capable of attempting an Atlantic crossing, even though the facilities for the four-man crew in the compact wheelhouse were minimal. However, the hull of the boat was damaged in rough seas near the Channel Islands during sea trials and she never made the record attempt.

All the other concepts for attempting the Atlantic record only got as far as drawings on paper. Most were developed in order to promote a particular development of marine technology and it was relatively cheap to get some ideas down on paper. The real challenge for any Atlantic record attempt is to get the required sponsorship that will pay both for building the boat and for making the record attempt. This is where the French are so good and there seems a much greater willingness in France to promote maritime ventures. This has been very noticeable in the sailing arena where the large multihulls such as *Banque Populaire* are very expensive but sponsors are willing to pay huge amounts for the resulting publicity. The *Virgin Atlantic Challenger* project was probably one of the best of the sponsored projects and the sinking of the first one so near to the finish line did more for the publicity of the project than if that first attempt had been successful. Richard Branson is a master of publicity and for the initial outlay estimated at around £1 million for the boat, it has been estimated that he got fifteen times that amount in publicity and he sold the boat afterwards.

Both the power and sail records on the Atlantic now stand at speeds that would have been thought impossible only a few years ago. Just to travel at 33 knots under sail is extreme and has only been achieved by a handful of people. To maintain that average speed over 3,000 miles of the world's toughest ocean is a remarkable achievement. It is the same with *Destriero's* average speed of 53 knots for the crossing. Few people have done that speed in the open sea but to keep up an average of this speed for 3,000 miles is exceptional. However, records are made to be broken and it may be only a few years before we see both of these records consigned to the dustbin of history. Around 100 years ago nobody thought that an Atlantic liner could make the crossing at 35 knots but fifty years ago it was done.

Chapter Ten

An Ocean in Turmoil

For seamen the Atlantic Ocean has an evil reputation. In the winter the storms that sweep across this ocean from west to east more or less follow the path of the main shipping routes. In the summer the low-pressure areas and their associated storms generally track further to the north but they never disappear and ships and yachts can never be assured a smooth passage across the Atlantic. To a certain extent this ocean turmoil has been tamed by the weather forecasters who can at least predict the weather with considerable accuracy but knowing the weather is one thing and avoiding it is another, and on this ocean there are only limited possibilities for weather routing when you want to get across to the other side.

For around 400 years since Columbus made his famous crossing of the Atlantic in both directions there was no access to weather forecasts. The captain of a ship would leave port to make the crossing of the Atlantic and from his own personal observations he would probably have some idea of what lay ahead in terms of the weather for the next twenty-four hours. After that there would be a day-by-day assessment of the weather hoping to get some idea of what might lie ahead, but this would only be from personal assessment and there was no help from the shore. Indeed, the Atlantic Ocean was a big unknown as far as weather forecasting was concerned and it was only when radio communications were established between the shore and ships out at sea that there could be any attempt at sending weather forecasts to ships at sea. It is only in the past 100 years or so that forecasts have become available to shipping and even then they were fairly rudimentary forecasts because there was so little information available about the weather measurements that could be sent in from ships at sea to help the forecasters improve the accuracy of their data. The open oceans were a blank page as far as forecasters were concerned and even in the 1950s when I went to sea we got entangled with a hurricane in Atlantic waters because it had not been seen or predicted by the weather forecasters.

The pace was stepped up considerably when steamships came on the scene. Now they could take the direct route to their destination without much regard for the wind, although even these ships would be slowed by storms. Weather forecasts for the ocean were still non-existent and while a captain might have clues about the weather changes from the visible signs, he would know little about the track of the depressions and the sort of weather that they might produce. When you add in the risks from fog and icebergs it is no wonder that ships disappeared without trace in those stormy waters. In a modern world where we know more about what is going on in the oceans than ever before, it is hard to picture what it must have been like to head off to sea only knowing what the weather had in store for twenty-four hours ahead if you were lucky. The introduction of the barometer to the science of weather forecasting gave ships' captains a slighter better insight into what the weather had in store but again it would only give perhaps twenty-four hours' notice of a drop in the barometric pressure that might indicate a storm ahead but very little information about how severe that storm might be and its extent.

Now we know a lot more about the weather with satellite pictures giving an update about what is going on in the oceans but satellites only tell you what is happening now and not what is going to happen. That was previously the role of the weather forecaster but it is a role that has now largely been taken over by some of the most powerful computers in the world which analyze in detail the turmoil of the winds and waves and forecast what they will do in the future. This can be done with considerable success and while it cannot change the weather, it does allow ships to find the optimum routes across the Atlantic to get favourable weather and to make the best time. Storms can be avoided if there is sufficient advance warning and there are now specialist weather routing companies that offer this service to shipping.

We have become familiar with the weather maps showing the isobars – lines of equal pressure – generated by the computers. We have also become familiar with the depressions shown by these isobars, the concentric rings that show the areas of low pressure where you can expect to find stronger winds. The closer the isobars the stronger the wind as a general rule and these depressions and their associated storms are a major feature of the North Atlantic weather.

Many of the major storm systems that sweep across the Atlantic take a more northerly route, starting off in the wilds of Eastern Canada and heading round the southern tip of Greenland and on to Iceland and the Arctic. This is a wild but relatively unfrequented part of the Atlantic Ocean, well off the line of the major trade routes, but it is a region where good fishing can be found. Countries have fought over the fishing rights in these wild waters and I spent some time in Icelandic waters in the winter on a large ocean-going tug when Britain was fighting Iceland over the fishing rights for catching cod in these waters. North of Iceland it was a good day when it was only blowing force 8, just an ordinary gale. On one occasion we were standing by a large French trawler that was on fire in a force 12 storm. They got the fire out but it makes

What might be described as a normal North Atlantic winter storm.

you realize how narrow the margins can become when you have mechanical or other problems in such extreme conditions when the safety margins are very small.

It comes as no surprise that the deepest depression ever recorded was found just south of Greenland in 1986. The central pressure in this record-breaking weather system was calculated at between 916 and 912 mb (millibars). When you consider that the average pressure at the centre of most depressions can range between 950 and 1,000 mb, you can get some idea of just how deep this particular depression was and as a general rule, the deeper the depression the stronger the winds revolving around it. This record-breaker was formed when two active depressions combined off the coast of Newfoundland and started to move east, creating a 'perfect storm' situation. Individually these two depressions had central pressures of 956 and 960 mb, which on their own represent very active depressions, but the combined system became explosive as it moved north-east towards Greenland.

A ship some distance from the centre of this monster recorded a pressure of 938 mb and later another ship recorded 920 mb and even that ship was not at the centre of the storm. The winds were blowing at 65 to 70 knots and this was a very violent storm. Later in 1993 a weather ship stationed to the west of Ireland recorded a pressure of 939 mb in wind speeds of 70 knots and this depression deepened to equal the record set in 1986. It seems likely that there are more very deep depressions lurking out there in the Atlantic but there are very few accurate recordings taken and ship readings may not be as accurate as those on land unless their barometer has been carefully calibrated. When you are in a storm of this magnitude reading the barometer may not be high on your list of priorities. There are some ship readings on record that go lower than these 'official' record lows with ships in the Atlantic recording 925 mb and 921 mb back in 1927 and 1870 but the accuracy of these readings may be suspect. Modelling by the British Met Office suggests that there may be even deeper lows out there with that 1993 storm going as low as 916. It is interesting to note that all these extreme lows have been recorded in the Atlantic, reinforcing its reputation as a violent ocean, and these extreme lows have only been exceeded by readings from the centre of violent tropical revolving storms, with one typhoon in 1979 producing a low of 870.

As a general rule, the deeper the depression, the stronger the winds. In the Atlantic at around 55°N latitude there are some areas where the wind can be blowing a gale on an average of 20–30 per cent of the time during the winter months. It is in this same region where there can be waves of 4 metres or more for up to 60 per cent of the time. A 4-metre wave is a significant sea for most ships and remember, that is the average with many waves much bigger. It is not hard to understand why the Atlantic has such a reputation for bad weather and it is difficult to imagine how the early explorers and seamen coped with these extreme conditions. Fishermen from Europe have been sailing across the Atlantic to the prolific fishing waters off Newfoundland, Greenland and Iceland for hundreds of years and they must have endured appalling conditions in their quest for fish. The death toll among the Grand Banks fishermen was very high and they not only had to contend with violent storms but also with extreme cold. I got a taste of these conditions when I was in the sea area north of Iceland during that Cod War voyage where there was the double jeopardy of storms combined with the threat of the ship icing up in the severe cold.

Ships tend to take the most direct route, the Great Circle line, across the Atlantic. A 'Great Circle' is a line that represents the shortest distance on the curved surface of a globe and that shows as a curve on the flat paper charts. On the Atlantic the Great Circle route takes a curve to the north so that ships are very much in the direct firing line of the storms whistling across the Atlantic. Weather routing should help them to miss the extremes of the weather and indeed this weather routing aims to find a compromise between the shortest route and the one in which the ship can maintain the fastest speed. Yachts that are not in a hurry tend to follow a more southerly route across the Atlantic where they engage with the Azores High and should get good sailing winds. This more southerly route may be longer but it also avoids the powerful and adverse Gulf Stream when heading west, which can slow progress considerably for a sailing vessel. Cruising yachts can afford this more leisurely progress but when racing or record-breaking, sailboats tend to work much closer to the weather limits. When record-breaking under power it is calm seas that you need but under sail you try to balance on the knife-edge between fast progress and wild seas. You want the strong winds for fast progress but you don't want the big seas that go with them as these waves can slow progress. It is a delicate balance between the two and record-breaking yachts look to hitch a ride on the back or front of a fast-moving depression where the wind is on the beam from the north or south. Trying to keep in the right position for the time required for a record requires good forecasting and on the one attempt I made on the sailing record we were riding the front of a deep depression. Unfortunately we got out of step with the weather pattern so the depression caught up with us and we were hit by the violent 70-knot winds of the most intense part of the depression and ended up having to be rescued.

No, the Atlantic is not an ocean to be taken lightly. I have crossed it in many types of boats and ships and I don't recall an easy or relaxed passage. Even when you skirt the edges of the Atlantic such as when heading along the shores of North America or crossing the Bay of Biscay, you can meet up with severe weather conditions. For centuries the Atlantic has been the main trade route of the world and it has taken its toll on ships and shipping. Anyone who takes the Atlantic and its wild weather lightly is likely to find themselves in serious trouble and the ocean floor must be littered with shipping that did not make it.

We have mentioned the extreme deep depressions and every so often the meteorological world goes haywire and the weather systems get totally out of step with reality. This is when forecasting can become a nightmare and when weather systems can combine to create meteorological mayhem. The wind and the waves can go off the scale and for anyone caught out at sea in these 'perfect storms' their life expectancy can shorten quite dramatically. Fortunately these perfect storms are rare but when they happen then watch out. The normal rules for coping with bad weather do not apply and survival can no longer be guaranteed.

The book *The Perfect Storm* follows the creation of just one such meteorological mishap where the forces of nature combined to create a fight for survival for the seamen and airmen caught up in the storm. It is a remarkable story of what it can be like fighting for your life in conditions that are beyond the comprehension of even most seamen. The world around you seems to have descended into total chaos and the normal rules do not apply. Everyone has their own way of coping when death comes knocking on the door and the remarkable thing about the story of the perfect storm event in the book is how so many of the participants did survive, while quite naturally the focus is on those who did not.

Perfect storms tend to happen mainly in temperate climes, probably around 30–45° north or south of the equator, and they tend to be formed from a meeting of two or more storm systems. One of these may be dying away but still have sufficient energy to vitalize and bring extra power to the system that it is going to meet. Often a vital component of perfect storms can be a hurricane, typhoon or cyclone that instead of following the general trend of moving away over land and dying out has maintained a course over water and is heading north or south away from the equator. By staying over water a tropical cyclone can pick up more energy from warm water, which allows it to perhaps deepen again and to maintain its intensity. These hurricanes can be diverted from their conventional track by the location of an active cold front over the land that doesn't welcome the intrusion of the hurricane into its territory.

So you have the remains of this tropical storm moving north out of the tropics and steadily weakening so that the wind within the storm may have dropped to a more manageable 50 or 65 knots, still strong but some way below hurricane force. Heading north it is moving into alien territory and in most cases it will become another low-pressure area that can join in the procession of low-pressure depressions that are a feature of the temperate latitudes. It may still retain its individual identity, although weakening all the time, and it tends not to join up with its adjacent low-pressure areas. However, if that cold front over the land on the western side of the ocean basin is very active there will be tremendous weather energy locked up there that is looking for release and that release may be seen first as a small kink in the line of the front, a kink that can gain enough impetus to start it rotating. Now you have the makings of a violent local storm that can play havoc with the normal flow of the weather. If this new very active low meets up with that hurricane that is heading north, then everything is likely to go off the scale and mayhem will result.

Like many of the more severe storms that plague the North Atlantic, the perfect storm of the book started with a small kink in a powerful cold front. On the weather chart a cold front looks like a nice regular straight line but in reality they are full of activity as cold and warm air mix, often in violent fashion. On a local basis this can generate thunderstorms but when a kink forms in the line of the front it can quickly move into a rotating motion like a mini-depression. Once the rotating motion has started and it picks up more energy, you have the start of a full-blown depression that can have a rapidly deepening centre. Immediately the wind strength increases and in *The Perfect Storm* this depression started out on a course to the south-east from a point up near the Grand Banks and as the story relates, the violent winds enveloped the swordfish fishing fleet that was still at sea. Further south the tail end of a hurricane was moving north and when the two storms met and amalgamated you had the perfect storm. Ships, yachts and fishing boats that were at sea were all caught up in the violent seas and screaming winds. This was a fast-moving weather pattern that was hard to forecast to warn vessels out at sea in good time.

One of the casualties was the yacht *Satori* that was caught up in the storm and it was the rescue of this crew that got coast guard boats and helicopters into trouble. I find it amazing that the coast guard ship *Tamaroa* even contemplated launching its RIB rescue boat in waves that were topping 60ft and in winds that were off the scale. Such is the traditional heroism of rescue services around the world and it is hard to just stand by and watch people die without trying to do something, but they were putting their own crew's lives at risk in this operation.

Although the book was called *The Perfect Storm*, this storm was known as the Halloween Storm and it caused enormous damage onshore as well as at sea. In official parlance the storm was known as an extra-tropical cyclone because it formed outside the tropics and when it picked up new energy from the warm waters of the Gulf Stream it reached full hurricane intensity. A side-effect of this storm was a huge tidal surge along the east coast of North America, creating some of the highest tides ever recorded.

The rescue of the crew of the *Satori* in the film *The Perfect Storm*. (*US Coast Guard*)

A perfect storm could be defined as any unusual storm event that generates unpredicted conditions. These are the storms that people both on land and at sea remember, the ones that get talked about for many years to come and tend to have a violence way beyond normal human experience. In some cases the storms themselves might not be that extreme but they can be extreme for the area in which they occur. The storm that hit the Fastnet fleet of yachts and caused such mayhem and loss of life could come into this category. This storm started as a very deep depression swinging in from the Atlantic towards Ireland but the mayhem started when the front associated with this depression swung across the area where many of the 300 yachts participating in the Fastnet Race were located. Not only did the passage of these fronts create a rapid increase in the wind but they also changed the wind direction, generating a confused and chaotic sea. Again the situation was compounded when a secondary low formed to the south of the main centre and because this did not show on the weather charts, its effects were not included in the forecast. This Fastnet storm qualifies as a perfect storm because of its two centres and the unforecast nature of the intense winds generated.

The Channel storm of 1956 started off as a summer depression moving in from the Atlantic towards south-west Britain. Nothing unusual there but when it encountered the land and headed up the Bristol Channel it deepened rapidly, with the high ground of the Welsh mountains thwarting its passage to the north. Here was an example of the way the high ground or mountains can influence the movement of storms and this storm was noticeable for the violence of the winds in the English Channel where there happened to be a yacht race in progress.

It appears that the English Channel experiences these perfect storms every few years and the Great Storm of 1987 had hurricane-force winds but most of the damage was caused on land rather than at sea, although a couple of yachts were in trouble having been caught out by the very sudden intensifying of the storm. This storm is remembered as the one that was not forecast, where the forecasters insisted that there was not a hurricane in the offing. Forecasters tend to be remembered for the ones they get wrong rather than the ones they get right.

Further north in the British Isles extreme winds are reported every year or two. Some of these are caused by the remnants of hurricanes that have survived all the way across the Atlantic and have picked up extra energy and ferocity on the way across. It is almost impossible to forecast storms of this intensity and they will probably appear in the forecast as storms with winds of 60 or 70 knots, bad enough but moderate compared with the damage that a 130-knot storm can do.

These perfect storms are mainly found in the Northern Hemisphere because here there are land masses that can change and influence the regular pattern of the flow of depressions. There can also be more extreme temperature differences over land than those found over seas and both high land and significant temperature differences can bring about short-term changes in the weather patterns that are difficult or even impossible to forecast in the longer term and so they fall into the category of unusual events. It is easy to sense the frustration of forecasters, wanting to understand and predict these unusual events but handicapped by the unusual nature of the event itself and the circumstances surrounding it. As a forecaster you do not get good marks for forecasting extreme events that then do not materialize.

Wild storms make for wild seas and for hundreds of years sailors have returned to harbour with tales of huge waves overwhelming their vessels. They may be called rogue waves or freak waves but these are really extreme waves, something way out of the ordinary as far as the regular pattern of waves is concerned. These extreme waves have often been considered to be folklore, the product of imaginative sailors' minds. Then authoritative reports started to emerge, followed by some dramatic photos, and the world of extreme waves became reality. Today there are sophisticated wave-measuring technology and satellite observations to help detect and determine these extreme waves and the world is waking up to the fact that the conditions out in the oceans can be much more extreme than was thought. The 100ft wave that was thought to be the product of science fiction has now been measured in the Atlantic and is a reality. For the sailor, the thought of such waves is a daunting prospect and these extreme waves are now recognized as a more frequent occurrence than previously thought.

Although there are no definitions about the terms, my feeling is that any wave over 20 metres in height is an extreme wave and waves on this scale can be divided into two types. There are the transient extreme waves, those that make a temporary appearance and then disappear, and those that form part of a wave train and exist for some period of time. Apart from their life span, one of the main differences between these two types of extreme wave is that it is more difficult to forecast the appearance of transient waves but those that form part of a more continuous wave train should be predictable. The science of extreme waves is still in its infancy in terms of how they are formed, how they can be forecast and how we can cope with them and the very transient nature of these waves makes them hard to study. The need to understand these extremes is vital for the offshore oil industry where platform structures tend to be built to cope with the 100-year wave, a wave that is predicted to occur only once every 100 years. Evidence is suggesting that these 100-year waves are occurring much more frequently than that, leading to a revision of the criteria used to design the platforms that now extend out into deeper Atlantic waters. Those 100ft waves are lurking out there and whether they are transient or longer-lasting, they present a considerable threat to man-made structures, both to shipping and to structures fixed to the seabed.

While there is a growing body of evidence about the existence of extreme waves and their increasing size, there is no doubt about the statistics. Figures from the British National Institute of Oceanography calculated using a Random Process formula suggest that if you take the average height of waves in a wave train, then one wave in twenty-three will be twice that average height and one wave in 1,175 waves will be three times the average height. Those figures will give seamen pause for thought but the additional chilling statistic is that one wave in 300,000 will be four times the average height. Think about that and you have the prospect of meeting a massive 20-metre wave when the average wave height is just 5 metres! However, to put this into perspective, 300,000 waves is an awful lot of waves and that equates to one wave every 6,000 miles or so, and those statistics only refer to one spot so if you move around then the chances are that you will miss the big waves altogether. It is fixed stations such as oil platforms that could be more concerned by these statistics and in one major hurricane in the Gulf of Mexico a number of platforms were damaged through wave impact on the underneath of the platform deck. This is the area of the platform that is designed to be clear of the water at all times, except possibly in that 100-year wave.

Also these extreme waves are only the highest in relation to their particular sea state and the average height to which they relate could be quite small, maybe in the region of a metre for the larger waves in the series. Such mini-extreme waves could pass almost unnoticed and be seen as little more than the wash of a passing ship. In my sixty years at sea I have only come across two extreme waves that caused concern and both were Atlantic-related. One was when we were searching for a fisherman who was reported washed off the rocks in the Bristol Channel. We were in a lifeboat searching just outside the surf line where a big sea was breaking in the north-westerly onshore gale. We would have gone inside the surf if we had seen something to rescue but the risk was too great during the searching period. As you can imagine, all eyes were turned towards the shore to look for the man in the water. I was on the helm and suddenly I was conscious of it going dark. I looked to seaward and there was this monster wave rearing up alongside us with the sun shining weakly through it. You know when the sun is shining through a wave that you don't want to be on the lee side of it and it looked like this near-vertical wall of water was going to curl over and crash over us. It was too late to do anything but pray and we went up the side of that wave like an express elevator and toppled over the crest just as the wave broke. That wave must have been three or four times the average wave height and so it had been just starting to break in the deeper water outside our path. It was just the one wave and we had a narrow escape and it brought home to me that there are always big ones out there and you need to allow margins for them.

The second extreme wave was found to the north of Iceland during the Cod War. Our big ocean-going tug was running before the big storm seas at slow speed and I was down on the low aft deck of the tug trying to get some good rough sea photos. I remember watching these big waves curling up behind us and then passing under the ship in a regular procession and then this monster wave reared up its ugly head like a vertical wall of water with the crest breaking. It must have been 40–50ft high, several times higher than the regular waves of the day. I took a quick photo and then ran for shelter as it crashed over the stern and swept over much of the forward superstructure. The seas off Iceland in the winter are not my favourite place and I got the feeling that that extreme wave was trying to tell us something.

I have mentioned the two types of extreme waves and of those it is the transient type that can be the most frightening and damaging. It is thought that these transient waves are caused by two phenomena and the really bad ones could be a combination of the two. Firstly, waves very rarely come in just one clean and tidy wave train with all the waves spread evenly and heading in the same direction. That could happen in an ideal world but in the real world there could be two or more wave trains in the same part of the ocean. There can be waves generated by the prevailing wind and there can be decaying waves remaining from a preceding storm or generated quite recently by the same storm heading in a different direction because the wind has changed. Look closely at the sea and you can pick out different wave trains and it is when the crest of two or more of these waves meet that the wave height can be increased dramatically. When two or more wave crests meet the height of each individual wave is added to the total, so three 4-metre wave crests meeting in the one spot could produce a 12-metre transient wave peak. It is transient because the height will drop as soon as one or more waves pass on but if you happen to be in that spot at that time you will experience a dramatic wave peak.

Then you can add into the mix the effects of currents or tides. If the waves are running against the current then the wave length will shorten and the waves will become steeper and often higher. This can generate some very nasty sea conditions with a succession of breaking crests and if this current factor combines with one of the transient wave crests then look out. You can get the same effect when waves approach shallow water. Once again the progress of the waves is slowed and they become steeper and higher and more

The damaged bridge of the *Lusitania* after encountering an extreme wave at speed.

prone to breaking. In extreme cases where a current is travelling at a quarter of the speed of approaching waves, the waves can stopped in their tracks and a mighty wall of water can build up that could prove fatal to small craft and dangerous to big ships. One of the earliest reports of a ship being lost to an extreme wave occurred 100 years ago when the steamer *Waratah* disappeared along with all her passengers and crew after leaving Durban heading for Cape Town and following the route of the notorious Agulhas Current.

The other type of extreme wave can occur when there is a very long fetch, winds that are blowing in the same direction for over 1,000 miles or more of ocean as can happen in the Atlantic. While the waves generated by these winds should be regular and even, it is thought that there can be a resonance in some waves that makes them travel faster than others so waves will over-take and cause extreme waves. A similar type of wave combination could occur when a depression deepens. The bigger the wave the faster it travels, so smaller waves occurring in the early stages of a depression forming could be overtaken by the larger waves formed later as the depression deepens. Again it would be when wave crests combine that extreme waves could form.

There is an increasing interest in extreme waves, which has led to research into this phenomenon. One thing the research has thrown up is that extreme waves occur with a much greater frequency than was previously thought, but then this is not hard to appreciate when you consider that just twenty years ago the detection of these waves relied entirely on ships sighting or experiencing them. A ship has to be in the vicinity of a wave for it to be detected and then at night the wave might not be seen or its size appreciated. Today there are more sophisticated means of detecting extreme waves such as radar scanning and satellite detection. Radar is used mainly from fixed platforms to detect and measure the wave heights around the platform and is used mainly to gather data from offshore oil platforms. Satellite detection can scan much larger areas of the sea and it is largely this satellite detection that has led to increased knowledge about the frequency of extreme waves.

Under a programme known as MaxWave that is funded by the EC, a programme of satellite detection of extreme waves has shown that not only do the waves occur more frequently than previously thought but that they occur in most sea regions. However, the increased detection frequency could be because in a revised specification for what constitutes an extreme wave they have used any wave just twice the significant wave height. Any seaman will tell you from experience that waves of this size are a relatively frequent occurrence and the statistics given above show this. Extreme waves are what the name suggests: waves that are extreme in size and therefore much larger than the more regular pattern of waves.

Reported encounters with extreme waves are relatively rare, and statistics are hard to come by. The MaxWave programme suggests that more than 200 large ships have been lost to rough seas and severe weather over the past twenty years. Whether this is due just to rough seas and damage or mechanical failure is not specified and the actual recorded encounters with extreme waves is much lower. Weather ships that have been cruising in open ocean waters on a continuous basis in the North Atlantic have recorded big waves, up to 75ft in height, and you might expect that if these extreme waves were a frequent occurrence then these weather ships would have experienced them. One instance of a weather ship meeting a recorded 90ft wave was in 2001 and this was one of the largest open ocean waves ever measured.

The officer on watch, Jan Erik Taule, takes up the story:

It was shortly after midnight, 11th of November 2001, that the 54-metre long MV *Polar Front* encountered a 27.2-metre wave in position N65° 55′ E002° 03′. For the last couple of days, the wind had been steadily WSW with gale force. The 10th of November the wind increased to storm force 10 and on into hurricane force 56 knots with gusts to 75 knots. At midnight 11th of November I relieved the captain at that time, Børge Misje, and got briefed about the weather conditions and especially the extreme height of the sea, which had raised to 18–22 metres. The ship log says at midnight – wind force 55 knots from W with snow and showery weather. In spite of the showery weather condition, it was a kind of bright night due to the moonlight between the showers.

I was sitting in the chair, having my coffee, when suddenly I saw a heavy sea rising in front of the ship, some distance away, and knew that this would be a nasty one. It looks quite scary in the moonlight with a lot of foam on top of the wave. I switched from autopilot to manual steering and at the same time gave more engine power, trying to meet the monster dead ahead. Luckily I managed to do so, and the wave lifted the ship bow in an abnormal angle. I felt that the vessel might have a problem climbing the wave, and gave full ahead forward. The vessel climbed slowly and suddenly the air was filled with a roaring noise and the air was nothing else than foam all around us. The ship shook and vibrated a lot when the propeller lost the water at the top of the wave. I myself was standing on my feet and grabbed my hands around the steering wheel, afraid of falling. 'Damn it' was the only thing I could say when the ship was over the top, and started falling down the other side of the wave. I felt myself hanging in the air and could hardly stand on my feet when the ship bow crashed into the next wall of water. The force of gravity was unlike anything I ever felt before.

The seawater smashed to the front of the vessel and found the way in to the accommodations through different air outlets. There was no damage to the vessel itself, but in cabins, galley, and other areas, furniture and loose parts was in a mess.

The crew itself took the incidence calmly – just another nasty bastard. That's all there is to say about it. Laying out here in the middle of the track from Atlantic lows it's a rough job, but a man gets used to whatever comes.

This 90-footer was measured by a wave height recorder on board the *Polar Front* and a similar device was fitted to the research ship *Discovery* when she encountered the first 100-foot wave ever recorded from a ship. Dr Penny Holliday was on board at the time and recounts the experience:

I wasn't asleep – no chance of that when your bunk appears to be trying to throw you out of it. I was trying to stay wedged into it, with my life-jacket stuffed under one edge of my mattress, and feet jammed against the wooden sides at the bottom. But there was no sleep. It was very noisy as you can imagine. As well as the sound of wind, and the sea crashing onto the side of the ship and swishing down the decks, I could hear general banging and crashing all around. The ship creaks and groans and as it flexes the fittings make a kind of he-he-he noise which in the middle-of-the-night paranoia sounds like your wardrobe is laughing at you!

At some point the chair in my cabin flew across from its position under the desk (where I thought I had carefully wedged it tight), bounced on the floor and jumped on top of me. So some of the time I was trying to sleep, and some of the time I was just lying awake hoping things would improve. Normally on a no-work-bad-weather-night I might wander up to the bridge to chat to whoever was on watch, but with the master, the chief engineer, two lookouts and the usual bridge officers up there, us scientists could tell that it wasn't a time for a social visit.

I couldn't honestly say I felt the biggest wave and knew what had happened, but during that night we had twenty-three waves that were over 20 metres, and I certainly could tell that this was no ordinary storm. I've been through some very bad weather several times before in the Rockall Trough and in the Iceland Basin – my worst previous being in 1996 when we had significant wave heights of about 13m south of Iceland. But the violence of the motion and the obvious very deep concern of the captain, engineers and bridge officers was something I certainly hadn't known before. A particularly alarming event happened the night after the biggest waves, when the storm was still raging but the waves had decreased a little. During the night, the starboard lifeboat came loose after a roll of about 35°, and was banging against the side of the ship. The noise of each bang was tremendous – somehow made worse by it being about 4.00am. Some extremely brave crew were dispatched to secure it until daylight and calmer seas. In many ways, this was the most frightening thing for me to see – the bosun and ABs having to go out into that weather to do a very dangerous job. I think that was when the seriousness of our situation was brought home to me. Wanting to keep out of the way, I stayed in my bunk, listening as the men with harnesses and equipment clinking, opened the watertight doors outside my cabin. I think I held my breath for most of the time they were out there. But they did the job and came back.

The *Discovery* was operating in the Rockall Trench, an area of deep water that lies between Iceland and the Shetland Isles. On the night in question the weather map showed the isobars lying west to east almost right across the Atlantic in a straight line. This created a fetch of over 1,000 miles for the waves to develop and the wave recordings were showing consistent waves of over 60ft with the winds blowing at around 50 knots. These are bad but not extreme conditions but the crew of the ship reported that they were experiencing violent seas. The huge 100ft waves are thought to have developed ahead of an active front that was traversing the area and the theory is that the extreme waves measured were created by resonance from this frontal system

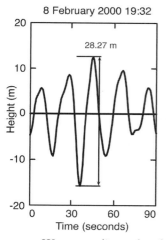
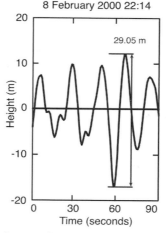
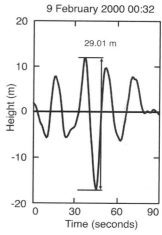

Wave recordings taken from the recorder on board *Discovery* when experiencing the extreme waves.

focusing and boosting the energy of the waves to create the monsters that were measured.

Most of the weather ships have now been replaced by recording buoys that are equipped with weather-monitoring equipment and they can send in continuous reports of weather and sea conditions. During some of the major storms that have occurred off the coast of North America these buoys are reported as having recorded waves of over 25 metres which is over 80ft and because these waves are associated with violent storm conditions it is thought that such waves are transient peaks created in the confused seas. The buoys tend to be moored in relatively shallow waters and this is likely to increase the height of the waves compared with those in the open ocean.

What is interesting about the recordings of that 100ft wave is that the trough is deeper below the median line than the wave crest is above it. We always talk about wave height and that is the distance between trough and crest and you picture a ship trying to climb over the huge crest of an extreme wave. In reality the chances are that it is the deep trough that comes either before or after the high crest that does the damage. These deep troughs or 'holes' are like the reverse of an extreme wave and when a ship or boat falls into them the chances of climbing out unscathed are small. This is when the ship is vulnerable and the following wave can deposit tons of active water on the deck to cause serious damage. This is what happened to the *Polar Front*. There is a chance that you might see an extreme wave crest some way off so that there is a chance to do something about it. You don't see one of these 'holes' until you fall into it and by then it is too late.

The holes exist in many types of sea conditions and there are many tales of ships and boats being affected by them. I found one in the dangerous Portland Race off the south coast of England when I was testing lifeboats. This race is

This ship will be just as concerned about what lies on the other side of this large wave as with the wave itself.

notorious for its waves with wild breaking crests created when strong tides meet shallow water in a gale of wind; perfect extreme conditions testing a lifeboat's performance in rough seas. We went over the first breaking crest quite happily and then there was this hole on the other side. The whole boat became airborne and then dropped into the hole where I swear you could almost see the seabed, and then the next wave fell on top of us. I was so grateful we were in a strong boat and we eventually rose clear with only superficial damage but the scary part of that 'hole' encounter was the total lack of warning.

As we start to get a better picture of these extreme waves and holes there are three types of extreme waves that are emerging. There is the 'three sisters' type where the wave is one of three very large waves and it is suggested that these are created by a secondary wave train being superimposed on the more regular waves. This may be the type of wave experienced by the *Discovery*. Then there is the wave tower: a sort of pyramid wave that exists as a single peak and could be caused in part by current focusing that causes large wave trains to cross each other at a shallow angle. Finally, there is the white wall: a huge wall of water approaching that looks vertical with the crest start to break. Several yachts and ships have reported this type of extreme wave and it must be one of the most frightening experiences of a life at sea.

Encountering any type of extreme wave in the Atlantic is likely to be a memorable experience, assuming the vessel survives. We hear the tales of survivors but how many ships and yachts have succumbed to these monsters of the deep? The *München* was a large modern ship and she disappeared without warning in 1978 in an Atlantic storm. There are many more stories of modern ships being damaged in storm conditions, so extreme waves could be the reason why ships disappear without trace and you have to ask how this can happen in times of modern technology and modern ship design.

There are two factors that seem to point to the cause. One is that many of the ships involved have had their bridge fronts well forward on the hull. Most passenger ships are built this way and the *München* followed this design style. It is not difficult to imagine what happens to these ships if they encounter an extreme wave with solid water coming over the bow and striking the vertical wall of the superstructure with incredible force. It is reckoned that the water in a major wave coming on board in this way could exert a force of 100 tons per square metre. Not many ships are built to withstand that and in the case of the *München* it could have wiped out the forward superstructure block and all the people in it. Passenger ships are regularly suffering from major wave damage and this is not new, with some major liners and cruise ships reporting wave damage at bridge level and above with the damage exacerbated by the speed of the ship.

Speed is the other factor and perhaps a more worrying one as large ships get faster and have to maintain tight schedules. A modern container ship or passenger ship can be 1,000ft long and may be travelling at up to 25 knots and because of the schedule there is a great reluctance to slow down to a safe speed just in case it meets an extreme wave. Equally, at their high speed there will be no chance of slowing down in time if an extreme wave is sighted ahead so they will always be vulnerable to these extreme waves. These large modern ships rely heavily on weather routing to avoid the worst of the weather and that seems to work in most cases, but weather routing tends to rely on forecast winds rather than sea conditions. There does not seem to be any prospect of being able to forecast the existence of extreme waves in advance with current technology and as in that case with the *Discovery*, the extreme waves were encountered when the wind was only blowing at force 10.

However, the estimated wave heights from some of these encounters still makes frightening reading. That wave that the *München* is thought to have encountered was estimated at 66ft high, while the Atlantic liner *Queen Elizabeth* reported a 90-footer in 1943. The German liner *Bremen* was completely immobilized and in severe danger of sinking after encountering an estimated 98-footer in the South Atlantic and there have been several cases in which modern cruise liners have suffered damage and passenger injuries from extreme wave encounters.

Yachts and small craft seem to be more cautious about extreme waves. Many yachts have experienced 50 or 60-footers but whether these were extreme among the general run of waves or whether the seas were generally very big is mainly a matter of conjecture. A small craft would tend to ride over the crest of an extreme wave and drop down the other side without much harm and when yachtsmen talk of extremes it is usually when talking about how steep the wave was rather than its height. A vertical wall of water that denotes a wildly breaking crest is a significant risk to a yacht. Its height is not so critical.

It is not just extreme waves that can cause concern but also extreme swells. Swells may not cause too much concern to shipping because they have a relatively gentle gradient but when they reach land or shallow water it can be a different story. In 2008 there was an extreme swell event recorded in the Atlantic when a low-pressure area moved away from the Atlantic coast of the US. Over a twenty-four-hour period this low deepened considerably as it moved north-east and then as it weakened it turned south-east. Then its movement stopped and the very strong winds from the north associated with this low pressure had a long fetch and this in turn generated a very heavy swell moving outward from the centre of the low. This swell extended over most of the North Atlantic and in Puerto Rico in the Caribbean breaking swells of 30ft were recorded and later as the swells developed the breaking surf reached 40ft in height. Swells of this nature may, on their own, have little impact on shipping but when a monster swell crest coincides with a big storm wave then you have the catalyst for an extreme wave situation.

I don't think that anyone doubts the existence of these monster waves and their random nature. As we learn more about them, it becomes a frightening scenario for ship-owners and ship-operators. No wonder the MaxWave project is trying to bring some order into this shipping chaos. If the possibility of encountering a 60ft wave could be quantified then ship designers could perhaps have a better idea of where the limits are and be able to design ships to cope and the captains of the ships could know when to slow down or take avoiding action. At present it is the poor old captain who has to take the responsibility of driving his ship safely in adverse conditions while still maintaining schedules, but he is put in an impossible position because he has so little information on which to base his judgement when it comes to extreme wave encounters. Extreme waves are still in the realms of the unknown and rarely experienced but when they hit, they hit hard and fast and there is no room for negotiation with this type of wave. It is significant that many of the reported extreme wave encounters have been in the Atlantic, possibly reflecting the high density of Atlantic shipping but also adding to the reputation of the Atlantic as the world's toughest ocean.

Chapter Eleven

Disasters on the Atlantic

The Atlantic Ocean is a dangerous place and throughout the centuries of Atlantic crossing history there is constant reference to the disasters and tragedies that have taken place in Atlantic waters. This should hardly come as a surprise when you look at the types of ships and boats that have attempted the crossing and the uncompromising weather and sea conditions that can exist on the Atlantic. While Atlantic disasters in recent times have been well-documented, in the days before radio communications so many of the Atlantic disasters went unrecorded. Ships simply sailed from harbour on a voyage and were never heard of again and the fate of their passengers and crew was never known. This sailing off into 'uncharted' waters was part of the risk associated with trading with the newly-discovered countries on the other side of the Atlantic. The potential rewards of such voyages must have been significant for seamen to take these risks and the trade across the Atlantic attracted a wide range of sailing ships with many of them being of rather dubious quality and condition.

It was not just the condition of many of the ships involved in the Atlantic trade that led to ships disappearing never to be heard of again. It was also overloading, because obviously the more cargo you carry the higher the return from delivering that cargo. The risks associated with overloading ships have been recognized for the past 4,000 years and the first official regulations relating to the loading of ships are thought to date back to regulations developed in Crete in 2500 BC. Vessels were required to pass loading and maintenance inspections before sailing and the Romans also brought in similar regulations. The first record of actual load lines showing how deeply a ship could be loaded with cargo before sailing are thought to have been developed in the Middle Ages in Italy when actual marks were put on the side of ships. It is not recorded how the position of these lines was calculated but it does indicate the concern about ships being overloaded.

Lloyd's Register of Shipping brought out recommendations for how much freeboard a ship should have when fully loaded. This Lloyd's Rule was introduced in 1835, mainly at the behest of underwriters who were insuring the ships and cargoes but it was in the 1860s that the concept of the modern

Plimsoll line was developed. The British MP Samuel Plimsoll managed to get a royal commission on unseaworthy ships to be established in 1872, and finally the Merchant Shipping Act of 1876 made the load line mark compulsory. A form of international agreement was established by requiring foreign ships visiting British ports to be marked with a load line but it was not until 1930 that full international agreement was reached requiring all ships to have a load line.

A load line is no guarantee of safety but at least it is a step in the right direction. The condition of the ship is equally important and the requirement for surveying ships at regular intervals goes some way to ensuring that a ship is in seaworthy condition. None of these precautions were established during the time when the Atlantic trade was developing in the seventeenth and eighteenth centuries and at this time there were few records kept. It has been estimated that during the twenty-year period around 1800 there were more than 2,000 shipwrecks each year on a worldwide basis. If you consider the high proportion of trade that was carried out on the Atlantic, then probably half of this number was lost on the Atlantic. Yet it was not just shipwreck that accounted for the high proportion of casualties. A succession of wars meant that ships carrying cargo and passengers were fair game if encountered at sea and many were captured by enemy ships, so if you did not succumb to storm

The Royal West India Line ship *Amazon* on fire in the Atlantic. (Illustrated London News)

and grounding there was a high risk that you might be captured by the enemy. Judging by the standards of modern shipping it becomes hard to comprehend why sailors and passengers even contemplated going to sea at all, but then of course these statistics have only emerged from historical research and the poor chances of surviving an ocean voyage were not known at the time. Every voyage set out with hope in the hearts and in many cases relied on the power of prayer for survival.

When we talk about disasters on the Atlantic, the *Titanic* stands out as a milestone event. With the loss of more than 1,500 lives in the cold waters of the Atlantic, this disaster highlighted more than anything else the high level of risk in making an ocean voyage across the Atlantic. In Chapter Five we saw the comments in a letter from one of the officers on an Atlantic liner about the effects of strain and tiredness on the ability of the officers to cope with the demands of navigating an Atlantic crossing at speed but the *Titanic* disaster had a much wider impact in terms of new safety legislation. One aspect of safety legislation for shipping is that it is always reactive rather than proactive – it responds to events rather than anticipating them – and when 1,500 people lose their lives then there will always be demands for changes. These changes came in the form of a requirement to carry enough lifeboats for all the passengers and crew on board and the establishment of the Ice Patrol to track and monitor the icebergs that might encroach into the shipping lanes so that shipping could take avoiding action. One of the problems associated with trying to legislate for improved safety in shipping is that you can only legislate for factors that can be measured. When it comes to factors such as the exhaustion of the officers on watch and the demands of keeping to schedules, these can be very subjective and equally hard to legislate for. Again as we saw in Chapter Five, the *Titanic* disaster did have an impact on safety but it did not stop shipping taking chances and aiming for higher and higher speeds and cutting safety corners to maintain the all-important schedules.

These were not the only factors that have been the cause of disasters on the Atlantic and disasters can be divided up into a variety of reasons for ships and boats not completing their voyages. Collisions, whether with icebergs or other ships, have been a significant factor, as have groundings which have mainly been caused by poor navigation information and techniques, fog and the lack of modern electronic systems. Storms have been a major cause of Atlantic disasters and continue to challenge the construction and operation even of modern ships. We will look at each of these in more detail high-lighting some of the more significant events, but for so many of the ships that have simply disappeared in the Atlantic over the years we will never know the cause of the disaster.

Collisions

The collision of the *Titanic* with an iceberg is the most high-profile collision to have taken place on the Atlantic and it has been so well-documented that there is no call to repeat it here. However, just three days before the *Titanic* disaster, the cargo ship *Niagara* passed between two icebergs just 10 miles from the *Titanic* iceberg but managed to stay afloat by continual pumping out of the water. That collision took place long before the days of radar that would have probably provided adequate warning of the presence of the iceberg long before the *Titanic* hit it. Ice still presents a collision risk in Atlantic waters but these days radar can detect the main icebergs without a problem and the collisions now tend to be ships hitting the smaller lumps of floating ice such as growlers and bergy bits that float at or just above sea level and so hardly show up on radar, the sort of ice that concerned us when we made the *Virgin Atlantic* crossing.

The *Titanic* was not the first Atlantic liner to hit an iceberg. Back in 1849 the 281ft-long paddle steamer *Pacific* was one of the fastest Atlantic ships of its day with a speed of 12.5 knots. She was built from wood and was ordered by the American Collins Line to outclass their chief rivals from the British-owned Cunard Line. *Pacific* set a new transatlantic speed record in her first year of service but after only five years in operation the ship, along with close to 200 passengers and crew, went missing without a trace on a voyage from Liverpool to New York. Although ships were sent out to try to find any sign of the *Pacific*, it was years later that a message was found in a bottle on one of the Hebridean islands off the west coast of Scotland suggesting that she was sunk after hitting an iceberg. The note was signed by W.M. Graham who was on the passenger list of the *Pacific* and who was a sea captain heading for New York to take command of another ship: 'On board the *Pacific* from Liverpool to N.Y. – Ship going down. Confusion on board – icebergs around us on every side. I know I cannot escape. I write the cause of our loss so that friends may not live in suspense. The finder will please get it published.'

Another iceberg collision mystery solved by finding messages in bottles was the liner *Naronic* owned by the White Star Line. She was reported to have left Liverpool for New York with seventy-four people, 3,600 tons of general cargo and more than 1,000 tons of coal on board in 1893. After she dropped her pilot on leaving Liverpool nothing more was heard from her but later that year about 150 miles north of where the *Titanic* sank, two lifeboats, one overturned and the other half-flooded with water, were the only wreckage found that could be traced to the *Naronic*. The White Star Line refused to accept that the *Naronic* might have been sunk after hitting an iceberg as it brought back too many memories of the *Titanic* disaster. Then over the next six months four messages in bottles washed up ashore, two on the US coast and two in the Irish Sea on the European side of the Atlantic. All the messages stated that the *Naronic* had struck an iceberg and was sinking but in spite of this evidence the authorities refused to accept that this was the fate of the *Naronic* as the signatures on the messages could not be traced to any known people on board.

Back in 1841, when on passage from Liverpool to Philadelphia, the sailing packet ship *William Brown* collided with an iceberg in a gale of wind. The collision took place 250 miles south-east of Cape Race in the area known as Iceberg Alley because so many icebergs tend to congregate there. The ship foundered along with thirty-three of the passengers and crew and the remainder took to the lifeboat which was seriously overloaded. There were none of the heroics seen when the *Titanic* sank and it is reported that seventeen passengers were thrown overboard from the lifeboat to lighten the load. The surviving crew members were later picked up by the sailing ship *Crescent* and transported safely to land.

In 1849 the Canadian-built emigrant ship *Hannah* on passage from Ireland to Quebec struck ice that holed the ship below the waterline. She is reported to have sunk in just forty minutes and the captain and two officers are reported to have commandeered the only lifeboat to escape, leaving 180 passengers and crew to fend for themselves. The survivors transferred to the ice and faced extreme cold in which many perished but luckily a passing ship found the survivors the next day and 130 of them survived. The captain and officers made it to the shore and were charged in court but escaped punishment by questioning the evidence of some of the witnesses.

Another emigrant ship, the *Maria*, had made numerous voyages across the Atlantic but in 1849 she had the misfortune to strike ice and was holed and sinking. Around twenty of her passengers and crew managed to jump on the ice but only nine of them survived the severe cold before being rescued by a passing ship. The year 1849 was a bad one for ice on the Grand Banks and adjacent waters and that same spring two other ships struck ice and sank in the vicinity but as these were cargo ships there seems to be much less concern about their fate.

Another example of inhuman behaviour came when the French sailing ship *Vaillant* struck an iceberg on the Grand Banks of Newfoundland in 1897. The *Vaillant* was on passage from St. Malo in France to the Canadian island of St. Pierre and was sailing in thick fog when the collision occurred. A total of seventy-eight lives were lost and it is reported that amid the chaos on board, seven people had managed to set sail in a boat that drifted for five days in the severe Arctic cold. Three of them died from starvation and cold and the remaining four were rescued seven days later. It is believed that the four survivors had resorted to cannibalism, eating the dead bodies of their comrades.

While the icebergs and ice floes were the danger to shipping, it was often the severe cold that was the killer. When the *John Rutledge* hit an iceberg in 1856 on a passage from Liverpool to New York she was well-equipped for survival and everyone on board managed to escape in the five lifeboats. They then drifted for nine days in the freezing conditions and when rescue finally came there was only one of the survivors alive to tell the story.

Many of the records of ships that have been in collision with icebergs or ice relate to ships carrying passengers and it is thought that there were many more collisions involving cargo ships where there were no survivors and the incident went unrecorded. With the prevailing fog, the rather random nature of iceberg locations and the lack of any detection equipment such as radar, the toll from iceberg collisions, particularly at night, was high. Without radio communications there was no way of calling for help in the event of a collision and it was the *Titanic* event that highlighted the use of radio in calling for assistance.

Even in relatively modern times there is still a risk from ice collisions in the Atlantic and the case of the Danish *Hans Hedtoft* that sank in 1959 still remains something of a mystery. Rather like the *Titanic*, she was hailed as 'the safest ship afloat' when she was launched. Designed to operate between Greenland and Denmark, she was on her maiden voyage returning to Copenhagen when she hit an iceberg about 20 miles south-east of Cape Farewell, the southernmost tip of Greenland. A German trawler responded to the distress signal but on arrival at the location no trace of the *Hans Hedtoft* could be found. Search operations continued for several days and months later the only evidence found was a lifebuoy washed ashore in Iceland. Some ninety-five people lost their lives in the sinking of the *Hans Hedtoft*, which still remains one of the unsolved mysteries of the Atlantic.

In 1991 the cargo ship *Finnpolaris* loaded with zinc ore hit what was thought to be a bergy bit off Greenland and sank. That same year the cargo ship *Marine Transport* suffered a similar fate and in both cases the crews were rescued. The *Marine Transport* was found to have close to half a ton of cocaine on board so although the crew was rescued they were immediately arrested for drug-smuggling!

Collisions between ships are quite rare on the Atlantic and the routing of ships making the Atlantic crossing on separated routes depending on whether they are east or westbound has tended to keep the ships apart. Historically, collision locations tend to be close to the pinch points at either end of the Atlantic route, around the Nantucket lightship/buoy on the American side and at the entrance to the English Channel on the European side, the areas where ships tend to be more concentrated and heading in both directions. The Nantucket lightship moored some 45 miles south of Nantucket Point was the focal point for ships heading in and out of New York and in 1933 was herself hit and sunk by an Atlantic liner, the *Olympic*, the sister ship of the *Titanic*. Three of the lightship's crew died in the collision which took place in thick fog. Lightships were being fitted with the new radio beacons that allowed ships to fix their position even in zero visibility and ships coming in from the Atlantic would home in on the beacon fitted to the lightship. The crews reported that they were constantly the victims of near misses in fog as ships homed in on their beacon until that fateful night when the collision occurred.

It was close to this lightship that one of the major collisions in the Atlantic took place in 1956, this one between two Atlantic liners that were both equipped with probably the best radar equipment of the time and this led to the phrase 'radar-assisted collision'. The ability of radar as a collision avoidance device had been questioned by some experts when it was introduced after the war. In 1956 it was still early days of the use of radar by ships and the techniques for collision avoidance were still being developed. The collision between the Swedish liner *Stockholm* and the Italian liner *Andrea Doria* took place 45 miles south of Nantucket Island in thick fog.

A total of fifty-one passengers and crew on board the *Andrea Doria* were killed in the collision, which ripped a great hole in the side of the Italian vessel. Miraculously, all the remaining 1,660 survivors on board were rescued from the severely-listing ship before she sank the next morning. Both ships were equipped with sophisticated radar systems, and authorities were puzzled as to the cause of the accident. Both were modern ships and with radar on board only slowed down slightly in the fog in order to maintain their schedules, confident in their ability to see and avoid other ships on the radar. The *Stockholm* was reported as being in the westbound lane to reduce the crossing time and she met the *Andrea Doria* coming westbound through the fog. Both ships picked up the other on radar while still miles apart but it was when taking incorrect avoiding action that the collision occurred.

The Norwegian tanker *Stolt Dagali* was sliced in two by the Israeli liner *Shalom* in 1964 off the coast of New Jersey, in an area that has been called Wreck Valley because of the number of shipping accidents that have occurred there. Some nineteen crew members on the tanker were killed when her stern was sliced off and the remaining twenty-four stayed afloat on the bow section that comprised watertight tanks. Fortunately the oil cargo on board was not highly flammable, which prevented a fire starting. Again this was an accident in thick fog and was blamed partly on the poor use of radar and look-outs.

The Italian liner *Andrea Doria* sinking off New York after colliding with the liner *Stockholm*.

Wartime when ships were running without lights at night created an additional collision hazard on the Atlantic. A cargo ship, the *Oregon*, was a few miles south of the Nantucket lightship in 1941 when it was struck by the US battleship *New Mexico*, also running without lights. Seventeen crew members of the *Oregon* were either killed or drowned and the remainder were rescued by a trawler fishing in the area.

The liner *Queen Mary* was another wartime collision victim when she collided with her cruiser escort north of Ireland. In late 1942 she was carrying around 10,000 US troops and running at close to 30 knots to avoid the U-boat threat and zig-zagging to make her course unpredictable. Her escort the cruiser *Curaçao* was running at 25 knots in a straight line and confusion on both vessels about who should give way made a collision inevitable, with the *Queen Mary* slicing the elderly cruiser in half. Some 337 lives were lost on the *Curaçao* and the *Queen Mary* with a damaged bow maintained speed as ordered, to dock in the UK. Not quite in the Atlantic but when on her way out of the St. Lawrence River to cross the Atlantic in 1914 there was a major disaster almost rivalling the *Titanic* collision when the Canadian Pacific liner *Empress of Ireland* was in collision with a collier when fog came down. Like the

The French liner *Normandie* capsized in New York Harbour after first catching fire when alongside during the Second World War.

Titanic, the liner sank quickly apparently due to portholes being left open and watertight doors not shut and around 1,000 of her passengers and crew drowned in the icy waters out of a total complement of 1,500. The collier was mainly held to blame for the collision.

Groundings

The two sides of the North Atlantic are very different in character with the American side being a maze of mainly shoals and low-lying land apart from the land well to the north where cliffs prevail, and the European side being mainly cliffs with some significant outlying rocks. Both hold significant dangers for shipping and one of the first reports of grounding was from one of the ships in Columbus' fleet of three ships in the Caribbean. Making a landfall on the US side when there was no electronic assistance and when navigators were challenged to even calculate the longitude which is vitally important to making a safe landfall was a high-risk operation. Sailing ships would heave to in the dark and then sail onwards in daylight in the hope that they would sight the low-lying land or at least sight the breaking waves on the shoals before they

Another Atlantic casualty – an unknown ship hits the rocks on the US coast when making a landfall.

hit them. The risk of grounding was heightened by the extensive fog banks that engulfed the northern coastline mainly during the summer months.

Heading eastbound, ships were perhaps better placed to make a landfall along the more distinctive high cliffs that featured on much of the European coastline. However, there were still significant dangers such as patches of off-lying rocks like Rockall and St. Kilda that remained unlit until quite recent times. In 1904 the Danish immigrant ship *Norge* struck an isolated rock in the vicinity of Rockall when on her way to America. Of the 800 people on board, 600 lost their lives because there were insufficient lifeboats and of those who were lucky enough to get in a lifeboat it was a long five days before they were picked up by a passing trawler, although one lifeboat made a navigation error and ended up in the Faroe Islands. The low-lying Scilly Isles represented a significant danger to ships heading for the English Channel and what was probably the largest British naval disaster occurred when Admiral Sir Cloudesley Shovell's flagship along with several other ships in his fleet ran aground on the Scilly Isles in 1707. More than 2,000 seamen were drowned that night due to a navigation error and it was this major disaster that was reported to have led to demands for developing a way for navigators to be able to establish their longitude.

Many of the ships of the Spanish Armada went aground on the west coasts of Scotland and Ireland when they were trying to find their way back to Spain, sailing around the north of Scotland after their defeat at the hands of the British. Atlantic storms proved too much for the tired and battered crews and many were driven onto the rocks. So many ships must have hit rocks or run aground on the shoals towards the end of their voyages with many of these unrecorded in the days before radio communications and electronic navigation aids. Ships and especially fishing boats just simply disappeared in the icy waters of the North Atlantic with little trace and no record of what happened.

I had my own experience of grounding back in 1952. It was not quite in the Atlantic but in the Sea of the Hebrides, just south of the passage between the Outer Hebrides and the mainland on the west coast of Scotland. It was winter and blowing a wild gale and snowing hard, blizzard conditions in which the visibility was close to zero. The ship *Tapti* was empty of cargo and so high in the water and very much affected by the strong wind which was on the beam, so we were going sideways almost as much as the engine was driving us forward. With no electronic systems to help us pinpoint the position, we were literally steaming into the blizzard blind. In the middle of the night there was this almighty crash and bang and the ship lurched to the point where I was almost thrown out of my bunk and we were hard and fast aground on the rocks. As we were not where we expected to be, we did not know where we were so it was a challenge for the authorities to send out help in the zero visibility. Eventually they were able to take bearings from our radio signals and to pinpoint the position so the Tobermory lifeboat arrived the next morning and took us ashore. From what I understood later we were in a high-risk situation and could have died that night if the ship had capsized but the whole crew was rescued and we lived to tell the tale. From that experience it is easy to imagine the situation of so many ships that have got into trouble on the coastlines of the Atlantic and never lived to tell the tale.

The immigrant ship *Tayleur* aground on the Irish coast in 1854 when 300 lives were lost.

The liner *Paris* aground on the Manacles Rocks off the Cornish coast in 1829. She was later refloated.

Among the liners, most managed to avoid grounding except in more recent times when the US liner *Manhattan* grounded off the Florida coast in 1931 and the Cunard liner *QE2* grounded near Martha's Vineyard in 1992. The latter was reported to be due to the ship striking an 'uncharted' rock and the squat of the vessel, the way the stern dips in the water when running at speed. Both ships suffered extensive bottom damage from the grounding but no casualties were reported so the event was more of an expensive embarrassment rather than a danger when modern ships ground in this way. The *Royal Majesty* was a cruise liner that grounded on the Nantucket Shoals in 1995, despite having all the latest electronic navigation aids on board. Her downfall came when the wire from the GPS antenna was damaged and the GPS display reverted to showing an estimated position rather than the true position. The navigator managed to reconcile this when he saw what he expected to see but the ship was actually 17 miles to the west of the main shipping channel into Boston and in shallow water. She was pulled off by tugs with bottom damage, wounded pride and a hefty bill being the main results. Analysis showed that no one on board had thought to compare the GPS positions with those shown by the Loran, an alternative electronic system, and no one had checked the depth-sounder which can give a good indication when the water becomes too shallow!

    While passenger ships with their high numbers of passengers hit the head-
lines when they get into trouble on the Atlantic, there is a new generation of
significant groundings in the Atlantic which are those that have caused extensive oil spills. The *Torrey Canyon* was the first tanker to hit the headlines when
she grounded on the Seven Stones Rocks off the Cornish coast while loaded
with 120,000 tons of heavy oil. This was back in 1967 when the techniques for
coping with major oil spills had not been developed and the black oil spread
for miles from the wreck contaminating extensive areas of pristine beaches
and contaminating the fishing grounds off south-west England. The wreck
stayed firmly on the rocks and in desperation the government ordered the
RAF and the Royal Navy to bomb the wreck in the hope that the oil would
catch fire and burn off, which did happen but only after thousands of tons had
spread over the adjacent seas and land.

    On the US side the *Argo Merchant* was the next major tanker disaster when
she grounded on the notorious Nantucket Shoals in 1976 but the amount of
oil released was small by comparison, just over 30,000 tons, and it was relatively light oil which was spread out into the Atlantic to evaporate rather than
drifting towards the sensitive shore and the equally sensitive fishing grounds.
The *Atlantic Empress* was a tanker that was in collision with another tanker

The tanker *Argo Merchant* breaking up after grounding on the Nantucket Shoals.

way to the south in the Atlantic when off the coast of Trinidad. She was loaded with over 300,000 tons of oil and this was a major disaster on the fringes of the Atlantic when the *Atlantic Empress* sank while under tow with major pollution resulting.

Back in the North Atlantic another headline-hitter was the *Amoco Cadiz* which suffered a loss of steering when rounding Ushant on the way north from the Bay of Biscay into the English Channel. Loaded with approximately 250,000 tons of crude oil, she drifted for some time with the engine still working so making progress but unable to point the ship in the desired direction. Other ships tried to help by attaching a tow line but the weather conditions prevented this and eventually the *Amoco Cadiz* hit the rocks and spewed oil along vast swathes of the French coastline. It was a major disaster that took years to clear up and along with the *Exxon Valdez* grounding in Alaska this was the event that finally persuaded the authorities that something had to be done to improve tanker safety.

It is hard to believe that the legislators could allow a tanker loaded with thousands of tons of oil to ply the oceans with just a single engine and a single steering system and with just an inch of steel plating separating the oil from the sea. The main changes that the legislators came up with were to insist that tankers had double bottoms and double sides, two layers of steel separated by a gap of about a metre or so that might offer some protection to prevent the oil from leaking out if there was a collision or grounding and to station large tugs at significant points on the coastlines to provide some form of towage capability if a ship became incapacitated. Routing systems also aimed to keep ships away from sensitive parts of the coast. We still have most ships roaming the oceans with just a single engine and a single steering system in the interests of cost and efficiency, so any engine or steering failure immediately raises the disaster level. While modern electronic navigation systems can improve safety they are not the total answer and human error is always lurking in the background as shown by the *Royal Majesty* grounding.

It is not just tankers that cause oil pollution. In 1986 the 900ft-long bulk carrier *Kowloon Bridge* was damaged in Atlantic storms and sought shelter in Bantry Bay in south-west Ireland. Worried about colliding with another ship also anchored in the bay, the *Kowloon Bridge* put to sea again in the storm conditions and when her steering failed she went ashore on the Stag Rocks off the south Irish coast where she became a total loss. She spewed out tons of fuel oil from her punctured tanks that devastated the local fishing grounds. The wreck of the *Kowloon Bridge* is still there today and I found it just below the surface at low tide when exploring the area in an RIB when we touched the mast, fortunately without damage.

Foundering

Ships sinking in the waters of the Atlantic were quite a common occurrence in the days of the sailing ships. Most of these 'ships' were quite small, probably under 100ft in length, and many of them were not in a good seaworthy condition. In hard financial times maintenance of the ships took second place to manning and stores and it might take just one Atlantic gale to seek out the weak points in a hull that had not been well maintained. As we have already quoted, there were times when it was reported that around half of the ships that sailed on voyages out of British harbours never returned. The reasons for their disappearance are not known in most cases and many of them did not disappear on the Atlantic but the reputation of this ocean and the fact that most ships leaving a British port had to venture out onto the Atlantic means that Atlantic storms could have been the reason for a ship's disappearance. The chances of being rescued if a ship was breaking up were small and would rely on a ship coming upon the wreck before the crew expired. This did happen but not often.

Probably the biggest cause of ships sinking in Atlantic waters was during wartime when ships were deliberately sunk either by gunfire or by torpedoes. In the two world wars hundreds of ships from both sides of the conflict were sunk on the Atlantic and the ocean floor must be littered with the rusting hulks of these ships. One of the worst war disasters was when the British battle-cruiser *Hood* was sunk by the *Bismarck*, resulting in more than 1,000 lives lost. The *Bismarck* herself later suffered a similar fate. Indeed, the seabed of the Atlantic is the resting place for thousands of ships and once oil became a cargo or a fuel for ships the level of pollution in wartime must have been high. However, the ocean has great powers of recovery and despite the vast quantities of oil that have been released, the ocean still survives.

One of the worst oil pollution events in the open waters of the Atlantic was when the tanker *Odyssey* broke in half around 700 miles west of Newfoundland after an explosion on board. The *Odyssey* was carrying 130,000 tons of heavy fuel oil from Scotland to Newfoundland when she was caught up in a severe winter storm. She sent out a distress message and then later an explosion on board caused her to catch fire, igniting the oil cargo. Despite a rescue ship coming to her aid within an hour, rescue could not be effected because the ship was surrounded by burning oil and all twenty-seven crew members perished.

There have been several ships that have either disappeared in unknown circumstances or, as in the case of the *Mary Celeste*, have continued to sail on with no crew on board. The *Mary Celeste* remains one of the great mysteries of the Atlantic but equally mysterious is the case of the *München*. The *München*

The cargo ship *München* that disappeared on the Atlantic virtually without trace.

was a modern cargo liner designed to carry special LASH barges that were floated off complete with cargo for onward transport. She was on passage from Germany to Savannah in the US in 1978 when she encountered severe storms with waves recorded at close to 50ft in height. Several distress messages were received purporting to come from the ship but reception was very poor and disjointed; however, a full-scale search for the ship or for survivors was started. This was the largest search and rescue operation ever mounted in the Atlantic and sixteen aircraft and more than 100 ships were involved. The only traces of the ship that were found were several life-rafts and one lifeboat but not one of the crew was picked up dead or alive. The enquiry into the loss put the cause down to severe weather but modern thinking suggests that the ship was overwhelmed by a rogue wave of massive proportions.

Another foundering drama on the Atlantic was the cargo ship *Flying Enterprise*. On Christmas night in 1951 this wartime-built ship was on passage from Germany to the US when she encountered severe gales in the Western Approaches. It is thought that some of the cargo shifted in the storm and the ship developed a 50° list. The passengers and crew were safely evacuated but Captain Kurt Carlsen remained on board. Ships came to the rescue and it was the British tug *Turmoil* that finally took the ship in tow a week later after the mate of the tug had jumped on board the *Enterprise* to help attach the tow line. The tow was heading back to Falmouth when just 60 miles out she ended her days by capsizing. Captain Carlsen at first refused any help except from

'The ship that refused to die' – the *Flying Enterprise* with a severe list in an Atlantic storm.

American ships and it has been speculated that the ship was carrying supplies and/or equipment for America's emerging nuclear programme. The whole saga of the rescue, the tow and the sinking were recorded on film and the rescue attempt dominated the headlines for a couple of weeks with the vessel being known as 'The Ship That Refused to Die'.

The Fastnet Storm was another event that took place in much the same waters and led to the deaths of fifteen yachtsmen and three people from rescue vessels. More than 300 yachts were taking part in this challenging yacht race that sees yachts head out from Cowes on the Isle of Wight into the Western Approaches to round the Fastnet Rock off the south-west coast of Ireland and then head back to Plymouth. Bad weather was forecast but nothing that a well-equipped yacht could not handle when the expected depression that was the cause of the bad weather started to deepen and developed into near hurricane conditions. Many of the yachts were in trouble in the severe conditions; five yachts sank and more than seventy reported capsizes. This was one of the most extensive rescue operations ever mounted on the Atlantic with six lifeboats, twelve helicopters and a vast array of ships of all types involved and the event led to a massive rethink of the safety requirements for yacht-racing. Another case of 'closing the stable door after the horse has bolted', reflecting on the continuing reactive response to safety at sea rather than a proactive one.

One would expect with all the modern technology available that ships breaking up or being overwhelmed in the Atlantic would be a thing of the past, but the container ship *Napoli* found that the Atlantic when it is angry can defeat the best efforts of such technology. In storm conditions in the Western Approaches this 900ft-long ship suffered cracks down one side of the hull and a flooded engine room. The crew abandoned ship into a lifeboat and were rescued and the ship was then taken in tow. Her condition deteriorated with further cracks in the hull and she was finally beached in Lyme Bay on the south coast of England. There the remaining cargo was discharged and the ship cut in half with the bow section going to the famous Harland and Wolff yard in Belfast and the aft section being broken up in situ. The *Napoli* disaster was investigated as a lesson in how not to handle serious shipping disasters and it appears that she was not the only container ship to suffer hull failure in this way, leading to questions about the validity of modern hull calculations and construction methods.

More recently there was the *El Faro* disaster off the islands of the Bahamas. Once again this brought into question the validity of modern technology or perhaps we should say its application in ship safety. The *El Faro* was a thirty-year-old ship that was on passage from Jacksonville in Florida to Puerto Rico in the Caribbean with a cargo of truck trailers and containers, her normal cargo. It was the hurricane season and a tropical storm was approaching the area and was forecast. This storm developed into a category 3 hurricane, quite severe on the hurricane scale, and the ship started taking on water and listing. Waves were in the region of 40ft high and the winds at around 100 mph and the last reported position of the *El Faro* was close to the eye of the storm. Engine power was lost, leaving the ship helpless to manoeuvre in the storm and then communications with the ship ceased and an extensive search was mounted that found some debris and a damaged lifeboat. Eventually the wreck was located in 15,000ft of water, lying upright and largely intact.

Months later with the aid of the latest underwater technology the black box of the ship was recovered. This recorded not only the full operating parameters of the ship, speed, course, etc. but also the conversations on the bridge of the ship, just as with aircraft black boxes. The mate of the ship is heard talking to the captain suggesting an alteration of course to avoid the worst of the storm but the captain continues on a course close to the centre of the storm. 'We'll be passing clear of the backside of it and the wind is giving us a push to increase our speed away from the storm.' The mate again suggested altering course as the ship was now just 22 miles from the centre of the hurricane. By 4.00 am the crew was struggling to pump out water and to right the ship and then the engine failed. At 0730 hours distress signals were sent out and the crew told to prepare to abandon ship. Minutes later a heavy rumbling was heard and then silence. All the crew, a total of thirty-three people, lost their lives that morning and once again modern technology had succumbed to the ravages of the Atlantic in one of its worst moods.

With the most detailed weather forecasts available to track the path of storms on the Atlantic it should be possible for ships to avoid the worst of the weather. This raises the question of whether modern ships are built to cope with extreme weather, instead relying on forecasts to allow ships to avoid storms. Then there are the pressures on ships' captains to keep to tight schedules that could affect their judgement when setting safe speeds and safe courses in storm conditions. The pressures on modern captains are high and the penalty for getting things wrong can be very high indeed and the Atlantic is always waiting to punish the unprepared.

Chapter Twelve

The Future

So can we tame the Atlantic? The technology of ship design is improving all the time and the meteorologists are getting bigger and better computers so they have a better understanding of the weather. Accurate position-fixing is now available at the touch of a button and modern electronic systems have taken much of the guesswork out of navigation and communications. The stage looks set for both ships and boats to cross the Atlantic with confidence but there is a strong feeling that for every step we take forwards in Atlantic technology we also take one backwards. It seems that we are using technology as an excuse to cut down safety margins and it is a bit like having a car fitted with improved brakes. You don't use these improved brakes to increase the safety of driving, you use them to drive closer to the car in front because you know you have better ability to stop! It is the same with shipping. The improved position-fixing is used to cut down the safety margins and navigate closer to dangers, while with improved weather forecasts you take a less cautious approach to the weather. Advanced ship design and construction are used to reduce costs rather than improve the safety margins. Nothing has really changed from hundreds of years ago when ship-owners, operators and designers focused on what they could get away with rather than increasing the safety margins. I would venture to suggest that a modern cruise ship operating on the Atlantic is no safer than the liners of a hundred years ago and accidents continue to happen.

Probably the biggest long-term worry about the future on the Atlantic is climate change. Climate change is an area of weather forecasting that has developed many contrasting opinions but among the forecasters the consensus seems to be that the Atlantic will grow stormier with more frequent hurricanes and deep depressions stirring up its waters. The problem is that the climate change forecasters tend to have a vested interest in forecasting changes that show more extreme conditions in the future. If the conditions are going to be more extreme, then the people out there who operate ships and boats want to know what the future holds and they turn to the forecasters for more information. This makes climate change forecasting a marketable product so it is in the interests of the climate change forecasters to forecast more extreme weather in order to generate business. This may be a tortuous argument but

Will the future see more and bigger Atlantic storms due to climate change?

there are certainly many question marks over what climate change has in store for the future in terms of Atlantic storms.

Some of the more extreme climate change forecasts suggest that the effect on the Atlantic will be more comprehensive. It could change the strength and direction of the Gulf Stream and thus the entire water circulation of the Atlantic Ocean. This could have long-term effects on the temperatures of the ocean and its surrounding coastlines. Perhaps one of the benefits of climate change on the Atlantic could be the melting of the Arctic ice and from that a reduction in the icebergs that flow down from the Greenland ice shelf. It does seem with climate change that almost anything is possible depending on who you listen to but whatever happens it is likely to be a slow-motion change rather than anything sudden and catastrophic.

Certainly the records show that there have been more hurricanes in recent years during the season that extends from March through to November and it also appears that this season of hurricanes is being extended. It is the same with the low-pressure areas and their associated storms that whistle across the Atlantic and the forecasters tell us that these are increasing both in frequency and in intensity. These changes have occurred in the past so this may be just a short-term aberration or it could be part of a long-term trend. Only history will show which of these is the correct forecast model.

Today shipping on the Atlantic has a wealth of information about storms and where and when they are forming and where they are heading. This means that the professional weather routers who help to plan the optimum routes for ships and boats across the Atlantic can enable ships to take avoidance tactics so that they bypass the worst of the weather. However, going back to that anomaly about the brakes on a car, this ability to route ships supposedly well clear of areas of storm on the Atlantic has tended to allow naval architects under pressure from owners to design ships that may be seaworthy in terms of what is required by the authorities but that can still be vulnerable if the weather routers get it wrong and they do happen to tangle with a storm in the wild waters of the Atlantic.

Take the modern cruise ship, for example. The latest designs of cruise ships are huge, probably around twice the volume of the historic '*Queens*', and they can carry upwards of 5,000 passengers. These mega-ships are designed as fine-weather ships with balconies open to the sea quite low down along the sides of the vessel and lifeboats suspended outside the hull in order to

An American aircraft carrier with a bow damaged when it encountered a severe storm.

Atlantic storms are forecast to grow worse with climate change.

maximize the internal space. They have effective stabilizers to reduce the ship's motion and so confident are the designers in the stability of the ships that much of the furniture is free-standing so could start to move about if the ship should start to roll.

The vulnerability of these ships was brought home by the experience of the *Anthem of the Seas*. This cruise liner, which is operated by Royal Caribbean, experienced extremely rough sea conditions after she sailed out of New Jersey in New York Harbour in September 2016. She was sailing towards Bermuda as part of a six-day round trip when she encountered storm conditions on the second day out.

The ship encountered the remnants of Hurricane Hermione which was whistling up the eastern seaboard of the United States. By the time it had travelled well north, the hurricane had been downgraded to a post-tropical cyclone which has less severe winds than those found in a hurricane but these are still challenging winds for a large cruise ship. It was reported that the ship experienced winds up to 90 mph, rain and high waves as it was rocked by the powerful storm.

With modern social media the conditions on board were soon reported around the world. Passengers reported being seasick and being confined to their staterooms to ride out the bad sea conditions. In situations like this, the crew will have to secure their departments to minimize any damage and gift shops will usually have to secure racks, stands and take everything off the shelves. Bars would have to be secured and the galleys will usually have procedures in place. It was reported that the ship was in virtual lockdown, but the average cruise ship passenger does not expect to find these types of conditions on what should be a luxury cruise.

Hermione was reported by the National Oceans and Atmosphere Association to have maximum sustained winds of 70 mph and to be moving at a very slow 3 mph. The storm-force winds extended out from the centre up to 230 miles so any ship in quite a large area would be affected. As always with hurricanes and their remnants in US water, the storm is well-monitored and forecast and it appears that the ship's captain, possibly under pressure from the owners, was expected to sail in the hope that the storm would pass through before the ship reached its area but the storm stagnated and virtually stopped moving, allowing the cruise ship to enter its intense wind arena. The rough sea caused the ship to slow its speed and this in turn meant that the stabilizers were less effective. Stabilizers are adjustable fins extending out from the side of the ship underwater and they rely on the water flow moving past the fins for them to be able to exert their stabilizing effect. The slower the ship goes, the bigger the reduction in stabilizing and so it was like a double whammy for the *Anthem of the Seas*. Slowing down to ease the stress of the ship in the waves and reduced stabilizing would give the ship an exaggerated rolling motion. This is the sort of gamble with the weather and the sea conditions that ships' captains have to assess and deal with all the time but in the case of a very large cruise ship the costs associated with delays or changes to schedules can be very high so there are considerable pressures to keep to the schedule whatever the weather.

The *Anthem of the Seas* is a 167,800 gross tonnage ship, roughly twice the tonnage of the liner *Queen Elizabeth*, and she can carry more than 4,100 passengers. Most of the damage caused by the excessive rolling was cosmetic involving furniture and fittings, but this incident does show just how vulnerable such ships can be if they are caught up in a storm. This was not the first storm experienced by the *Anthem of the Seas* and shortly after she entered service in 2015 she was damaged when she encountered a major storm off Cape Hatteras a little further south along the US Atlantic coast. With so many of these large cruise ships now operating in waters that are frequented by hurricanes and storms, you have to question both the pressures that they operate under because of the high costs of any delays or changes in itineraries and the risks of a major disaster involving one of these ships. Perhaps in this case they expected the storm to be moving north at a fast rate as most of them do and they were caught out when it became slow-moving or virtually stationary, and you have to wonder whether it was the forecasters who got it wrong or the captain of the ship.

The cruise liner *Anthem of the Seas* which suffered damage when it encountered the remnants of hurricane Hermione.

Cruise ships can be particularly vulnerable in this way because of their large human 'cargo' but modern container ships can be equally vulnerable. With speeds of up to 25 knots and cargo in the containers being valued at perhaps over £1 billion, these ships can also be vulnerable if they encounter storm conditions. Their speed equals that of many modern liners and with the containers piled high on deck they could be vulnerable in storm conditions or in a rogue wave encounter. Those containers piled high on deck rely on the connections between each container for security and so can be vulnerable to wave impact and it is not unknown for the container lashings to fail and for containers to be lost overboard or for part of the stack to topple. A recent incident demonstrated the vulnerability of these ships when the 100,000-ton container ship *Bremen Express* had to stop in mid-Atlantic to fix a fault with its engine. Once stopped, the ship turned beam-on to the heavy seas and was rolling heavily. This excessive rolling put a heavy strain on the container lashings and some failed, causing the ship to lose a considerable number of containers overboard.

It is not hard to picture the same thing happening to a cruise ship, although they do have multiple propulsion systems so a complete shut-down is less likely. However, slowing down could cause excessive rolling which in turn could lead to equipment shifting and passenger injuries. Both container ships and cruise liners can be vulnerable in adverse conditions if things go wrong. Of course, the ships can slow down in adverse conditions but both these types of ship tend to operate to tight schedules and there is a lot of pressure to

How seaworthy is a modern container ship in storm conditions?

maintain those schedules. More and more ships are relying on the expertise of weather routing companies to keep them out of weather extremes and the faster the ship the easier this can be but that scope for deviation can be limited by the need to keep to the schedule. With these large container ships, some over 1,000ft long, and the huge cruise ships now in operation there was the hope that size could provide a cushion for operating at speed in adverse conditions, but experience has shown that increasing size only gives a small advantage in rough seas and any advantage seems to be taken up by the designers trying to maximize the payload.

So for the future the role of the weather forecaster on the Atlantic is going to be vital. Not only must the forecaster get it right for several days ahead to enable longer-term route planning, but they must also be accurate. You get no medals for forecasting storm conditions that don't materialize, in the same way that you don't get medals for missing the development of storm conditions. Weather forecasting will become a challenging occupation and even with the extremely powerful modern computer-generated forecasts it can still be challenging to forecast those extremes that are so critical to shipping safety. We may not be able to change the weather on the Atlantic but at least if it can be forecast with accuracy it can help shipping to cope. Storms are just part of the weather forecasting requirement and hopefully in the future the forecasters will be able to pinpoint areas where rogue waves can be expected so that ships, particularly fast ships, can take avoiding action. Rogue waves are probably the biggest risk to shipping in the North Atlantic, particularly those ships travelling at higher speeds. As part of the constant demand to improve the accuracy of forecasting in the Atlantic, NASA has launched a series of small Earth science satellites that will be capable of measuring surface wind speeds at up to four times per second and a new design of satellites that can analyze storms using laser probes. These are mainly aimed at improving knowledge of hurricanes and this information might have warned the *Anthem of the Seas* in time to take avoiding action.

Since the last days of the Atlantic liners when commercial ships were crossing the Atlantic in less than four days there has not been much focus on high speed in Atlantic waters apart from various record attempts that have had little commercial focus. The emphasis on higher speeds has switched from passengers, who are well catered for by airlines, to moving cargo across the Atlantic at high speed. Short transit times can become important for high-value cargoes and the choice for shippers has been between air freight which is very expensive and shipping by container which has a much lower cost but which can take many days or even weeks. In order to try to fill the gaps between these two extremes there have been proposals for high-speed cargo ships to make the Atlantic crossing.

A consortium called FastShip Atlantic, Inc. had plans to build four container vessels to transport high-value, perishable and other time-sensitive cargo at twice the speed of conventional ships. It would have made the transatlantic crossing from Philadelphia to Cherbourg in France in less than four days, and the plan was to provide a door-to-door service between the US mid-west and Central Europe in seven days. These ships were to have had a semi-planing type of hull with a length of 860ft and be capable of carrying 12,000 tons of cargo at speeds of up to 40 knots. To achieve these speeds the FastShip vessels would be powered by five Rolls Royce marine gas turbines coupled to water-jet propulsion, delivering a total of 335,000 hp. This propulsion system would have been the most powerful ever fitted into a ship and in some respects the record-breaking vessel *Destriero* that currently holds the record for the fastest crossing used a similar propulsion system but with only three turbines and jets.

It was claimed that the unique hull design of these ships would enable them to maintain full speed in waves up to 25ft high, which in the light of current experience seems an incredible claim. However, despite the very high fuel costs that these ships would have had to sustain and the possible overestimation of their sea-going capabilities, this project came close to fruition partly because these was some military backing when it was demonstrated that the ships could be quickly converted for military transport operations. Back in 2003 this project was costed at over £1 billion and it is likely that this figure would be at least doubled in today's market. The FastShip project kept going right up until 2012 when the company filed for bankruptcy. It was remarkable how this project developed a life of its own with many major investors and even the government allocating funding but it is hard to imagine that the claimed speeds and performance in adverse Atlantic sea conditions could have been realized and it seems likely that there could have been serious structural damage when trying to maintain schedules in adverse conditions. The Atlantic is not very kind to high-performance ships in winter storms.

Another project that started at about the same time was the Pentamaran. This high-speed initiative was started by a European ship-owner who asked the British design team BMT if they could develop a fast container ship that could cope with ocean conditions and combine this with speeds of up to 40 knots. The study included a wide variety of concepts and it was narrowed down to a long slender hull with supporting side sponsons. Initially it was thought that a trimaran could provide the solution but with development it was found that the Pentamaran was a better solution. A Pentamaran is a strange-looking vessel with a central long slender hull that is stabilized by two slim sponsons on each side whereas a trimaran has only one on each side. By having two, the performance in waves is improved and this is thought to be a better solution for an ocean-going ship. Development led to a variety of Pentamaran concepts and one that looked really promising was to utilize the concept to transport road trailers down the east coast of the US to help relieve the pressure on the roads. This project was well-developed but as always seems to be the case, when it came to providing funding for the construction of the ships the money dried up.

The Pentamaran was also developed in a form for ocean travel and like the FastShip the idea was to create a high-speed cargo ship running at around 40 knots. A big difference between these two projects was that the Pentamaran could achieve its high performance by using conventional medium-speed diesel engines similar to those already in use on many ships. Not only did this reduce capital costs compared with the expensive gas turbines of the FastShip but it also reduced the fuel consumption. The FastShip required a lot of power because the whole wide hull was being lifted in the water to make it a semi-planing type of vessel whereas the Pentamaran with its long narrow hull was slicing through the water. Long narrow hulls can achieve high speeds with modest power provided they are long enough and slim enough and this combined with the stabilizing provided by the side sponsons was developed to create an efficient hull shape. Sadly, as with so many projects, there was not a ship-owner who was brave enough to move away from conventional concepts to invest in this new technology and the patent on this hull concept has now expired so the technology is available out there.

Mention should be made of an interesting high-speed concept that was primarily developed to set a new Atlantic record under power. To qualify for the Hales Trophy such a vessel was required to have 'some commercial purpose' and in this case this was to carry high-speed cargo. The record vessel would be a small prototype to test the concept and, unlike the FastShip and the Pentamaran, this new design would be largely based on tried and tested technology. Constructed from aluminium, the hull would be a deep V-design to help cushion the impact with waves at high speed. The hull would be long and narrow so that it would be partially wave-piercing and to reduce the contouring over the waves. This meant there was every chance that the hull would be going through waves which meant that solid water could be coming down the deck at speed and this could destroy anything in its path. To counter any problems, the deck was designed with steep sloping sides so any water would have an easy path back into the sea and the controlling bridge structure was raised on stilts so that water could pass freely underneath. The legs of this structure would contain the air inlets and exhausts from the three gas turbines required to give the vessel a top speed of over 60 knots. It was a novel but practical design that never got built but it did show a possible route to developing a high-speed vessel to take on the might of the Atlantic. At about the same time an American team developed a cargo-carrying side-wall hovercraft that was designed to set a new record as well as being the prototype for a very fast cargo vessel, but again funding for this project never materialized.

All these concepts were aimed at the market for carrying time-sensitive cargoes across the Atlantic and the time may come when the demand for this grows but you can't help feeling that the market for high-speed cargo will never quite materialize. Are shippers prepared to pay a higher premium on their transport costs in order to save a couple of days' time for the transit? That is one question to which the answer appears to be no and indeed it does appear that even the modern fast container ships are operating at slower speeds than they were originally designed for to reduce fuel costs. There was never much doubt about speed of transit when it came to passengers but with cargo it does appear that the situation is much more negotiable and there is a reluctance to pay the premium for a fast transit. This means that the technology is waiting in the wings if the demand does materialize and the Pentamaran does seem to offer a more cost-effective solution than the FastShip concept. Moving cargo at high speed does not have the same glamour as moving passengers, particularly when many of the passengers can be high-profile on the social ladder.

Currently there is only Cunard, now owned by Carnival Cruises, that offers transatlantic passenger voyages as part of the itinerary for their passenger ships but these voyages are a shadow of the former fast schedules. Certainly they are more of a cruise than a fast transit with the aim of trying to recreate some of the past glamour of the Atlantic voyages and not for those who have to make the crossing in a fast time. For speed, air travel is the way to go with time measured in hours rather than days, but there has been an attempt to offer sea travel across the Atlantic at high speed with a new concept of high-speed vessel. This is far removed from the vessels that have been proposed for high-speed cargo operations and the aim was to offer a crossing of the Atlantic in two and a half days at high speed.

This timing would allow for a return voyage every week and in order to achieve such a schedule not only was a high-speed ship required but a shorter route was selected. By sailing from the River Clyde and ending the voyage in Boston rather than New York some 500 miles of steaming could be saved. It was felt that such a fast schedule could prove attractive to those who did not like flying, those who wanted a taste of what it was like to travel by sea across the Atlantic and those who simply wanted a new travel experience. The challenge was to find a vessel design that could achieve this type of schedule.

For the design the prospective operators turned to the New Zealand design team of Craig Loomes Associates who have a long history of designing advanced high-speed craft. They decided that a trimaran design would be appropriate for the North Atlantic conditions and came up with the concept of an 800ft-long design based around a long slender central hull with aft stabilizing sponsons. Equal attention was paid to the design of the top of the vessel to ensure that there were no projections that would interfere with the

A huge trimaran design aimed at a high-speed Atlantic crossing and capable of carrying 1,000 passengers.

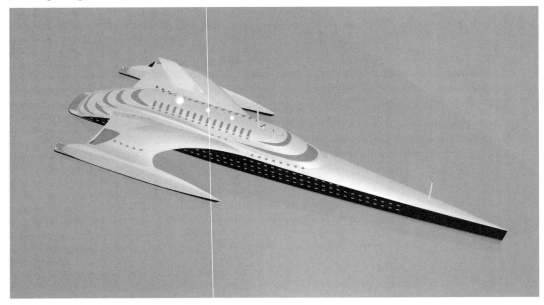

water flow both above and below the waterline. The aim was to have a design that would be wave-piercing so that rather than contouring the waves in an Atlantic storm the vessel would simply go through the wave to give what was hoped would be a fairly level ride, even in storm conditions. Unlike a conventional ship's hull where the buoyancy of the hull causes it to lift as a wave approaches the bow, with this trimaran design there was minimal buoyancy at the bow allowing the vessel to keep at a virtually level attitude even in big waves.

Accommodation could be provided for up to 1,000 passengers in this revolutionary design which was probably an optimistic number for those wishing to cross by water rather than by air. The public rooms would be located in the raised aft section and items such as lifeboats would be installed in protected parts of the stern of the ship. The proposed power was three gas turbines that would be coupled to water-jet propulsion and it was this power plant that was mainly the cause of this project not getting off the ground. Gas turbines tend to be very thirsty when operating at sea level and with something like 200,000 hp required to maintain a 50-knot speed, the fuel bills would be very high meaning that fares would have to be pitched considerably higher than competing air fares; this was not likely to attract the number of passengers required to make the service viable.

All these advanced concepts have been developed to take on the might of the Atlantic and it is possible that they could work as long as there is careful weather routing that would allow the vessels to maintain high speeds. However, one of the problems with Atlantic weather routing is that many of the low-pressure areas that dominate the Atlantic weather during the winter months are large and can embrace considerable areas of the North Atlantic. This means that the options to find an alternative route with less severe weather may be limited and could entail a considerable deviation with the extra distance involved negating the reduced transit times possible with high speed. This is one of the reasons why it seems likely that any attempt to try to introduce high-speed cargo ships on the Atlantic may be some way off. Other reasons are, of course, the high cost of fuel for maintaining high speeds and the relatively high cost of building the innovative ship designs required for high-speed operations. The time may come but it is probably a few years away at this stage.

One possible solution for high-speed Atlantic travel that has been proposed is the Wing in Ground (WIG) craft. These are to all intents and purposes an aircraft but one that flies very close to the surface of the sea where it can generate a lot more lift than is possible when flying high in the sky and so be more efficient. WIGs can fly at relatively high speeds of over 100 knots and they can be good load-carriers, opening up the possibility of carrying cargoes

A huge Wing in Ground (WIG) craft that could possibly take on the Atlantic and offer a high-speed crossing.

or passengers across the oceans at a more leisurely pace than is possible with aircraft. I have flown a small WIG on the River Rhine and it is an interesting experience flying at around 80 knots just above the surface of the water. The Russians have built very large WIGs but their performance figures are restricted and experience in operating them over open oceans and in rough seas is limited so they are probably not an option for Atlantic travel at this stage.

Weather is so often the limiting factor for Atlantic travel and perhaps one possible alternative to the ships currently in use is submarines. By travelling underwater a submarine would be immune from the weather on the surface and so would be able to maintain a schedule without difficulty. It needs more power to move a submarine at the same speed as a comparable ship because the resistance is higher and getting air to the engines and the exhaust back up to the surface are problems to solve with nuclear power being the logical solution so no air or exhausts are needed. Currently submarines are confined to military applications apart from a few small sport submarines but the potential for cargo transport is considerable and may be the solution in the future if the climate change people are right and the Atlantic Ocean gets wilder with more frequent storms. Submarines are unlikely to appeal to passengers who would probably prefer their high-speed metal tube in the sky rather than a much slower metal tube underwater.

More immediate to Atlantic shipping is a new threat looming on the horizon. With modern electronic navigation using advanced position-fixing there should no longer be any excuse for ships to run aground even in the densest of dense fogs that can prevail along the coasts on both sides. We have now been blessed with the ability of the Global Positioning System (GPS) to fix the position of ships reliably and with an accuracy measured in metres anywhere in the world. It is impressive technology that should mean that ships know exactly where they are at all times, night and day and in any visibility and it is only when mistakes are made such as happened with the *Royal Majesty* cruise ship that things might go wrong. However, GPS can be vulnerable because the signal that comes down from the GPS satellites is extremely weak. Some experts say it is like looking at a light bulb from 100 miles away. This weak signal can be easily swamped by a powerful signal sent out nearby on or close to the same frequency. GPS jamming, either accidental or deliberate, is becoming a considerable menace and it can provide a simple way for the bad guys to interfere with ship navigation in sensitive waters. Just one terrorist in a boat armed with a powerful jammer that he has bought on the internet for a few hundred dollars could cause a major shipping catastrophe.

This may be the new threat on the Atlantic taking the place or perhaps adding to the weather threats such as storms and fog. Jamming is one type of this new cyber threat to navigation but much more sinister is the threat from GPS spoofing. Jamming the GPS signal simply means that it is not available and this should be recognized quickly by the navigators on board. There are plans to provide a back-up Loran system working on different frequencies that would step in if the GPS was not available. With GPS spoofing a signal is still available but that signal has been modified to give an alternative position. This can be done gradually so that unless the position is monitored very carefully the change may not be detected and the ship could be led astray. Jamming has to be done relatively close to the ship being affected but spoofing can be done over considerable distances and could lead a ship into dangerous waters, possibly without the crew realizing the danger. This is a troubling new development for Atlantic shipping just at a time when it looked like things were becoming safer.

Certainly things have come a long way since those early exploratory voyages across the ocean. Gradually the technology has evolved to improve things but it has to be said that much of the technology of shipping is aimed primarily at improving efficiency rather than safety. The Atlantic has always been a challenging place for shipping, combining long steaming distances with challeng-

Can the Atlantic storms get much worse than this?

ing sea conditions, and the legislators have always been playing catch-up with the rules and regulations to try to maintain an acceptable level of safety as ship-owners and operators have tried to push the envelope of efficiency and speed. The history of the Atlantic has been littered with disasters, some passing almost unnoticed in the greater scheme of things, while others such as the *Titanic* have led to changes in the safety requirements for shipping. Maybe the time is coming when there will be another major disaster in Atlantic waters that will lead to further changes and it is not hard to suggest that this will involve one of the new generation of massive cruise liners.

In building and operating these mega-ships it looks like we are sleepwalking into disaster. As a seaman it is not hard to imagine the difficulty in coping with trying to rescue 6,000 people from a sinking cruise ship, even if this occurs close to land. Out in the middle of the Atlantic this would be a major disaster that would have to rely on passing ships for rescue and modern ships are ill-equipped for rescue work as I know from personal experience. So could a modern cruise ship get into trouble in mid-ocean? Fire on board has been one of the frequent perils afflicting cruise liners and this can disable the ship and leave it at the mercy of a storm. We saw how when the *El Faro* lost power she was then overwhelmed by the hurricane seas so picture that scenario with a major cruise ship. The designers and operators will argue that the modern ships are capable of weathering the storm but as a seaman I find that difficult

Storm waves hit the rocks at the Round Island Lighthouse in the Scilly Isles.

to believe and disasters usually start with small things going wrong and then the situation escalating. You can have back-up systems for when things go wrong but disaster seems to come much closer when two or more things go wrong at the same time. At sea, experience shows that you have to expect the unexpected. With the *Titanic*, passengers and crew could have been saved if there had been enough lifeboats but the combination of hitting the iceberg and not having sufficient lifeboats was what caused the escalation of the disaster.

History shows that the Atlantic is not an ocean to be taken lightly. It can have its wonderful moments of moderate seas and sunny skies but equally it can change its mood into some of the roughest seas and highest waves in the world. We may be getting better at understanding the weather and how it affects the seas but we cannot control the wind and waves and the long-term forecasts are that these will get worse over the next decade or two. Will modern ships be able to rise to this challenge on the Atlantic and can the Atlantic be tamed?

Select Bibliography

Primary Sources

Barton, Humphrey, *Atlantic Adventurers* (1953).
Benstead, C.R., *Atlantic Ferry* (1936).
Bombard, Alain, *The Bombard Story* (1953).
Brinnins, John, *The Sway of the Grand Saloon* (1972).
British Admiralty, *Ocean Passages of the World* (1950).
Britten, Edgar, *A Million Ocean Miles* (1936).
Brooks, Clive, *Atlantic Queens* (1989).
Drummond, John, *Gap of Danger* (1963).
Farrington, Karen, *Shipwrecks* (1999).
Flaykat, William, *Perils of the Atlantic* (2003).
Fox, Stephen, *TransAtlantic* (2003).
Hekell and O'Grady, *Ocean Passages and Landfalls* (2005).
Hughes, Tom, *The Blue Riband of the Atlantic* (1973).
Junger, Sebastian, *The Perfect Storm* (1997).
Kediker, Marcus, *The Slave Ship* (2007).
Lubeck, Basil, *Western Ocean Packets* (1977).
Maginnis, A.J., *Atlantic Ferry* (1892).
Maxtone-Graham, John, *The North Atlantic Run* (1972).
Merrien, Jean, *Madmen of the Atlantic* (1961).
Miller, William, *SS* United States (1991).
Nicolson, Adam, *Atlantic Britain* (2004).
O'Hagan, Andrew, *The Atlantic Ocean* (2008).
Postma, Johannes, *Riches from Atlantic Commerce* (2003).
Ridgely-Nevitt, Cedric, *American Steamships on the Atlantic* (1981).
Ridgeway and Blyth, *Fighting Chance* (1966).
Rogers, Stanley, *The Atlantic* (1930).
Sandler, Martin, *Atlantic Ocean* (2008).
Severin, Tim, *The* Bredan *Voyage* (1978).
Smith, Billy Gordon, *Ship of Death: A Voyage That Changed the Atlantic World* (2013).
Winchester, Simon, *Atlantic* (2011).

Secondary Sources

Atlantic Monthly	*New York Times*	*Ships Monthly*
Lloyd's List	*The Rudder*	*The Sunday Times*

Index